127624

Effective
Business Communication

SECOND E

ASHA KAUL

Professor
Communication Area
Indian Institute of Management Ahmedabad

D1331334

PHI Learning Private Limited

Delhi-110092

2015

ST. HELENS
COLLEGE

658·45
KAU

127624

June 2015

LIBRARY

₹ 225.00

EFFECTIVE BUSINESS COMMUNICATION, Second Edition
Asha Kaul

© 2015 by PHI Learning Private Limited, Delhi. All rights reserved. No part of this book may be reproduced in any form, by mimeograph or any other means, without permission in writing from the publisher.

ISBN-978-81-203-5072-4

The export rights of this book are vested solely with the publisher.

Nineteenth Printing (Second Edition)   ...   .   **January, 2015**

Published by Asoke K. Ghosh, PHI Learning Private Limited, Rimjhim House, 111, Patparganj Industrial Estate, Delhi-110092 and Printed by Raj Press, New Delhi-110012.

To
My Family

Contents

9. Writing to Communicate   208

List of Exhibits

Preface

Fourteen years have passed since the first edition of the book was completed. Much has changed in the domain of communication. It has now become more scientific with an urgent need for effectiveness in the discipline. Not only is the micro environment clamouring for change but also the macro! For instance, on one hand, we have the corporate requirements, and on the other, changes in government policies and encouragement to foreign investments. All this has made it imperative that precision and correctness in the what, why and how of communication be maintained. While the need has been articulated, how do the processes get established?

As the title suggests, let us restrict ourselves to business communication only. We find that companies are grappling with techniques and tactics of effective communication and are attempting to standardise processes and procedures. However, the underlying question in all these efforts remains unaddressed, which is, "Does one size fit all?" The book **Effective Business Communication** is an answer to many such queries of a similar nature. The book presents situations and proposes solutions, which though not comprehensive given the nature of the output, definitely give a direction and point to correctness and effectiveness in oral and written communication.

Though not a new concept, the relevance of communication can be understood from the fact that we are communicating almost 80 to 90 per cent of the time either formally or informally. We are either sending or receiving messages. If we have been communicating and are still *doing communication* wherein lies the need to read a book and develop skills? Can it not be learned on-the-job? The answer to both these questions is a yes and a no! A 'yes' because skills can be learned and developed when in action. A 'no' because our attempt is to move beyond the narrow confines of mediocrity to zones of excellence. Definitely then, the choice is not tough!

There have been changes in the speaking and documentation styles. Though the basic concepts and principles have not changed, application has become varied. Keeping this fundamental in mind, I have added select, current situations and examples from my interaction with the corporate world and students at IIMA. Though the names have been changed to maintain anonymity, the additions are real life requiring effectiveness in oral and written communication. As the title of the book suggests, the emphasis is on formal business communication situations. The aim is to articulate a systematic process and structure of communication in multiple situations. Wherever necessary, illustrations and exhibits have been provided for exemplification of concepts.

STRUCTURE OF THE BOOK

Beginning with an overview of business communication, the book leads the reader through the principles of communication—oral and written. There are nine chapters in the book. The first two deal with oral communication and the other seven with different forms of written communication. The first chapter, *Principles of Communication*, post a definition of communication, details the process in simple terms, discusses the basic purpose of communication and types. For the sender and the listener to be in sync the chapter outlines the rules to be adhered to. To emerge as an effective communicator, there should be familiarity with the role adopted so that suitable strategies can be appropriately applied in all situations. The differences between oral and written communication are also presented.

Chapter II, *Oral Communication*, discusses required techniques for effectiveness. How can communication be improved by understanding and removing sender and listener oriented barriers form a major part of the chapter. Strategies for listening, once the barriers are removed, are discussed in detail followed by appropriate methods for giving feedback. What is telephone etiquette? The focus of the last section in the chapter is on techniques of making the telephonic message more appealing

Moving from oral to written communication, the third chapter, *Mechanics of Writing* presents the basics of writing. Explaining techniques of composing business messages, the chapter presents fundamentals as preparing notes, following a certain style and tone, managing punctuations and removing dead wood from the text. Additionally, the chapter explains methods for identifying errors and correcting the same with the use of the dictionary and the thesaurus. It suggests ways to improve the vocabulary and make the writing style simple and reader friendly.

The fourth and fifth chapters in the book are *Report Writing* and *Sections of the Report*. These two chapters are crucial as they emphasise a form of writing, namely reports, which is extensively used within organisations. Be it an inter or intra organisational report, the focus is on techniques for communicating to create impact. Both the content and the style should be immaculate and possess the capability to appeal and convince.

The next chapter, *Circulars, Notices, Agenda, Memos and Minutes* presents styles of writing official documents. The focus in this chapter is on accuracy, clarity and style. The procedures and processes of writing these forms of internal communication are explained with clarity and samples provided to help the student/practitioner adopt techniques with ease and speed.

Chapter 7, *Writing Letters* deals extensively with different types of letters and how they should be drafted. Telegrams, telex, facsimiles and emails are also presented in this chapter. Though telegrams and telexes are gradually losing significance, they have still not completely lost ground. This chapter provides room to comprehend the different forms of letter writing.

While applying for a job, the CV and Resume—the manner of drafting and making a pitch—are important. We may wish to shoot out a solicited or unsolicited letter when in the process of job hunt. To create the desired impact and ensure that the CV/Resume is not trashed, content needs to be written in a specific manner so that there is an organisational fit and documented skills and capabilities appeal to the recruiter. This forms the crux of the eighth chapter, *Applying for a Job*.

To be able to write and convince, the content should be error free. Chapter 9, *Writing to Communicate* presents incorrect use of language and phrases that rob the text, be it a report or a letter, of authenticity and credibility. The chapter also presents correct use of the examples and the rationale or logic is also provided in the form of explanations. This makes it comprehensive and strengthens the student grasp on topics as logic, logical rigour, reader orientation, syntax and semantics. This chapter is an addition to the first edition of the book.

Asha Kaul

Acknowledgements

It was difficult getting back to the first edition of the book after almost fourteen years. Where did I begin? In the classrooms! In interaction with students, and Academic Associates (AAs), I found immense scope of revising the book and sharing examples and short anecdotes with potential readers. Then began the process of revision. The AAs were roped in for collation of material. Ms. Pooja Susan Thomas was the first AA (IIMA) who made substantial contributions in terms of going through the original text and making suggestions, which were undoubtedly good. Dr Rahul Shukla, AA (IIMA) after assisting me in an elective course almost immediately got down to providing examples for the ninth chapter. I would like to give credit to both these AAs, who despite their busy schedule stuck by me and the new edition of the book. Thanks Pooja and Rahul!

Acknowledgements are also due to Ms. Bindu P. Thachapully who joined IIMA as an AA and was with us for a very short while. In her short stint at the Institute she was able to contribute anecdotes and quotes to three chapters. Her speed and accuracy acted as a constant reminder to me that I too need to get back to the revision. I would like to also thank my PGP students, IIMA who provided examples to me and made the entire process of writing vibrant.

In a chance meeting with Mr Ashwin Pandya, an old friend, I discovered in him the talent of sketching, painting and designing. Hey Presto! Before he realised he had committed to designing the cover. Thanks Ashwin for your late yet timely entry!

Last but not the least my gratitude to family members who have been kind and supportive and have survived my eccentricities in periodic spells of hibernation. I would like to thank my mother Mrs. Vimla Kaul, a hard critic and my father Late Shri G.N. Kaul for always encouraging me. Acknowledgements to my mother-in-law, Dr. K.K. Kaul whose silent support has always acted as an impetus to achieve and excel. Harsh, Anand, Rupa and Rohini—thanks for understanding and being there. One of these days, we will make up for the lost time!

Asha Kaul

CHAPTER

1

Principles of Communication

CONTENTS

- Introduction
- Definition of Communication
- Process of Communication
- Turn-Taking System
- Basic Purpose of Communication
- Communication Network
- Types of Communication
- Difference between Oral and Written Communication
- 7 C's and 4 S's

LEARNINGS

After reading this chapter you should be able to:

- ➢ Comprehend the process of communication
- ➢ Understand the role played by each component in the process
- ➢ Pick up cues and signals to steer the communication to a desired end
- ➢ Use appropriate channels of communication
- ➢ Visualise your place in the communication network

KEYWORDS

Communication, Channels/Medium, Cues and Signals, Communication Network, Decoding, Diagonal Communication, Feedback, Horizontal Communication, Message, Oral Communication, Perception, Processes of Communication, Receiver/Decoder/Listener, Sender/Encoder/Speaker, Transmission, Turn-Taking System, Verbal Communication, Vertical Communication, Written Communication

INTRODUCTION

What is communication? Communication, derived from the Latin word *communis* means "to share, ideas, concepts, feelings and emotions". The science of communication is almost as old as man. From time immemorial, there has been a felt need to share or to communicate. As a result, different vehicles/channels were identified and subsequently improvised for the purpose of transmission of ideas and concepts. What is the importance of communication? Why should it be studied? Why should the vehicles/channels be analysed and examined?

The importance of communication can be gauged by the fact that we are communicating in some form or the other almost every moment of our lives. Whether we are walking, talking, playing, sitting, or even sleeping, a message is being formulated and transmitted. Man, in the generalist sense, is a social animal, and is constantly interacting with other individuals. Hence, it is essential to understand the art of communication and apply or modify it in a suitable manner. The ability to communicate is much more than a composition of certain physical attributes, vocal chords, and articulators. It is the ability to symbolise or to understand concepts in terms of images or symbols which facilitates communication. In other words, communication is much more than an understanding of the spoken or written language. It is a composite of symbols, gestures, and illustrations that accompany either the spoken or the written word.

DEFINITION OF COMMUNICATION

TOPIC OBJECTIVES
Identify the elements in a communication process
Map the flow of communication

"The older I grow, the more I listen to people who don't talk much."   —Germain G. Glien

Communication is a two-way process in which there is an exchange and progression of ideas towards a mutually accepted direction or goal. For this process to materialise, it is essential that the basic elements of communication be identified. These elements are:

1. Sender/Encoder/Speaker
2. Receiver/Decoder/Listener
3. Message
4. Medium
5. Feedback

Sender/Encoder/Speaker

The person who initiates the communication process is normally referred to as the **sender**. From a personal data bank the sender selects ideas, encodes

| Encoding of message |

and finally transmits them to the receiver. The entire burden of communication then rests upon the sender or encoder. The choice of images and words, and the combination of the two is what compels the receiver to listen carefully.

In this process a number of factors come into play, primary among them being an understanding of the recipient/s and their needs. If the message can be formulated in accordance with the expectations of the receiver, the level of acceptance is higher.

> For example, a consultant wishes to communicate with the HRD manager of a company. The objective is to secure consultancy projects on training of personnel. If the consultant wishes the HRD manager to communicate with him, he has to ensure that their goals converge. He has a tough task ahead of him. The manager has been interacting with many consultants. Why should he pay heed to the proposal of this consultant?

In a situation such as this, a good strategy to be adopted is to expand the purview of the proposal and make it *company specific*. The result can be highlighted and spelt out in terms of increase in sales. If sufficient preparation has been done, the message too will be formulated in a manner conducive to the interests of the HRD manager.

Receiver/Decoder/Listener

The listener is now faced with the task of decoding the message.

This process is carried on in relation to the work environment and the value perceived in terms of the work situation. If the receiver views a similarity in the goal of the sender there is high receptivity. The

| Decoding of message |

decoding of the message is done in almost entirely the same terms as was intended by the sender. In the example cited above, as soon as the HRD manager realises that the proposal of the consultant is going to result in tangible benefits, there is high receptivity and interest in the communication is reinforced.

Message

Message is the encoded idea transmitted by the sender. The formulation of the message is very important, for an incorrect patterning can turn the receiver hostile or make him/her lose interest.

At this stage the sender has to be extremely cautious. What is the order in which ideas should be presented? Suppose there are four points to make.

Should the sender (a) move in the stereotyped manner of presenting them in a sequence or (b) be innovative and proceed in a creative way? Probability is high that in case (a) there may be some monotony and in case (b) a wrong spot may be touched. How then should the message be formulated and transmitted? The ordering, as stated earlier, should be based on the requirements of the listener so that its significance is immediately grasped. As soon as the receiver finds a link between personal goals and the codified message, there is interest generated and responses are as per expectations. In such a situation, we can affirmatively state that the message has created the desired impact.

> *Formulation of message*

Medium

Another important element of communication is the medium or channel. It can be oral, written or non-verbal. Prior to the composition of the message, the medium/channel should be decided. Each medium follows its own set of rules and regulations. For example, in oral communication one can afford to be a little informal, but when using the written mode, all rules of communication need to be observed. It must be remembered that anything in writing is a document that would be filed for records or circulated to all concerned.

> *Choice of medium*

Feedback

> *Feedback completes loop of communication*

Feedback is the most important component of communication. Effective communication takes place only when there is a feedback. The errors and flaws that abound in business situations are a result of lack of feedback.

Rajat and his team have been working on Advance Traffic Management System (ATMS) of U.P. state government for the past three months. It had been decided that after three months there would be a review meeting of the ATMS project in the head office. The review meeting is to be held in the head office where Rajat and his team will present their project agenda and discuss the progress, so far.

They are worried about the review and the feedback they might get. General Manager (GM) reviewing the presentation tells Rajat and his team that their agenda is good, but the current working approach needs further improvement. He also makes some sweeping personal remarks that hurt the team members. Moreover, they are left confused about what is good about the agenda presented by them, and feel that the GM's comments may be insincere and only a padding for the criticism to follow. Being told that their current approach needs improvement would not help them identify shortcomings in the approach. They feel that they don't deserve the criticism and are left feeling unappreciated and demotivated.

If feedback is solicited on all occasions, errors in communication can be minimised or even completely done away with.

Warning! Fallacious statements or erroneous conclusions are made because of lack of confirmation through feedback and discrepancy between the message encoded and decoded.

PROCESS OF COMMUNICATION

TOPIC OBJECTIVES
Understand the process of encoding and decoding
To convey the right message to the right person

"What is the shortest word in the English language that contains the letters: abcdef? Answer: feedback. Don't forget that feedback is one of the essential elements of good communication."   —Anonymous

The sender, according to his or her ideas, behaviour pattern and intention, selects a message, encodes it, and transmits it to the receiver through a medium— be it oral, verbal or non-verbal. The receiver decodes the message and gives an internal response to the perceived message. It is noteworthy that the response is not in relation to the actual content, but rather to the "perceived content" of the original message. This completes the first phase of the communication process. It is interesting to note that words in themselves have no meaning. It is the *perception* of a particular word and the *intention* behind it that assigns a meaning to the encoded message. Variations in perception of the same word between the sender and the receiver often give rise to misunderstanding and differences in communication.

First Phase:
↓
Encoding
↓
Transmitting
↓
Decoding

In the second phase, the receiver formulates the message, encodes and transmits it to the original sender-now-turned-receiver. This stage is referred to as *providing feedback,* and is most crucial. Unless there is feedback—be it in the verbal or the non-verbal form, we cannot say that effective communication has taken place. If the feedback is in tune with the original intent of the sender, communication proceeds without a hitch. However, there can be instances when the receiver does not agree with the message of the sender. This does not mean that there is breakdown of communication. We can, in such instances; state that effective communication is stalled for the time being. It can resume after clarifications are sought in subsequent discussions.

Second Phase:
↓
Providing feedback

For the process of communication to be effective, there should be a well-defined goal in the mind of the sender. Harmony between the goals of the two communicators makes for good and easy progression of ideas and concepts.

"Good communication is as stimulating as black coffee, and just as hard to
sleep after."   —Anne Morrow

Whatever be the initial situation, the sender necessarily needs to adhere to
the following stages:

1. Create awareness in the mind of the receiver on the topic.
2. Propose point of view with clarity and preciseness so as to eliminate
    possibilities of confusion.
3. Enable smooth flow of discussion through observance of communi-
    cation strategies.
4. Reinforce or correct ideas in the mind of the receiver concerning the
    goal of communication.
5. Achieve the goal of communication.

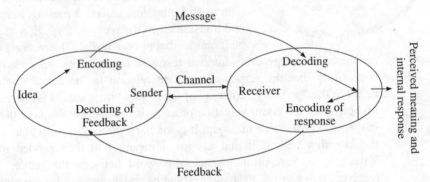

Exhibit 1.1   Model of communication.

At the time of transmission and reception of message, all our five senses
play an important role in grasping the intent. The sense that is predominantly
active at a particular stage helps in a higher degree of absorption. For
example, in the course of the communication, if the visual sense at a
particular moment is highly active, we respond only to the visual cues.

TURN-TAKING SYSTEM

TOPIC
OBJECTIVES
Understand the process of
turn-taking
Enable and control
communication

"A conversation is a dialogue, not a monologue.
That's why there are so few good conversations:
due to scarcity, two intelligent talkers seldom meet."
                                        —Truman Capote

Ethnomethodologists have identified different
organisational features in a piece of conversation.
Seven such aspects have been identified. The first is
of direct relevance as it helps in facilitating the process of communication.

The first rule states that: A turn-taking system allocates turns to the speakers in the following manner:

1. The first speaker selects the one to talk next (by asking questions/tag questions, etc.) or
2. The speaker who self-selects continues speaking for a whole turn

The entire process of communication hinges on this rule. The sender has to chalk out strategies by which the receiver is led to agree to the underlying goal. For this, many strategies need to be planned, e.g. transmitting visual signs or cues that prompt a receiver to pick up the thread and begin communication or fill in the gaps or conclude. These signals form an essential part of the entire process. Together with identification of these signals, there should also be an accurate interpretation and response. A wrong step or a move at an incorrect moment can abruptly bring communication to a close.

> *Controlling communication*

On meeting Bhaskar at the coffee machine, Abhishek enquired from his colleague, "Hey, where is Jacob?" Without looking up from the cup he was filling, Bhaskar replied, "He has been working hard to please the boss." Abhishek was taken aback, but recovers quickly and responds with a chuckle,
"That reminds me, do you know if the boss wanted our project file by this evening?"

Bhaskar makes an unwarranted statement which does not speak very highly either of Jacob or himself. Abhishek is sensitive and has picked up the cues and signals being emitted to him. He has also realised that the turn has perforce been allocated to him. In this instance, we gather that Abhishek does not wish to displease Bhaskar for some reason. Without reacting to Bhaskar's statement, Abhishek has responded with a chuckle and changed the subject.

Abhishek could have responded in a similar vein with an additional sarcastic remark. Or he could have reacted to Bhaskar's statement and defended Jacob. A number of factors come into play when a statement of this kind is made and communication still carries on: the relationship between Abhishek and Bhaskar, the urgency to get on with higher goal issues, and a desire on the part of Abhishek to not displease Bhaskar.

Identification of the cues and signals helps in turning the discussion in the desired direction. Hence, it becomes imperative that the turn-taking system be thoroughly understood so that the sender can juxtapose comments and suggestions at the right moment and steer the communication along goal-oriented channels.

> *Cues and signals*

Note: It is the speaker/sender who is primarily responsible for effective communication.

BASIC PURPOSE OF COMMUNICATION

TOPIC OBJECTIVES
Analyse the uses of communication
Distinguish various kinds of communication networks

"The problem with communication is the illusion that it has occurred."   —George Bernard Shaw

"What is the purpose of (formal) communication?" A response to a query of this nature will be more beneficial if attempts were made to understand the business situation where success or failure of issues is always measured in terms of man-hours spent in the completion of a task. Let us take an example.

Suppose the boss issues instructions to the subordinate to complete a certain project in a particular manner within a stipulated timeframe. The subordinate complies and completes the task as per the perceived dictate and personal ability. However, the end result is a miserable failure because the manner of completion does not match with the expectations of the boss. A lot of time has been wasted as a result of miscommunication on the part of the two members of the same organisation. In fact, more time will now be spent on rectifying the errors that had crept up in the first instance. If the amount of time used in completion of this particular task is calculated, it would be seen that almost double the amount of time has been taken.

The example of miscommunication, cited above, is one of the most common and prevailing examples in organisations resulting from a lack of feedback. This, however, is not the only criterion that qualifies for an in-depth study of communication. Let us take a look at the communicative competence required at three different levels in an organisation.

In the *business situation* the role of a manager, with progressive seniority is to coordinate, issue instructions, collate information, and then present the same. All these activities require effective communication skills. The

Helps in coordinating, collating, and issuing instructions

sooner these skills are honed, the easier it is for the manager to accomplish tasks. Similar is the case of the junior manager vying for a quick promotion. As work in the organisation is always done in coordination with other people, effective communication skills become a necessity.

Two junior managers going up the ladder of success possess almost the same academic qualifications and almost similar personality traits. Only one of them would be able to make it to the Managing Director's chair. Who would it be?

Without doubt it would be the manager with excellent communication skills. Prior to entry in any organisation, certain communicative abilities are also looked for in candidates. Ability to speak, conduct oneself properly in an interview, get along with others, listen carefully and accurately, make

Brings improvement in speaking abilities, listening, interacting, writing, convincing and persuading

effective presentations, prepare good yet brief report, make proposals, sell ideas, convince and persuade others are some of the attributes looked for in a candidate. If an individual possesses these attributes or can train for excellence, there will be self-realisation of how easy it is to secure a comfortable position in an organisation and to achieve success.

COMMUNICATION NETWORK

"The two words 'information' and 'communication' are often used interchangeably, but they signify quite different things. Information is giving out; communication is getting through."   —Sydney J. Harris

TOPIC OBJECTIVES Communicate effectively through internal and external networks Comprehend the significance of horizontal, lateral and diagonal networks

An organisation is a composite of many individuals working together, towards its growth. They are constantly interacting with each other and with people outside the company. The communication network in an organisation is of two types:

1. Internal
2. External

Internal Communication

Interaction between members of the same organisation is called *internal communication*. It can be both formal and informal. Large organisations with hundreds of people working find it very difficult to have direct interaction with each and every one. They adopt a number of strategies, e.g. newsletters, annual reports to communicate the essential message. In such large setups, it is neither possible nor necessary to transmit all information to every member.

Formal communication

Informal communication

Informal communication is prevalent in organisations with an initial manpower of approximately 20 people, all of whom have direct interface with one another on a daily basis. Almost all messages are volleyed back and forth in an informal manner.

The channels of communication may be as follows:

- Vertical
- Horizontal
- Diagonal

Vertical communication

Upward and downward

Upward and downward flow of messages constitutes vertical communication. Information is transmitted from the top management to the employees working in the organisation or vice versa. As it is not possible to have a direct interface on all occasions, especially when the number of people working is high, messages traverse or percolate down with the help of a go-between or an opinion leader. In such situations, probability is high that the message may get distorted as it travels from one person to another.

> In the game "Chinese whisper", you whisper a message to the person next to you and that person in turn whispers it to the next and so on. When the last person to receive the message announces what he/she has heard, everyone realises, amidst a lot of fun and laughter, that the final message is completely different and nonsensical.

The intent of the original message keeps changing as it travels from one person to another with the addition or deletion of words. If the learning from this game was translated into the organisational set-up, it will be seen that messages similarly get distorted when they travel upward or downward.

Distortion of original message can be avoided when information that travels is not fragmented and the number of people who pass the information is reduced. Further, efforts can be made to ensure that there is one-to-one communication within the departments. The heads of the various departments can form a close link and share information. Besides, distortions can be minimised with the usage of the electronic media and e-mails.

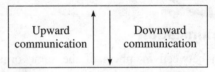

Exhibit 1.2   Vertical communication.

Lateral/Horizontal communication

Interaction with peers or colleagues is referred to as *lateral/horizontal communication*. This can prove to be the most effective form of communication, as peers are not hindered by "chain-of-command" techniques. The volume of horizontal communication that a company enjoys will be contingent upon the interdependence of various departments. In fact, if work is done keeping the functioning of various sections in mind, communication gets richer and more comprehensive.

Communication with colleagues/ peers

Without lateral communication, once again, there cannot be fruitful progression at the organisational level. In such situations, there will be lack of coordination and cooperation and many frustrated attempts will be made to conjoin activities of one department with another. Further, it can also result in duplication of work and messed up employee relationships.

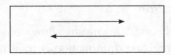

Exhibit 1.3   Lateral communication.

Diagonal communication

In an organisation, communication does not necessarily traverse along a stipulated path. While vertical and lateral forms for transmission of messages are important, there is yet another mode to be taken cognisance of, that is, the *diagonal*. In this type of communication, there is no direct path for information transmittal either planned or chalked out. It can, at certain stages, take on the upward path, then a lateral direction and, finally, move downward, or it can even skip certain stages.

> Informal, can travel in any direction

This channel proves to be very effective as hierarchies are done away with and communication flows irrespective of position or status. It also helps in building relationships and binding ties between the superior and the subordinate. In fact, in many countries managers are being trained to move in the midst of employees at work to remove the fear of status and position. This channel can, however, give rise to gossip, grapevine and rumour. As no one is directly responsible for the flow of information, no one is willing to take responsibility. Only a prudent manager, in the midst of rumours and gossip, can sieve through the information, decipher the intent of the sender and arrive at a definite conclusion.

This channel can, however, prove to be slightly problematic for the managers who wish to control flow of information. They may feel threatened that their controlling authority is under surveillance. But this is a temporary phase and, with constant and mature interaction, can be rectified.

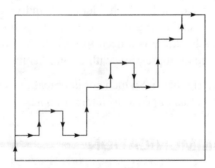

Exhibit 1.4 Diagonal communication.

Warning! Use the lateral and diagonal mode of communication selectively.

External Communication

Communication is an *ongoing process*. It does not only take place with people within the organisation but with people outside the organisation as well. If a company has to survive in the competitive environment, it also has to adopt the latter form of communication. The image of the company is dependent on the relationship that it maintains with people outside. External communication can take on a number of forms:

1. Advertising
2. Media interaction
3. Public relations
4. Presentations
5. Negotiations
6. Mails
7. Telegrams
8. Letters

External communication can again be oral or written. The first three forms of communication mentioned above, viz. advertising, media interaction, and

Communication with external customers

public relations, fall mainly within the domain of corporate communications. Establishing good relations, negotiating or conducting a deal, interacting with clients, issuing tenders, soliciting proposals, sending letters are all part of external communication. This is a difficult task as interaction takes place and varies between a host of people belonging to different disciplines, with different personalities and expectations. As communication proceeds with external customers, almost all skills needed for adept communication have to be brought to the fore to avoid any embarrassment or lapse in performance.

While communicating at the internal level, an individual can, on a few occasions, be slightly lax. The same would not hold true if communication was for the external stakeholders. As individuals are representatives of the companies, they need to be cautious while interacting with external stakeholders for there is a need to protect the image of the organisation and create a positive impression with a long-lasting impact.

Note: The rigour with which communication is carried out may be different for an external as opposed to internal context.

TYPES OF COMMUNICATION

TOPIC OBJECTIVES
Differentiate between various forms of communication
Select the most appropriate based on the situation and the requirements therein

"The more elaborate our means of communication, the less we communicate."   —Joseph Priestly

We can categorise communication under three heads: oral, non-verbal, and written.

1. Oral communication
   (a) Words
   (b) Articulation
2. Non-verbal communication
   (a) Body language
   (b) Signs and symbols
   (c) Territory/Zone
   (d) Object language

3. Written communication
   (a) Reports
   (b) Illustrations
   (c) Memos
   (d) Telegrams
   (e) Facsimiles (FAX)
   (f) E-mails
   (g) Tenders
   (h) Others

Oral Communication

Encoding of message

Anything emanating from the mouth is referred to as *oral*. Within this component will fall words and the manner in which they are pronounced. More important than the words is paralanguage or voice articulation. The listener pays more attention to voice modulations than the spoken words. It has been found that the listener pays heed to the verbal content only seven per cent of the time, 38 per cent of the time there is a focus on voice articulation and modulation, and 55 per cent of the time the attention centers around body language or body sport. If all these three components are in harmony, the listener has no problem in grasping the import of the message. If there is some dichotomy between the two, it creates conflict in the mind of the listener and there is higher belief in the interpreted message derived from voice modulation and the body language than words.

> The manager of a textile company visits the house of a newly joined executive trainee. The trainee is about to go out for a party. Even as she invites the manager into her house, she realises that she cannot leave without offending her superior nor can she stay back happily. The conflict in her mind is reflected in the difference between her words, which are full of typical welcoming phrases, and her tone which lacks the same warmth.

Words both connote and denote a meaning

In oral communication, words should be very carefully chosen. Words both denote and connote a meaning. The former would almost be the literal translation of the word, something like a dictionary meaning. The latter would be the implied meaning. Whenever there is difference between the two, it can lead to what we refer to as a "sarcastic remark". This is also evidenced in tone and voice modulations.

> A business executive plunged in heavy work is disturbed by a friend who drops in without an appointment. The executive makes a statement of the following nature, "I am delighted to see you" with an edge to the voice. Through this statement it is clear that she is denoting how happy she is to meet her friend. However, the underlying connotations too are evident: "Did you have to drop in at this moment?"

It is the intention of the sender behind the words or the connotations that are more important. These are also supported by the voice modulations.

Warning! Your tone and expression will give the intended connotation of your message away.

Non-verbal Communication

Non-verbal communication is an integral part of us and helps in communicating effectively. The way an individual positions his/her own self, holds hands, tilts head, all transmit volumes about the individual. As discussed in the section on oral communication, a receiver observes non-verbal communication 55 per cent of the time, which is much more than listening merely to the words and the voice articulation. Lack of emphasis in this area is due to paucity of material and lack of expertise. However, the 'feel' for an understanding of body language is present in all, e.g., a novice cannot figure out exact correlates for a particular body sport, but is able to generate an impression and feeling about an individual that he/she believes more readily than words. Let us take an example:

| Body sport |

> A subordinate might have an important issue that she wishes to discuss with her boss. The boss pays her attention for the first five minutes, after which he removes his spectacles, turns in his swivel chair and looks at the ceiling. The superior has not said a word that would indicate his desire to discontinue the interaction. The subordinate however, senses the disinterest, her pace of speaking becomes slower and she finally stops with probably a feeble statement.

Every time there is some talk of body language, perforce we are driven into the domain of proxemics: understanding the relationship between two people through their observance and respect of each other's zone or territory. As communication is a two-way process, the distance maintained between the two interactants displays the relationship shared by them. Each individual is surrounded by four zones or territories: the intimate, personal, and social and public zone. Depending on the relationship enjoyed with the other participant, entry in the various zones is permitted, e.g. if the receiver is an acquaintance, entry into the intimate zone of the sender is prohibited. In case of accidental entry in the intimate zone, there will be a sudden moving back on the part of the other participant, as a non-verbal signal, which screams: Stay away!

| Proxemics or territory or zone |

The clothes that an individual wears, the accessories on the self—all communicate a message. Have we ever wondered why is it that we always change before going to our workplace? Why do we have a different set of clothes for office and for home? The primary reason is that even through our dress code we are transmitting a message.

The significance of non-verbal and oral communication can be best understood by an example.

> Suppose we are waiting for a client, and a car halts outside our office window and we happen to be looking across. How is the first impression created in our mind? The model and make of the vehicle prepare the ground for creating the first impression. This is reinforced or corrected when the car owner gets down. By now, we have taken a look at the clothes and the things being carried. Next, we observe the gait. If it is quick and nimble, impressions of an agile and alert client come to our mind. On the contrary, if the gait is laboured, we probably turn our face and carry on with our work. When the external customer approaches us, involuntarily we make a note of the physical distance that is maintained. What ultimately help us in judging the client are the words used and their impact. What is being said, how is it being said, are some queries that automatically get sorted out in our mind.

In this example, there was no deliberate attempt on our part as an expert to segregate the various components of communication and analyse the client. It was an involuntary exercise but one that helped us in judging an individual of capabilities and competencies.

Note: Our self-presentation also communicates a message.

Written Communication

Written communication takes on a number of forms. The writer has to be extra cautious at the time of formulating a message, if it is of a formal nature. Whatever is written is in black and white is used mostly for documentation of information or circulation to all concerned. Therefore, there are very few chances of the writer trying to shift stand and take a different position. There could, as in oral communication, be errors in understanding of the script, but the chances should be minimal for clarity is to be ascertained.

Written communication— Formal, conventional

Written communication is the most formal of all types of communication. It is also bound by the dictates of the organisation. Many companies have their typical manner of functioning and sending written messages. They are accustomed to a set pattern, and any deviation from the norm can create a disturbance in the normal functioning of the company. Further, with the progression of technology, written communication has widened its horizon to encompass electronic means of communicating messages. E-mail is an excellent example of this. Transmitting of written messages within the company or outside can be done easily and in a short span of time.

Warning! Since written forms of communication are also used for purposes of documentation, the writer must formulate his message with care.

DIFFERENCE BETWEEN ORAL AND WRITTEN COMMUNICATION

TOPIC OBJECTIVES

Learn the importance of oral and written communication

Decide on the form of communication to impress

"Good communications, written or oral, begins with an understanding of the audience. If you can get inside their heads, you can find a way to connect."
—Debra Bennetts

Though both oral and written communication are part of one discipline, there are major differences between them. It is this characteristic that makes a communicator adopt them separately on different occasions. Oral communication is interactive, while written communication is non-interactive. In the former, interaction between the sender and the receiver through words is what characterises and differentiates it

Oral communication

from written communication. It is fluid and without boundaries. If the sender feels that the goal is not being met, there can be an attempted change in strategies. However, the same is not true for written communication. The medium is frozen. Whatever has been written finally gets transmitted as a complete picture in itself. If it is incomplete, it is

Interactive, fluid, brief, non-restrictive in place, immediate feedback

reworked. Complex issues are best sorted out through written communication. On the contrary, oral communication looks only at basic issues. The minute they start getting convoluted, the normal reaction is to request the recipient to pen down the ideas for greater clarity. As it takes a comparatively long time to formulate ideas and put them down, written communication normally enjoys a longer time frame than oral communication which is aimed at being brief and succinct.

"Writing, the art of communicating thoughts to the mind through the eye, is the great invention of the world...enabling us to converse with the dead, the absent, and the unborn, at all distances of time and space."
—Abraham Lincoln, *Speeches and Letters of Abraham Lincoln, 1832–1865.*

Oral communication has the distinct advantage of being conducted almost any place where the two participants meet. The same does not hold true for written communication. The places where they are received are highly restrictive. Despite this disadvantage coupled with the cost factor that is rather high when compared to oral communication, written

Written communication— Non-interactive, restrictive in place, non-immediate feedback, longer with respect to time

communication is still preferred in many situations. Probably one of the reasons for this is that written messages have a greater impact. The same things when stated orally may not create the same impression. Finally, there is the difference in terms of feedback. In the case of oral communication, feedback almost always is immediate. On the other hand, for written communication it is not immediate. If the time span in providing feedback exceeds the normal timeframe, conclusions are almost always arrived at: company is not interested, references are being worked at, and people are influencing and swerving the direction of the feedback. It is because of these differences that oral and written communication are used on different occasions and situations. Both have their advantages and disadvantages. However, none can replace the other. Both are essential and needed. What can, nevertheless be done, is develop awareness of the disadvantages and make attempts to improvise and make the best of the situation.

Note: Adopt verbal or non-verbal means of communication according to the demands of the context.

7 C'S AND 4 S'S

TOPIC OBJECTIVES
Use 7 C's and 4 S's to communicate effectively
Be wary of complex communication techniques

"I've learned that people will forget what you said, people will forget what you did, but people will never forget how you made them feel."   —Maya Angelou

---

May I Smoke?

Jack and Max are walking from the religious service. Jack wonders whether it would be all right to smoke while praying.
Max replies: "Why don't you ask the Priest?"
So Jack goes up the Priest and asks: "Priest, may I smoke while I pray?"
Priest says: "No, my son, you may not, that's utter disrespect to our religion."
Jack goes up and tells his friend what the good Priest told him.
Max says: "I'm not surprised. You asked the wrong question. Let me try."
And so, Max goes up the Priest and asks: "Priest, may I pray while I smoke."
To which the Priest eagerly replies: "By all means my son, by all means."

—Anonymous

---

7 C's

In any business environment, adherence to the 7 C's and the 4 S's helps the sender in transmitting the message with ease and accuracy. Let us first take a look at the 7 C's:

1. **Credibility.** If the sender can establish credibility, the receiver has no problems in accepting statement. Establishing credibility is not the outcome of a one-shot statement. It is a long-drawn out process in which the receiver, through constant interaction with the sender respects credibility and is willing to accept the statements as being truthful and honest.

    Builds trust

2. **Courtesy.** Once the credibility of the sender has been established, attempts should be made at being courteous in the expression. In the

Improves relationships

business world, almost everything starts with and ends in courtesy. Much can be accomplished if tact, diplomacy and appreciation are woven in the message.

Example

> **Type I Rohini:** "You can never do things right. Try working on this project. If you are lucky you may not have to redo it."
>
> **Type 2 Rohini:** "This is an interesting project. Do you think you would be able to do it? I know last time something went wrong with the project, but everyone makes mistakes. Suppose we sat down and discussed it threadbare? I'm sure you would be able to do wonders."

The two statements convey totally different impressions. While the first statement is more accusative, the second is more tactful and appreciative of the efforts put in by the receiver at an earlier stage. The crux of the message in both the statements is the same: You want an individual within an organisation to undertake a project. The manner in which it is stated brings about a difference in approach. Further, expressions that might hurt or cause mental pain to the receiver should, as far as possible, be ignored. For this it becomes essential that the "I"-attitude be discarded in favour of the "you"-attitude. Development of interest in the "you" will perforce make the other individual also see the point of view of the other. At the time of emphasising the "you-attitude", only the positive and pleasant "you-issues" should be considered. If it is being used as a corrective measure, then the results are not going to be very positive or encouraging.

3. **Clarity.** Absolute clarity of ideas adds much to the meaning of the message. The first stage is clarity in the mind of the sender. The next stage is the transmission of the message in a manner which

Makes comprehension easier

makes it simple for the receiver to comprehend. As far as possible, simple language and easy sentence constructions should be used, which are not difficult for the receiver to grasp.

4. **Correctness.** At the time of encoding, the sender should ensure that knowledge of the receiver is comprehensive. The level of knowledge,

Builds confidence

educational background and status of the decoder help the encoder in formulating the message. In case there is any discrepancy between the usage and comprehension of terms, miscommunication can arise. If the sender decides to back up communication with facts and figures, there should be accuracy in stating the same. A situation in which the listener is forced to check the presented facts and figures should not arise. Finally, the usage of terms should be non-discriminatory, e.g. the general concept is that women should be addressed for their physical appearance whereas men for their mental abilities. This, however, is a stereotype and at the time of addressing or praising members of both the sexes, the attributes assigned should be the same; and similarly for occupational references. In the business world almost all professions are treated with respect. Addressing one individual for competence in profession but neglecting the other on this score because of a so-called 'inferior' profession alienates the listener from the sender.

5. **Consistency.** The approach to communication should, as far as possible, be consistent. There should not be too many ups and downs that might lead to confusion in the mind of the receiver. If a certain stand has been taken, it should

Introduces stability

be observed without there being situations in which the receiver is left groping for the actual content or meaning. If the sender desires to bring about a change in understanding the shift should be gradual and not hard for the receiver to comprehend.

6. **Concreteness.** Concrete and specific expressions are to be preferred in favour of vague and abstract expressions. In continuation of the point on correctness, the facts and figures presented should be specific. Abstractions or abstract statements

Reinforces confidence

can cloud the mind of the sender. Instead of stating: "There has been a tremendous escalation in the sales figure", suppose the sender made the following statement: "There has been an escalation in the sales figures by almost 50 per cent as compared to last year." The receiver is more apt to listen and comprehend the factual details.

7. **Conciseness.** The message to be communicated should be as brief and concise as possible. Weighty language definitely sounds impressive but people would be suitably impressed into doing precisely nothing. As far as possible, only

Saves time

simple and brief statements should be made. Excessive information can also sway the receiver into either a wrong direction or into inaction. Quantum of information should be just right, neither too much nor too little. For example,

In most cases it has been seen that the date of the policy...

Usually the policy date...

In the first example, the statement is long and convoluted. However, the second example is crisp, concise and to the point.

C's	Relevance
Credibility	Builds trust
Courtesy	Improves relationships
Clarity	Makes comprehension easier
Correctness	Builds confidence
Consistency	Introduces stability
Concreteness	Reinforces confidence
Conciseness	Saves time

Exhibit 1.5   7 C's.

4 S's

"Put it to them briefly, so they will read it;
clearly, so they will appreciate it;
picturesquely, so they will remember it; and, above all,
accurately, so they will be guided by its light."   —Joseph Pulitzer

An understanding of the 4 S's is equally important.

1. **Shortness.** "Brevity is the soul of wit," it is said. The same can be said about communication. If the message can be made brief, and

    Economises

    verbosity done away with, then transmission and comprehension of messages is going to be faster and more effective. Flooding messages with high sounding words does not create an impact. Many people harbour a misconception that they can actually impress the receiver, if they carry on their expeditious travails. Little do they realise how much they have lost as the receiver has spent a major chunk of time in trying to decipher the actual meaning of the message.

2. **Simplicity.** Simplicity both in the usage of words and ideas reveals

    Impresses

    clarity in the thinking process. It is normally a tendency that when an individual is confused that there is attempt to use equally confusing strategies to lead the receiver in a maze. Reveal clarity in the thinking process by using simple terminology and equally simple concepts.

3. **Strength.** The strength of a message emanates from the credibility

    Convinces

    of the sender. If the sender believes in a message that is to be transmitted, there is bound to be strength and conviction in the statements made. Half-hearted statements or utterances that the sender does not believe in add a touch of falsehood to the entire communication process.

4. **Sincerity.** A sincere approach to an issue is clearly evident to the receiver. If the sender is genuine, it will be reflected in the manner of communication. Suppose there is a small element of deceit involved in the interaction or on the part of the sender. If the receiver is keen and observant, he/she will be able to sense the make-believe situation and, business transactions, even if going full swing, would not materialise.

> Appeals

Note: Apply the 7 C's and 4 S's to business contexts to achieve greater ease and accuracy in communication.

S's	Relevance
Shortness	Economises
Simplicity	Impresses
Strength	Convinces
Sincerity	Appeals

Exhibit 1.6   4 S's.

SUMMARY

Communication is a two-way process in which there is an exchange and progression of ideas towards a mutually accepted direction or goal.

The sender, according to his/her ideas, behaviour pattern and intention, selects a message, encodes it, and transmits it to the receiver through a medium—be it oral, written or non-verbal. The receiver decodes it and gives an internal response to the perceived message.

The sender, if he/she desires to control communication, has to chalk out strategies by which the receiver is led to agree to the goal.

All of the above activities require effective communication skills.

With reference to an organisation, communication can be internal or external. Depending on your position in the communication cycle and the organization's hierarchy, internal communication can be vertical, horizontal/lateral or diagonal.

There are both advantages and disadvantages in oral and written communication.

The 7 C's and the 4 S's help the sender in transmitting the message with ease and accuracy.

CHECKLIST

Do's	Don'ts
Format the message in accordance with the receiver's expectations	Communicate without a well-defined goal
Choose the right medium for your message	Overlook the disadvantages, rules and regulations in the choice of a particular medium
Solicit feedback	Provide or seek ill-timed feedback
Use electronic media, share information, form more lateral communication networks within an organisation	Maximize distortion of the message by fragmenting the message or by increasing the number of communicators
Use channels that help bind the superior to the subordinate	Encouraging grapevine, rumor, gossip
Choose your words carefully	Be careless with tone and voice modulation
Formulate a written message with care	Use the written medium where immediacy of interaction is required
Appreciate people's different personalities while communicating	Use one-size-fits-all communication approach
Respond to the message	React to the message
Adhere to the 7 C's and 4 S's	Use a language and style that violates the principles of communication

RAPID REVIEW

A. Pick Your Choice

1. The response received to a message is called
    (a) encoding   (b) channel   (c) feedback
2. Very often, the
    (a) loud   (b) non-verbal   (c) written
    message is more important than the verbal one.
3. Effective communication
    (a) takes up a lot of time   (b) saves time   (c) is a waste of time
4. Communication network in any organisation is
    (a) internal and external   (b) verbal and written;
    (c) oral and non-verbal
5. Listener pays heed to the verbal content
    (a) 7%   (b) 38%   (c) 55% of the time
6. Body language is
    (a) structured   (b) faked   (c) involuntary

7. Message is the
   (a) raw   (b) structured   (c) encoded
   idea transmitted by the sender.
8. (a) Ethnomethodolists   (b) Communicators
   (c) Researchers
   list seven aspects in the turn taking system.
9. Ability to communicate effectively
   (a) is inborn   (b) can be developed
   (c) cannot be developed
10. Upward and downward flow of messages constitute
    (a) vertical communication
    (b) horizontal communication
    (c) diagonal communication

B. Match the Following

A	B
1. Feedback	(a) Involuntary
2. Cues and signals	(b) Cyclical
3. Vertical communication	(c) Upward and downward
4. Horizontal	(d) Non-interactive
5. Body language	(e) Between peers
6. Voice articulation	(f) Territory/Zone
7. Proxemics	(g) 55%
8. Non-verbal communication	(h) Given by the receiver
9. Written communication	(i) Help in processing communication
10. Process of communication	(j) 38%

C. True or False

1. Feedback must always be carefully interpreted.
2. Communication is the exchange of ideas.
3. The encoder is the receiver of ideas.
4. Input is another word for channel.
5. Encoding is the process of interpreting the message.
6. Feedback is the message sent by the decoder to the encoder.
7. The vertical channel of communication is used much more frequently in most organisations than the horizontal channel.

8. Communication is the transmission of verbal and non-verbal ideas, feelings and attitudes that produce a response.
9. The channels of communication are vertical, horizontal and diagonal.
10. The receiver and the decoder are one and the same person.

Answers

A. 1. (c) 2. (b) 3. (b) 4. (a) 5. (a) 6. (c) 7. (c) 8. (a) 9. (b) 10. (a)

B. 1. (h) 2. (i) 3. (c) 4. (e) 5. (g) 6. (j) 7. (f) 8. (a) 9. (d) 10. (b)

C. 1. True   2. True   3. False   4. False   5. False
      6. True   7. True   8. False   9. True   10. True

QUESTIONS FOR DISCUSSION

1. What happens when a message is sent and received?
2. The role of the sender is tough as he/she necessarily needs to adhere to certain stages for the completion of his/her goal. Briefly discuss these stages.
3. What is a turn taking system? What is its relevance to the entire communication process?
4. Specify the different types of communication. Which type is the most common and which has the greatest impact and why?
5. What is oral communication? What factors need to be kept in mind at the time of formulation of the message?
6. Define proxemics. How does it help in the comprehension of the message?
7. Compare and contrast oral and non-verbal communication.
8. Classify and elucidate the different channels of communication.
9. What is the I-attitude? What are the ways in which correctness can be observed while formulating a message?
10. How important are credibility and conviction to the reception of the message?

EXERCISES

1. Indicate the process of communication with a simple drawing. Label all parts.
2. Switch on your favourite channel on TV and play it on mute. Try to understand the message being transmitted. List at least ten non-verbal gestures that helped you to comprehend the message.
3. Divide the class into two. One group synchronises words, expressions and voice modulations while the other concentrates only on words. On the

basis of the exercise examine the question, "Is how you say something as important as what you have to say?"

4. As an observer dispassionately give this advice to five students you select: "If you have a message to transmit—simply state it." Carefully observe the effect of this piece of advice on five receivers. Note down your observations.

5. List ten areas in communication that you feel are the most sensitive ones and state why they are so.

6. Pick up any two students in your class. At random give feedback to both of them—positive to one and negative to the other. Note down their verbal responses and body language. Is there any difference between the responses of the two students? If yes, what is it? What strategies can be used to even out the differences?

7. Divide the section into two groups with two observers. Both the groups are numbered and further subdivided into senders and receivers. It is decided beforehand that the message transmitted in the first group is meaningful and in the second, a mere exchange of social pleasantries. Observers to list down the criteria that help them to determine the significance of the message—whether it is meaningful or being used to while away the time.

8. Observe the non-verbal cues in a piece of communication. How do these cues affect the meaning of words? What is their impact on the receiver?

9. Select two students and a message to be transmitted through three different media. List the similarities and dissimilarities between all the three media.

10. Give verbal feedback in which you yourself do not believe. Is the dichotomy between words and feelings or actions evident to the sender?

C H A P T E R

2

Oral Communication

<table>
<tr><td>

CONTENTS

- Introduction
- Features of Oral Communication
- Noise
- Barriers to Communication
- Listening
- Feedback
- Telephonic Messages

</td><td>

LEARNINGS

After reading this chapter you should be able to:

➢ Use IMPRESS for effective communication

➢ Understand the barriers to communication

➢ Learn ways of overcoming barriers to communication

➢ Reflect on your role as sender and receiver

➢ Learn to listen and give appropriate feedback

➢ Strategise communication to ensure effectiveness in the process

➢ Know how to effectively communicate with technology

</td></tr>
</table>

KEYWORDS

Barriers, Confirmatory Feedback, Corrective Feedback, Decoding, Empathy, Good Listening, "I" Attitude, IMPRESS, Internal Response, Physical Noise, Psychological Noise, Telephonic Talk

INTRODUCTION

> "To speak and to speak well are two things. A fool may talk but a wise
> man speaks."
> —Ben Jonson

Communication is a composite of speaking and listening. Honing skills in both these areas is absolutely essential if the communicator wishes to impress the receiver. The initial impact is made by the speaking abilities of the sender. However, it is the accurate listening which ensures well-defined responses and effective communication. If the overall effectiveness of these two components is considered, it would be seen that the ability to listen rather than to speak fluently creates a better impression.

FEATURES OF ORAL COMMUNICATION

**TOPIC
OBJECTIVES**
Define communication using
IMPRESS Identify the source of
noise in communication

The two activities, viz., speaking and listening, cannot be segregated. Both are closely intertwined and an overall impact is created if both these skills are used effectively. Let us use the word "IMPRESS" as an acronym to understand the basic features of communication or concept which, if once understood, would definitely help us to impress the co-interactant.

I—Idea. The first step in the process of communication is to decide on the idea to be communicated. There may be a host of ideas flitting through the mind of the sender. Depending on the situation and the receiver, the speaker selects the idea best suited to the occasion and audience.

M—Message. Once the idea has been selected, it is garbed in a language that is comprehensible to the receiver. The encoding of the message is done keeping a number of factors in mind. What is it that needs to be stated? What is the language that is going to be understood by the receiver? Does the idea necessarily pertain to the interests of the receiver? What is it that the receiver actually needs to know? Framing of the message, if done (keeping answers to these questions in mind), will definitely create an impact on the receiver.

P—Pause/Paragraphs. The significance of pauses cannot be underestimated. Pauses should be juxtaposed at just the right minute so that the receiver can assimilate the impact of the message. The use of pauses can be best understood in the context of a presentation. The presenter should, at the time of making a presentation, use this device suitably. Excessive use of this technique can make the presentation boring and monotonous. The right use of pauses actually stimulates the audience. The impact is often so great and forceful that the receivers actually lean forward in their chairs when the presenter pauses, as if urging to resume the presentation. This technique, in the course of the interaction, lasts for barely a few seconds. However, the impact is long and meaningful. In written communication, pauses get translated into commas. If the decision to use a certain number of commas in a paragraphs is right and the division of points in paragraphs is also correct, then written communication becomes meaningful and creates a positive impression.

Note: The right use of pauses and punctuations aid the intended meaning of the message.

R—Receiver. The receiver is the most important person in the process of communication who could, also prove to be the most difficult. In order to draw the attention of the recipient, it is imperative that there be an extra plus to retain interest. To satisfy this criterion the sender should address the needs and expectations of the receiver. Formulating the statements according to a mutually accepted goal is a good way of drawing and retaining interest and attention.

E—Empathy. In communication, empathy should be used to help understand the other individual, the strategies that are adopted and the responses given at a particular moment. It would be worthwhile to note that all communication is situation bound. The same individual in two different situations may use the same words but intention may be totally different. The exact meaning of an utterance can be gauged when we literally put ourselves in the shoes of the other person and try to understand the situation from the perspective of the sender.

Each individual, as a sender has, what we refer to as, a 'logic bubble' that enables formulation of message/s in a particular order. The same holds true for the receiver or the listener. The higher the *empathy* between them, the greater the overlap in the logic bubble, and the level of understanding and more the receptivity to messages and ideas. Empathy needs to be differentiated from, "sympathy", which is different in connotation. Sympathy is placing the self on a higher pedestal and viewing the other in a sympathetic light.

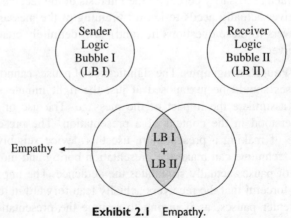

Exhibit 2.1   Empathy.

S—Sender. The communication process hinges on the sender who initiates the interaction and brings forth ideas and concepts to be shared with the receiver. The role of the sender is critical as the success or failure of interaction depends on the strategies adopted to transmit the message. A cautious sender will understand that there is a difference between the mental frames of the interactants. Such a difference can be a result of discrepancy in interpretation of words, perception of reality, and attitudes, opinions and emotions. Message, if formulated, with awareness along these areas, is sure to bring success to the sender in message receptivity.

S—Security check. Effective communication necessitates that the receiver listens carefully to the utterances of the sender so that the end results are positive. The primary rule is: *never be in a rush to commence communication.* Sufficient time and effort should go into formulating the message. Suppose the sender wishes to communicate five points. The sequencing and necessary substantiation of points with facts and figures should be done prior to the actual beginning of the communication process. This would build authenticity in the message and eliminate all possibilities of errors.

To sum up, the sender, in order to impress the receiver should, in the beginning have an idea encoded in the form of a message. At the time of encoding, a thorough security check is done to ascertain that all points have been included in a desired order. The message is then transmitted to the receiver with the required voice articulations and pauses so as to heighten the impact. Finally, the response of the receiver is viewed empathetically. Once all these factors have been addressed, it proves easy to prevail upon the receiver.

There could, however, be moments when, in spite of efforts being made to make the interaction informative and meaningful, all communication links fall apart and the process ends in a meaningless rumble of words and sounds. This disturbing or distracting factor is what we refer to as *Noise*. This may be on the part of the sender or the receiver and can be voluntary or involuntary.

Warning! Never rush to send a message without having taken the time and trouble to formulate it!

NOISE

TOPIC OBJECTIVES
Identify factors creating noise
Learn techniques for minimizing noise

"I have long held the opinion that the amount of noise that anyone can bear undisturbed stands in inverse proportion to his mental capacity and therefore be regarded as a pretty fair measure of it."
—Arthur Schopenhauer

Noise can be defined as a physical sound or a mental disturbance that disrupts the flow of communication as the sender or the receiver perforce gets distracted by it. According to this definition, noise can be classified into two categories:

1. Physical   2. Psychological

Physical Noise

Physical noise is that sound which emanates from the surroundings and hampers the listening process. For example, while speaking on the telephone, disturbances may hinder the smooth transmission of message or just at the time when the sender wishes to transmit an important point, there may be an undesired telephonic sound. The question is, how does one address noise? Physical noise is not all that difficult to manage and at the time of communication can be done away with. For instance, the practice followed by companies is to maintain sound-proof rooms for discussion.

Psychological Noise

While care may be taken to eliminate possibilities of physical noise, problems arise at the time when psychological noise plagues either the sender or the receiver. Whenever there is psychological noise, it results in (un)welcome ideas or thoughts crowding the mind, which are of more relevance than the ensuing communication to either of the participants. Listening, as a result, is hampered and responses are not well-formulated. Some of the common forms of noise are mental turbulence, preoccupation, ego hang-ups, anxiety, tiredness, pre-conceived ideas and notions. These are mostly involuntary and no specific cause can be assigned to them.

Let us take the example of a young married couple with a new born baby. If the child is unwell, it maybe difficult for either of the parents to concentrate at work.

It is important to gradually develop awareness of noise generating factors. To further elaborate, if the sender is aware of the mental turmoil and knows that it would disturb the listening process he/she may decide to jot down points on a piece of paper and also jot down points or comments of the receiver. On the other hand, the receiver may also be distracted by psychological noise. Outward manifestations of this disturbance can be in the form of restless tapping on the table, looking in other direction, shifting restlessly, changing positions, etc. These are just some of the means through which the sender can gauge the presence of psychological noise in the mind of the receiver. To make more meaningful and successful communication, the sender should attempt to secure the attention of the receiver. This can be done by entering into a question/answer session or asking for advice. Both these devices will, to a great extent, remove the element of psychological noise.

Types	Causative factors	Remedies
Physical	Disturbances and distractions in the environment	Ensuring that all channels are clear and free of noise
Psychological	Mental turbulence, preoccupation, ego hang-ups, anxiety, tiredness, preconceived ideas and notions	Entering into Question/Answer sessions, securing advice

Exhibit 2.2   Noise.

BARRIERS TO COMMUNICATION

"To be able to ask a question clearly is two-thirds of the way to getting it answered."
—John Ruskin

TOPIC OBJECTIVES
Distinguish various barriers to communication
Discuss rules and remedies that help overcome barriers

An activity as complex as communication, is bound to suffer from setbacks if conditions emerge that are contrary to the smooth functioning of the process. They are referred to as **barriers** for they create impediments in the progress of the interaction. Identification of these barriers is crucial. According to the role observed by the two participants, let us categorise the barriers as:

- Sender-oriented
- Receiver-oriented

Sender-Oriented Barriers

Sender-oriented barriers can be voluntary or involuntary. At any cost, efforts should be made on the part of the sender to identify and remove them. If the interaction gives rise to barriers, communication comes to a grinding halt. Some of the sender-oriented barriers are as follows:

1. **Badly expressed message.** Not being well-versed in the topic under discussion can create problems of this nature. The sender

   Concrete ideas and well structured message

   may not be able to structure ideas accurately and efficiently. What he/she wishes to say and what is finally stated may not be the same. The discrepancy emerges as soon as the words are uttered. In fact, one of the important criterion at the time of initialising a piece of communication is that ideas should be concrete and the message well structured. The receiver should not feel that the interaction is a waste of time. The moment this feeling crops up, the listener totally tunes off and the process of effective communication ceases.

Let us consider the example of Ram, a young graduate, who has been called for an interview in a prestigious Corporate house. The interviewer asks Ram to tell the panel something about himself. Ram, unprepared for the question, blurts out school and college details, some pleasant and some unpleasant. His statements are punctuated with, "I am sorry", "No, this is not what I meant!".

The overall impact is negative!

Go prepared for any meaningful interaction!

2. **Loss in transmission.** This is a very minor issue, but is one that gains in magnitude when it leads to inability in transmitting the actual message. Once again, if the choice of the channel or medium is not right, the impact of the message is lost. This is mostly a physical noise. The responsibility lies with the sender, to ensure that all channels are free of noise before commencing communication.

Correct choice of medium/ channel

3. **Semantic problem.** High and big sounding words definitely look and sound impressive. But if the receiver is not able to comprehend the impact of these words, or if they sound 'Greek' or 'Latin', the entire exercise of communication proves futile. This problem could arise in the interpretation of the words or overall meaning of the message. This barrier is also related to the understanding of the intention behind a particular statement. For instance, the sanctity associated with the word "white" for the sender may be violated when the receiver uses it in a careless fashion. The idiosyncrasies of the receiver should be well understood by the sender if barriers are to be avoided. The look on the face of the listener should be sufficient to warn the sender that limits have been crossed or the message has been misunderstood.

Simple words and accurate understanding of intention

Mind, free of bias

4. **Over/Under-communication.**

> Coolidge was known for his terse speech and reticence. A woman bet her friend that she could get Coolidge to speak to her, which was something he was reluctant to do. She went up to him and said: "Hello, Mr. President, I bet my friend that I could get you to say three words to me." "You lose," Coolidge replied dryly, and walked away.
> —Unknown

As stated in Chapter 1, the quantum of communication should be just right. Neither should there be excess information nor should it be too scanty. Excess information may confuse the receiver as to the exact import of the message, and scanty information will create the need to grope for the actual intent of the message. The sender should, as far as possible, try to get the profile of the receiver so that a mental assessment can be done on how much material is needed and how much can be done away with. Suppose the sender begins with information already available with the receiver, the latter may lose interest as it is a mere repetition of what is already known. By the time the sender reaches the core of the message the receiver is tuned off.

Quantum of information should be right

JAM: Is your message just right? Is there too much of information to throw your reader off?

5. **'I'-Attitude.** Imagine a piece of communication that begins and ends with the pronoun "I". How tedious it is going to be for the listener to sit through the entire interaction. If the sender starts every sentence with "I", it gradually leads to what is referred to as the *I-syndrome*. This "I-centric" individual will not be receptive to changes, if suggested by the receiver; for changes will go against personal biases.

Avoid I-attitude

6. **Prejudices.** Starting any piece of communication with a bias or know-it-all attitude can prove to be quite detrimental to the communication process. Though easier said than done, when communication commences, all sorts of prejudices should be done away with, and the mind should be free of bias. This will enable the sender to formulate the message, keeping only the receiver and communication needs in mind. Thoughts like "Last time he/she said this..." or "Last time he/she did this..." or "He/she belongs to this group..." can totally warp the formulation of the message. This barrier can also be extended to the receiver. If the respondent begins with prejudices in mind, there will be inability to listen or understand the intent of the message. The messages will be understood with prejudices, if any, that a receiver harbours against the sender.

Mind, free of bias

Warning! Avoid complicated 'Greek and Latin' messages if you want to communicate effectively!

Participant	Barrier	Causative factors	Remedies
Sender/Encoder/ Speaker	1. Loss in impact	Badly expressed message	Think prior to speaking
	2. Ineffective grasp of message	Loss in transmission	Remove physical noise
	3. Misunderstood statements	Semantic problem	Use simple language
	4. Groping for the right message	Over/Under communication	Make the quantum of communication just right
	5. Lack of collaborative effort	"I-attitude"	Minimise usage of "I"
	6. Biased communication	Prejudices	Formulate messages with an open mind

Exhibit 2.3 Sender-oriented barriers.

Rules for overcoming sender-oriented barriers

These barriers are not insurmountable. Care and constant practice on the part of the sender can remove them. Some of the rules for overcoming sender-oriented barriers are as follows:

1. **Plan and clarify ideas.** Ideas should be carefully formulated/ thought out before beginning any kind of communication. This can be done by following a few steps. Primary among them is to test thinking by communicating with peers and colleagues. It is said that two minds are always better than one. Ideas, when discussed aloud with another person, necessarily take on a shape and form. Errors of logic, if any, get sorted out. In this process the thoughts of others can also be collated and incorporated to make the communication richer and more fruitful. As these steps require pre-planning and extra time, the sender should be highly motivated. Unless there is sufficient motivation, the sender will not spend extra hours in planning the message and clarifying it by facilitating discussions with other members in the organisation.

   > Test thinking, discuss, collate and pre-plan

2. **Create a climate of trust and confidence.** In order to win the trust and confidence of the receiver, the sender has to put in extra effort through which the trust and confidence of the recipient is won. This is what we normally refer to as establishing sender credibility. If the receiver is convinced that the sender has good intention and best interests at heart, there will be a willingness to pay attention to all that is being said and an attempt will be made to grasp the import and intent of the message.

   > Empathise

3. **Time your message carefully.** Different occasions and hours necessitate a variation in the encoding of the message. The sender has to be careful of the time *when* and the place *where* communication commences. As all communication is situation bound, a statement made at an incorrect moment, or a wrong place can stimulate an undesired response. The most prudent step is to measure the import of the message in relation to the situation and then impart it.

   > Keep the 'where' and 'when' in mind

4. **Reinforce words with action.** Whatever statements are made, should be reinforced by action on the part of the sender. The receiver should not feel that there are two codes at play, one for transmittal and the other for action. If there is harmony between the two, the decoder is mentally at peace, for the grasp is more accurate and thorough.

   > Harmonise words and actions

5. **Communicate efficiently.** The effectiveness of the communication can be ascertained through feedback provided by the receiver who is also wary when requested for feedback. Soliciting and receiving feedback is the simplest and surest way of removing any barriers that might crop up in the course of communication as a result of either over-communication or a semantic problem.

> Solicit feedback

Once all barriers to communication have been overcome, communication, it can be said, has been *meaningful* and *purposeful*.

Note: To help plan for your message, test your ideas on peers and colleagues.

Receiver-Oriented Barriers

The receiver too can be guilty of erecting barriers in the course of the interaction. Although the role is passive in the initial phase, it gets activated once assimilation and absorption of information begins to take place. He/she is equally to blame if the situation goes awry and communication comes to a stop, or there is miscommunication. Some of the receiver-oriented barriers are as follows:

> Jot down points

1. **Poor retention.** Retention is extremely important during interaction. If the receiver has poor retention capability, the message will probably get lost in the course of the proceeds. There will be no connection between what was said initially and what is being said now. The receiver may counter statements instead of seeking clarifications that may lead to clamping on the part of the sender. If the decoder feels that retention is not good, a judicious strategy is to jot down points. It does not project a poor image. On the contrary, it shows conscientiousness to get the message right.

   > Encourage juniors to come up with ideas and listen

2. **Inattentive listening.** The mind has its own way of functioning. It is very difficult to exercise control over the mind. Listening is more an exercise in controlling the mind and exercising it to assimilate messages. The errors in listening arise primarily because the receiver is either not interested in what is being said, or has other things to concentrate on. The art of listening is an exercise in concentration. If this skill can be honed, barriers to communication will not be erected.

   > Improve concentration

3. **Tendency to evaluate.** Being judgemental and evaluative can both lead to miscommunication. Remember, the mind cannot perform two activities at the same time. If it is evaluating, listening cannot take place. Evaluation

   > Delay evaluation

should always be a sequel to the listening process. It cannot be done simultaneously with listening. If the listener begins to mentally pronounce judgements as soon as the speaker begins to speak, a major part of the content is missed out on. Responses, then are either incorrect or reflect misunderstanding.

4. **Interests and attitudes.** "I am not interested in what you are saying" or "My interest lies in other areas". Starting any piece of communication with this kind of indifference can

| Develop interest |

thwart any attempts at communication. Fixed notions of this kind should be dispensed with. It is not possible to be interested in all that is being said. But to start any communication with this notion is hazardous.

5. **Conflicting information.** Dichotomy in the information that the receiver possesses and the one which is being transmitted can create confusion and result in miscommunication. Conflict

| Confirm with feedback, clarify |

between the existing information and fresh one results in elimination of the latter unless the receiver is cautious and verifies with the sender the reliability and validity of the message. The sender should convince the receiver that whatever is now being said is correct and relevant to further proceedings.

Warning! If you are not able to convince the receiver or capture interest, you have entered into a conflict zone!

6. **Differing status and position.** Position in the organisational hierarchy is no criterion to determine the strength of ideas and issues. Rejecting the proposal of a subordinate or

| Encourage juniors to come up with ideas and listen |

harbouring a misconception that a junior cannot come up with a "eureka" concept is not right. In fact, many companies have started encouraging youngsters to come up with ideas/solutions to particular problems. These ideas are then discussed among the senior managers and their validity is ascertained keeping the workings and the constraints of the company in mind. The basic purpose of this upward traversing of ideas is that fresh and innovative minds can come up with unique solutions. If an individual has been working in a particular company for some years, it is natural that

According to one manager, "When I go to tell my boss that I have a problem and what I've done with that problem, there is never any feedback like 'that was a good thing to do'; or 'not bad, I think I would add this other aspect'. The boss only states 'here are the things you have to do', with no comment on what the manager has done. This could either indicate lack of confidence in the subordinate's ideas or might indicate that the boss has confidence only in his/her own ideas, and does not wish to encourage new ideas.

the mind gets conditioned in a particular manner. Challenging newcomers to innovate as a part of company policy takes care of ego problems that may arise if this is not the accepted norm.

7. **Resistance to change.** Fixed ideas, coupled with an unwillingness to change or discuss, hampers listening and results in

> Be flexible

miscommunication. Novae concepts that require discussion before they can really materialise, if rebuked, fall flat. The onus lies directly on the receiver who is unreceptive and unwilling to change. People with dogmatic opinions and views prove to be very poor communicators and erect maximum barriers.

8. **Refutations and arguments.** Refutations and arguments are negative in nature. Trying to communicate with the sender on the premise that

> Enter into healthy discussions

refutations and arguments can yield fruitful results would prove to be futile. Communication is a process in which the sender and the receiver are at the same level. The minute refutations or arguments begin, there is a shift in balance between the two participants, after which the receiver moves to a perceived higher position while the sender remains at the same level. In case there are some contradictions that need to be resolved, discussion is the right way to approach. Sequential process to be followed should be listening to the views of the other, trying to understand or at least showing that there has been understanding, and appreciation and, finally, positing own views. The strategy adopted should not make the sender feel small or slighted.

JAM: Do you still continue to evaluate **and** listen? Are you resistant to change?

Participant	Barrier	Causative factors	Remedies
Receiver/ Decoder/ Listener	1. Dichotomy in reception and comprehension	Poor retention	Jot down points
	2. Partial grasp of topic	Inattentive listening	Keep the mind open
	3. Distancing from the speaker	Tendency to evaluate	Delay evaluation
	4. Lack of interest	Differences in interests and attitudes	Find an area of interest
	5. Mental turbulence	Conflicting information	Check reliability and validity
	6. Superior attitude	Differing status/Position/ Self-experience	Listen to ideas
	7. Mental block	Resistance to change	Be open to change
	8. Lack of provision of correct feedback	Refutations and arguments	Enter into healthy discussions

Exhibit 2.4 Receiver-oriented barriers.

Most of the barriers that are receiver-oriented are best overcome by improving listening skills and learning strategies of giving feedback. While the sender definitely facilitates communication, it cannot be termed as a one-man show. The process is also of interest to the receiver. Before we proceed to take a look at decoding and giving a response, let us concentrate on the fundamental stage of the communication process,that is, listening.

Note: The receiver is also responsible for enabling effective communication.

LISTENING

TOPIC OBJECTIVES

Understand the process of listening

Identify the essentials for and deterrents to listening

"The older I grow the more I listen to people who don't talk much."   —Germain G. Glien

Listening can be defined as the accurate perception of what is being communicated. Accuracy, it may be stated, is never 100 per cent. Because of the differing perceptions of individuals, there are sure to be variations in understanding the intent of the message. The process of listening is two-fold:

1. Decoding
2. Giving an internal response to perceived message.

Decoding

The process of decoding begins as soon as the message reaches the receiver. While the mind is literally open for message receptivity the question is how much of the information he/she decides to use or considers as relevant is contingent upon perception of the message. Words and statements are best understood when there is an understanding of the context. If the sender has been careful, the usage of terms will be easily comprehensible to the receiver. However, if certain links have been missed out on in the belief that the receiver would be familiar with them, the decoding process suffers. The decoder views the utterances from a personal perspective and then gives a response.

Internal response to perceived message

Moving on the presumption that the decoding has been accurate or exactly as desired by the sender, communication progresses to the second stage, that is, giving an internal response to perceived message. This would entail the stage where the receiver will probably try to weigh the utterance with respect to his/her own needs and expectations. If there is harmony between the two, the response is going to be well formulated and conducive to the growth of communication.

In this two tier process of listening there are three embedded steps that help in information assimilation.

1. Levelling
2. Sharpening
3. Assimilation

Information or messages collect in the mind of the receiver like a garbage heap. The mind automatically sifts through the material and picks up areas or ideas on which it would prefer to focus. These would pertain to the level of interest and expectations of the receiver. Finally, it assimilates only those issues that it thinks are of direct relevance to it.

Note: Decoding of the message is dependent on the receiver's perceptions.

Essentials for Good Listening

Listening is a skill that needs to be mastered. Everyone cannot be a good listener. One of the primary essentials for developing good listening skills is

| Ability to concentrate |

cultivation of a positive attitude. It is difficult to listen objectively to what the other person is saying if listening begins on a negative note. A positive inclination enables the receiver to be open to suggestions and statements made by the sender. A closed mind and unwillingness to listen to reason or ideas that suggest a deviation from the norm, lead to an unreceptive attitude.

Developing a positive stance alone will not suffice. It needs to be coupled with the ability to concentrate. The mind possesses tremendous capacity to swing in more than one direction. Control needs to be exercised

| Positive attitude |

to prevent mental moves in unwarranted directions. The entire process can be compared to meditation. The same degree of rigour and concentration needs to be applied. The reason for discrepancy in sender intent and receiver grasp can be explained scientifically. The speaking capacity of an individual is approximately 180 to 250 words per minute. The capacity of the individual to process words is approximately 400 to 600 words per minute. If there is a small deviation or digression on the part of either the sender or the listener, the mind takes a swing. By the time it resumes its original position, the sender has already transmitted a major chunk of the message. Hence, arise errors in communication leading to what is commonly referred to as "miscommunication". If by extreme discipline the receiver can listen attentively, these errors would be minimised.

However, there can be instances when the mind gets exhausted and stops paying attention. In such instances a prudent move will be to indulge

| Enter into Question-Answer sessions |

| Maintain eye contact |

in question-answer sequences. When a recipient directly asks a question, the normal tendency of the sender is to look deep in the eyes of the person and respond. Under the direct gaze of the sender it is very difficult for the mind to stray. Much is revealed as well as concealed by the eyes. If the eyes are subject to the scrutiny of the sender, it is tough for the listener to doze off or stray. This technique is a very useful one as it stalls errors in the listening process.

Note: Question and answer sessions prompt the receiver to stay alert.

The body language at the time of listening should also be conducive to the communication process. Leaning back or sitting slumped in the chair are gestures through which the listener increases the distance from the sender. If an upright position or a slight lean in the chair is sported the receiver narrows the distance. Chances are high that there will be an improvement in the listening.

> *Conducive body posture*

JAM: Is your body communicating the right message?

Essentials	Resultant features
Positive attitude	Acceptance
Concentration	Receptivity
Question-answer sequence	Concentration
Direct eye contact	Direct connect
Conducive body posture	Attention

Exhibit 2.5   Essentials for good listening.

Deterrents to the Listening Process

Listening is a very difficult process. It does not take much effort to lose track of what the sender is trying to communicate. Awareness of the deterrents to the listening process heightens consciousness on the part of the receiver of the errors that may crop during the interaction. Some of the deterrents to the listening process are now described:

Ego. The biggest stumbling block in the process of communication is the *ego.* Superiority complex coupled with the desire to suppress the other or force to listen, totally warps the listening process. All ideas or concepts to be discussed are bypassed, ignored or not listened to. The mind is closed to anything that the sender suggests if it is not in accordance with what the receiver wishes. The reason for this could be simple: the receiver considers the self as superior and is not willing to listen to the other person who is regarded as a subordinate.

> *Hone listening skills*

> Some managers can be so oblivious to the needs of others that they're almost impossible to be around with. "I'm just too good to be true. Can't take my eyes off me... At long last brains have arrived. And just thank ME I'm alive..." A bad manager who acts as if the universe was created solely for self-gratification, is only going to lose out on the rest of the team members.

Involvement with the self/preoccupation. Excessive involvement with the self leads to the centring of emotions and feelings around "I". In these situations it is difficult to listen to what the other person is trying to say. If the messages of the sender revolve round the expectations and needs of the receiver, there is higher receptivity to what is being said.

> *Look beyond the self*

All other issues pertaining to non-involvement of the self are of no consequence to the receiver.

Warning! If you wish to ascertain that your message is not rejected, you must amend your information to the needs and expectations of a self-involved reader.

Past, present and future. Excessive emphasis on completed activities in the past and anticipated results in the future leaves little time to concentrate on the message of the encoder. Past imperfect, present tense and the future (which is uncertain) act as a web. For example, if the receiver has been reprimanded for a project in the past, he/she is tense while interacting with the same individual in the present. As the concentration is on the possible repercussions in the future, there will be inability to listen attentively in the present.

> Do not get trapped in the vicious cycle of time

Fear. The biggest deterrent to the listening process is the element of fear. It alienates the receiver from the sender. Even before communication can commence, the mind of the receiver is blocked. Should or should not a personal view be posited? What is going to be the general outcome? Would he/she be viewed in a positive light? All these flood the mind. When the actual process of communication begins, the process of trying to find a solution to the problems messes up the entire process. By the time actual focus on the message begins, almost half the communication is over, and again the crucial elements have been missed out on. This deterrent is a pre-communication factor that spills into the actual process and hampers listening.

> Eliminate fear

Note: Fear can close the mind of the receiver even before communication can commence.

The familiarity trap. "I know it all" is a trap in which many of the receivers fall. Quite often conceived knowledge on a particular topic can hinder the listening process.

> Learn that there is more than you already know

The receiver may become complacent about the issue to be discussed. Closing the mind to the current proceedings merely because of the familiarity trap can create major listening errors. It should be borne in mind that even if it were the same individual repeating the same message there are sure to be additions and deletions to the original messages.

Stress. Working under stress can again create barriers to the listening process. However, stress is a variable that can have both a positive and a negative impact. There are a lot of people who cannot cope with stress and are not able to perform to the best of their abilities. Then there are others whose skills are sharpened when they are under stress and any work that they perform is always positive with extremely satisfactory results.

> Do not work under stress

Awareness of these deterrents is crucial. If the individual feels that interaction with other individuals can be hampered because of the presence of these traits, the rough edges should be trimmed to make interaction a profitable and enjoyable affair.

JAM: Are YOU aware of what deters you from better listening?

Deterrents	Behavioural patterns
Ego	Will not listen
Involvement with self	Wallow in self-sympathy
Imperfect past, present tense, and future which is uncertain	Unable to listen
Fear	Closed mind
The familiarity trap	Assured of self
Stress ... negative impact	Prone to being hyper-tense

Exhibit 2.6   Deterrents to the listening process.

FEEDBACK

TOPIC OBJECTIVES

Learn tactics of giving strategic feedback

Analyse confirmatory and corrective feedback

"Two monologues do not make a dialogue."

—Jeff Daly

Moving on the presumption that listening has been accurate, the receiver is also expected to provide feedback. This is the most important part of communication that completes the entire process. If it is missing, chances are high that interaction may be incomplete or inaccurate. A good strategy of giving feedback is to follow a three-tier process:

1. Listen carefully to what the sender is trying to communicate.
2. Repeat the crux of the message to ensure that sender intentions have been rightly understood.
3. Give a response to the message.

The second step is the most critical. At the time of interacting, the participants acknowledge the message by probably a nod of the head or a "yes". Wherein lies the assurance that whatever has been said has been understood with the same intention? The same words used in two different contexts could have two different interpretations. Moving on the assumption that a stereotyped meaning can be applied to all situations can lead to inaccuracies.

Feedback can be of two types:

1. Confirmatory
2. Corrective

Confirmatory feedback ascertains the moves and actions of the sender. Whatever is being stated is accepted and the receiver agrees to the statement. The situation is happy, as there is no scope for dissent. Both the participants are at accord with one another. Problems arise when the feedback is corrective. How should the statements be

Confirmatory feedback

formulated so that they do not offend the speaker? Words have to be picked and used carefully so that there is no misunderstanding. Chances are high that there has been miscommunication at some stage or the work input is much below expectations for which corrective feedback is being given. In these situations it is always prudent to follow any of the following steps in giving feedback.

The feedback should not be strongly worded. If it begins with a negative phrase, it will close the mind of the receiver to what is being said. He/she may wallow in self-sympathy or seethe in anger and in the process may miss out on the actual content. Feedback should start with a positive statement that shows appreciation of what has been done or an understanding of the current situation. This would keep the participant alert and more receptive to the feedback. Most of the time corrective feedback is given by superiors in the organisation. A healthy culture of establishing good relationships with subordinates can be cultivated. If the junior is convinced because of existing relationship with the senior that the latter has the best interest in mind, there will be no hostility at the time when corrective feedback is being provided. Empathy, as described earlier, is needed not only at the time of communication but should be applied throughout the interaction so that it builds or improves relationships.

| Corrective feedback |

Many a time the agenda for the feedback is not clear to the receiver. Being corrected on an issue without any clue can antagonise the interactant. The purpose for which corrective feedback is given should be spelt out right in the beginning to avoid miscommunication.

| Clarify agenda |

> Ashok was due to go on a vacation. Unfortunately, the deadline for a new project was looming near. Ashok decided to designate Ramesh, a junior research fellow, with the responsibility of completing the project report in his absence. When Ashok returned to work, a few days away from the deadline, he found that Ramesh was not even half-way through. An angry Ashok called Ramesh for a meeting. When Ramesh entered the office, Ashok flared up and yelled at him, "What is this Ramesh? This is very upsetting!

At the time when the agenda is being specified, the focus should be more on giving specific examples than speaking in the abstract, e.g. making a statement of the following nature: "Your behaviour really upsets me" does not prove to be of much help to the receiver. Instead, it can be rephrased in the following manner:

| Empathetic behaviour |

> "Your inability to hand in the project report on time caused a great deal of embarrassment to me as I was also not able to submit to the superiors on time. The end result was that we just had to shelve the meeting. Decisions concerning sanction of funds will now only be taken a week later. This means that I stop further research as there are no funds."

A number of factors emerge when feedback of this type is given. Not only does the recipient realise the fault but is also made aware of the gravity of the consequences. As great emphasis is placed on the behaviour that led to unhappy consequences the impact of feedback is greater.

Note: Structure corrective feedback by opening with appreciation and following it up with critical commentary.

In corrective feedback "I-messages" are used as it is one person correcting the other for some error in performance. Even in instances when the communication is "you-centric", it is not pleasing, as the tone is reprimanding. As stated earlier, in communication we avoid the "I-attitude" or "I-message" but at the time of giving feedback we have to make use of these messages. Further, specific examples concerning slips or errors in performance need to be provided so as to make the feedback concrete and specific. This would add to the gravity of the interaction. Specific examples relating to behaviour need to be cited to heighten the impact of the feedback.

| Use "I-messages" |

| Give specific examples |

Finally, there is a need to check for clarity of feedback. As the intention behind a statement is more important, the communicator providing feedback should check for correct comprehension of message. If the intention is misunderstood, the entire purpose of providing feedback is defeated.

| Check for clarity of understanding |

Warning! Carefully choose the words for corrective feedback! Make sure your intention is clear to your receiver!

Manner of providing feedback	Results
Empathise	More receptive
Specify agenda	Higher concentration
Describe behaviour	Greater understanding
Quote specific examples	More involvement
Concentrate on actions	Greater awareness
Use "I-messages"	Higher degree of involvement
Spell out consequences	Greater focus
Ensure clarity of understanding	Greater understanding of the situation

Exhibit 2.7   Feedback.

TELEPHONIC MESSAGES

TOPIC OBJECTIVES

Strategise while communicating via technology

Distinguish between face to face and telephonic talk

"This 'telephone' has too many shortcomings to be seriously considered as a means of communication. The device is inherently of no value to us."
—Western Union telegraph company memo, 1877

With the advancement of technology, more and more changes are being brought about in the manner of communicating. Telephones, cellulars, pagers, facsimiles, e-mails, whatsapp, sms, etc.—all give the sender the satisfaction that the communicator is 'plugged in'. Messages can reach from one corner of the world to the other almost immediately. However, these latest technological advancements do not have the advantage of face-to-face interaction.

The most common and frequently used form of technological transmission of a message is the telephone. Messages are delivered and received immediately. However, there are certain factors that need to be cognised. While direct communication does not involve any cost, telephonic messages are not cost effective. Time is definitely another important factor to be kept in mind while formulating messages. What strategies should be adopted? How should messages be formulated are just some of the queries that emerge. Many of the strategies are the same as are observed in face-to-face interaction but concentration needs to be higher as there is nothing apart from words and voice articulation to capture the attention of the receiver. In telephonic communication there is no direct eye to eye contact and there is almost no chance of deciphering the message through body language. Therefore, strategies need to be well planned at the time of conducting business communication using these technological devices. Let us take a look at some of the strategies that can be adopted by both the sender and the receiver.

> *Factors to be kept in mind— Cost, time, strategies to be adopted, voice articulation*

Note: Plan agenda and content before you make a call.

Sender-Oriented Strategies

The individual who makes the telephone call will, in this instance, be termed as the *sender* or initiator on whom rests the onus of steering the communication in a mutually accepted direction.

1. **Planning.** Identify the purpose of your call. What is it that you wish to communicate? Who is the recipient? Would the person be interested in the call? What is the time when the call is being made? Is it information that is being provided or is it a request for action? Answer to all these queries will form part of the initial process of planning. We can divide this stage into four parts: purpose, listener, content to incorporate, and organisation of the information.

   Identify purpose of call

   The purpose determines, to a large extent, the nature of audience participation. For instance, if it were to provide information, the listener will be less receptive as the role in the interaction will be passive. Another criterion for enlisting receiver support is the time when information is being shared and its relevance to the receiver. A simple statement as, "We are a new software company and I would like to tell you something about us" will probably elicit a response of the following nature, "Not right now. I am busy. Probably at a later stage you can come and see me. Fix an appointment with my secretary." The mission has fallen flat because the response is not desired or expected. Contrast this with the following statement, " I recently heard that you were looking for software professionals for..." If this statement is backed with company research and their current openings you have already won a receptive audience over to your side. Check and recheck about your listener—name and designation—and what is it that you can promise to deliver.

In the case of a request, the challenge is higher than the previous example as a greater level of participation from the receiver is solicited. Why should the request be granted? If the sender has chosen an opportune moment to float the request keeping in mind the expectations chances are steep that the request will be granted. Communication that is going to result in an inane exchange of formalities should not be attempted.

> Sangeeta needed two extra days to complete a project assigned to her. Sangeeta had no clue how to proceed as her boss was rigid and the matter was of some urgency. However, she knew that her boss was amenable to reason and had some amount of faith in the quality of work Sangeeta delivered.
>
> Sangeeta should not start her request in the following manner: "Could you possibly grant me two extra days as I have not been able to complete the project." Contrast this statement with the following message "I have been able to complete the project almost eighty per cent. I was keen to hand it over to you by tomorrow. However, at the last minute there was a virus that corrupted the entire data. I have a hard copy of it and to feed it again I would require two more days. Do you think it is possible to grant me two extra days?"

Sufficient preparation has gone into this statement and the result of it will, in all probability, be positive. Let us analyse the message step by step. Presentation of facts, keenness to complete it on time, explanation why it cannot be done, and, finally, desire to seek advice. The ball is now in the court of the receiver and on more occasions than one, there will be empathetic listening and the request will be granted. The last of these steps—seeking advice—tilts the balance in favour of the receiver by leaving the option open to agree or disagree. Prior to making the request, the sender should have collated information concerning the following: What is the urgency of the task? What will be the repercussions if the task were not accomplished? How will the receiver view the request? If the task is of extreme urgency, there is no sense in requesting for extension as the response is going to be a big NO. If the receiver were slightly flexible, small concessions may be granted, but if rigid, the request will fall flat!

Steps: Present facts, show keenness; explain why it cannot be done, seek advice

At the time of providing information or making requests, the sender should be honest in making statements. A false or incorrect utterance will automatically close all channels of further communication. For there to be precision in the dialogue questions

| Be honest and sincere |

or the points to be discussed should be jotted down in advance so that little time is wasted in thinking before making an honest statement.

Warning! Do not be ignorant of what your purpose is and who your listener might be!

Another important factor to be managed is the quantum of information. The sender should focus on one idea as it is not possible

| Quantum of information should be right |

to manage a leisurely business conversation over the telephone. Message should be brief and crisp. The timing should also be right. If it is an overseas call, the time should be checked prior to making a

call. Early in the morning, more specifically on a Monday morning or late in the evening when it is time for the office to close or Friday evening, are inopportune moments to make a call. The reason why a call should not be made on a Monday morning is that the receiver needs some time to settle down, probably issue instructions, and coordinate activities for the week. Extraneous issues at this time of the day are unimportant. Similarly, at the time when the office is about to close or all work for the day or week has been wound up, a request for a telephonic talk, which has not been solicited, will be viewed very positively.

2. **Delivering.** This stage is as important as the planning stage. There should be a paper and pencil handy so that suggestions and comments

| Start with a smile |

can be jotted down. When the sender begins to speak, there should be a smile on the face. The receiver on the other side of the telephone line will be able to hear the smile. A grumpy start to the subject is going

to put off the decoder. This is similar to face-to-face interaction. A receiver much rather prefers to interact with a sender who has a pleasant countenance than one who looks stern and rigid. The encoder should first introduce self and if it is a long distance call, must specify immediately the place of the call. If the message is urgent and personal, the same should be specified with coordinates of the caller.

Note: Time your call well, start it with a smile, and remember to introduce yourself!

At the time of delivering the message, establish rapport with the called by

| Talk of areas of common interest |

talking of areas of common interest so as to solicit the attention and cooperation of the called. Finally, in an enthusiastic voice reveal the basic purpose of making the call. Remember that the purpose should be stated in a manner that reveals a link between the interest of the caller and the called. Listen carefully to the receiver's voice and ideas. Do not interrupt in between.

As you listen to the voice, pay special attention to the tone. Does it sound bored, indifferent, annoyed or angry? The right cues should be picked up and further discussion should be modulated keeping these signals in mind.

At the need of the call paraphrase the ideas of the receiver to ensure

> *Listen carefully to the voice and ideas*

that there has been no error in receiving the message. There can be impatience on the part of the receiver and unwillingness to communicate subsequently with you if there is misinterpretation of the message.

Finally, the close should be on a cordial note: a thank you for sparing the time, a reiteration of the main idea and a promise to get back at a time convenient to the receiver, and a brief pause to allow the called to disconnect

> *Close on a cordial note*

first. This step will mostly be observed if the communication has gone at a smooth pace. If there have been ups and downs in the course of interaction, this process may not be observed. Probably the receiver will disconnect or bring the communication to an abrupt end.

JAM: Have you picked up the right cues to discern whether your listener might be interested?

Receiver-Oriented Strategies

> In a call center environment, the minute the person picks up the call, the body language in the traditional sense disappears. But, since the customer will 'hear' body language in "the tone of voice", the tone accounts for a major part of the total communication, while words account for the remaining.

The role of the receiver in telephonic communication is more relaxed than it is in face-to-face interaction. Many of the politeness rules that are

> *Spell out name, ask for purpose of call*

adhered to in the latter case need not be followed, e.g. direct eye contact, feigning interest, slight forward lean are all strategies that receivers normally adopt in interpersonal communication. If the receiver wishes to evade a sender, instructions can be given to the secretary not to put the call through. The role of the secretary in telephonic communication is very important. She should, on receiving the call, specify her name After that there should be a request on her part asking the caller how she can be of help to him. She should also request for information concerning the call so that she can apprise her boss of the intentions of the caller. When telephone calls are in excess, she is selective in connecting calls to the superior. She does this after finding out the basic purpose of the telephone call.

For telephonic talks to be effective, listening skills should be well-

> *Listen attentively*

honed. In case it is a message which the secretary is taking for her boss, she should paraphrase the substance of the message and repeat the contact number so as to eliminate any possibility of error in listening. The basic rule of etiquette, when communicating on the telephone, requires

> Cordial tone, correct language and courtesy

the receiver to clearly state his/her name on picking up the phone from the cradle. The tone and the language used and courtesy go a long way in building an image of the receiver and the company.

Note: Telephonic etiquette influences the image of the company.

As the sender in telephonic communication is not present to influence the receiver by body sport, the caller can pay more attention to the message

> Paraphrase crux of message

and chalk out concrete statements with direct relevance to the issue. When information is transmitted, it is always presented in chunks and is followed by a brief pause. The receiver should utilise this moment and paraphrase, repeating the substance of the message. This can be done periodically, to ensure that there has been no error in the understanding of the message.

Warning! An intermediary such as a secretary must repeat the substance of the message to eliminate possibility of error.

Similarities	Dissimilarities
Sender needs to prepare well in advance	There is no direct eye contact
The needs and expectations of the receiver need to be well researched on	Body sport does not distract the receiver
The organisation of the points should be logical and appealing	The receiver can evade further communication
Clarity and courtesy should be strictly adhered to	The communication is very brief
The voice articulation and tone should be pleasing and convincing	Only one idea is focussed upon

Exhibit 2.8   Similarities and dissimilarities between face-to-face communication and telephonic talk.

SUMMARY

To establish effective communication with the receiver, the sender should, at the beginning have an idea encoded in the form of a message. After encoding, a security check is done to make sure all points have been dealt with in a desired order. The message is then transmitted to the receiver with required voice articulations and pauses so as to heighten the intended meaning of the message.

The feedback or response of the receiver should always be viewed empathetically.

Noise can be defined as physical or psychological disturbance that disrupts the flow of communication as the sender or the receiver perforce gets distracted by it.

Barriers create impediments in the progress of the interaction. Identification of barriers is extremely important to enable better communication. According to the role observed by the two participants, barriers may be categorised as 'sender-oriented' and 'receiver-oriented'. By following the rules for overcoming barriers, by improving listening and feedback skills most of these barriers can be overcome.

Listening is the accurate perception of what is being communicated. Because of the differing perceptions of individuals, there are sure to be differences in understanding the intent of the message.

There are two components to the listening process—decoding and internal response to perceived message. Awareness of the deterrents to listening allows for better communication.

Feedback is an important part of communication that completes the entire loop of the process. It comprises listening to the sender, repeating the crux of the message, and giving a response.

Feedback can be of two types: confirmatory and corrective.

Techniques need to be well-planned at the time of conducting business communication using technological devices.

CHECKLIST

Do's	Don'ts
'Impress' your listener	Be in a rush to start communicating
Seek the attention of your receiver	Let psychological noise crowd your conversation
Get the profile of the receiver to determine quantum of information	Begin every sentence with 'I', or start your sentence with a prejudice or know-it-all attitude
Jot down points when the message is being transmitted	Use organisational position as a criterion to determine validity of ideas
Maintain eye contact while communicating	Look at inane object, ceiling or the floor
Clarify the agenda for the feedback	Neglect to clarify your intention during corrective feedback
Establish a good rapport with subordinates	Let the past and the future influence the present context of communication
Focus on one idea during a telephonic conversation	Clutter your call with multiple points
Understand who your listener might be and what is it that you promise to deliver	Remain focussed on the self
Close telephonic talk with thanks, a reiteration of the main idea and a promise to get back	Be curt and abrasive in the closing of the telephonic talk

Role Play[1]

India Aeronautics (IA)
Group 1

Background Information

India Aeronautics (IA) was established on January 1, 1960. Presently, IA is running 19 Production Units, 10 Research and Design Centres at 8 locations in India. The company holds an impressive track record—15 types of Aircraft/Helicopters manufactured with in-house R&D and 14 types produced under license. IA has manufactured over 3658 Aircraft/Helicopters, 4178 Engines, upgraded 272 Aircraft and overhauled over 9643 Aircraft and 29775 Engines.

In the past years the company has also delivered aircrafts to Indian Air Force (IAF). However, in the last few years, it has not been able to manufacture and deliver the aircrafts to Indian Air Force in time. The company is handling multiple projects, which could also be one of the reasons for not completing production on time. This has, to some extent, eroded company reputation both nationally and internationally. Employees have begun to feel discouraged.

The Chairman has called for a meeting with General Manager, Operations to discuss the modus operandi.

Role Play: Chairman, P.K. Mahajan

You are the Chairman, IA. You have finished going through the recommendations provided by Mr. A.K. Mehta with respect to project management. Though you find the measures effective on paper, you do not find them feasible to be adopted. The recommendations may, as per your estimate, result in heavy loss to the unit. You are of the view that Mehta has done a rushed job. He could have spent more time on assessing the merit in the recommendation. You have called him for a meeting to discuss the approach and express your dissatisfaction with the work.

India Aeronautics (IA)
Group 2

Background Information

India Aeronautics (IA) was established on January 1, 1960. Presently, IA is running its 19 production units, 10 research and design centres at 8 locations in India. The company holds an impressive track record—15 types of aircraft/helicopters manufactured with in-house R&D and 14 types produced under license. IA has manufactured over 3658 aircraft/helicopters, 4178 engines, upgraded 272 aircraft and overhauled over 9643 aircraft and 29775 engines.

In the past years, the company has also delivered aircrafts to Indian Air Force (IAF). However, in the last few years, it has not been able to manufacture and deliver the aircrafts to Indian Air Force on time. The company is handling multiple projects, which could also be one of the reasons for not completing production on time. This has, to some extent, eroded company's reputation, both nationally and internationally. Employees have begun to feel discouraged.

As General Manager, Operations you have detailed information on the project. Based on the data, you had generated a report and put down your recommendations. The Chairman is seemingly not convinced with your recommendations and has called for a meeting.

Role Play: A.K. Mehta, General Manager, Operations

You are a General Manager, Operations. You have been called by the chairman Mr. P.K. Mahajan to discuss the measures provided by you for project management. In the rush to complete the report, you had jotted down recommendations which you knew looked good on paper, but could not be implemented. Prepare yourself for receiving feedback from the chairman. Mentally prepare the argument that you will like to put forward to justify your stand.

---

[1] Written by Mr. Rahul Shukla, Academic Associate, Communication Area, IIMA.

RAPID REVIEW

A. Pick Your Choice

1. In listening it is important to give attention to
   - (a) what is said
   - (b) what isn't said
   - (c) the non-verbal
   - (d) all the earlier stated points
2. Biased listening is a result of
   - (a) prejudices
   - (b) semantic problems
   - (c) arguments
   - (d) discussions
3. Mental blocks can be removed by
   - (a) giving correct feedback
   - (b) listening carefully
   - (c) being open to changes
4. Element of fear in the mind of a person leads to
   - (a) closed mind
   - (b) lack of proper feedback
   - (c) negative attitude
5. Empathy leads to
   - (a) greater receptivity
   - (b) more involvement
   - (c) greater focus
6. The closing in a telephonic message should be
   - (a) short
   - (b) cordial
   - (c) abrupt
7. In telephonic talk the message should be
   - (a) brief
   - (b) convoluted
   - (c) evasive
8. Semantic problem relates to
   - (a) badly expressed message
   - (b) meaning associated with words
   - (c) intention of the speaker
9. Poor retention can be overcome by
   - (a) repeating the message again and again
   - (b) entering into a question/answer session
   - (c) jotting down points
10. Lack of interest in a topic is a
    - (a) sender oriented barrier
    - (b) receiver oriented barrier
    - (c) none of the above

B. Fill in the Blanks

1. We must learn to listen for both _____ and _____.
2. Listening is a _____ process.
3. Noise can be _____ and _____.
4. As far as possible words should be reinforced with _____.

5. _____ at the time of listening should be conducive to the communication process.

6. Listening involves _____, _____ and _____.

7. Feedback is of two types: _____ and _____.

8. To tip the balance in your favour never _____ advice but always _____ advice.

9. To ensure that listening has been very careful always _____ and then _____.

10. Two strategies for eliminating psychological noise in the self are: _____ and _____.

C. True or False

1. We can concentrate on more than one thing at a time.

2. We can learn to listen effectively.

3. Communication is a game of listening only.

4. If our vocabulary is good, we are skilled communicators.

5. The "I attitude" as far as possible should be adopted.

6. Evaluation should be done simultaneously with listening.

7. At the time of giving feedback "You attitude" is important.

8. A dull and boring speech delivered with sufficient voice articulations can, to a great extent, capture the attention of the audience.

9. As communication is a two-way process, preparing in advance is a waste of time.

10. Providing excessive information is always good as it helps the receiver to sift and sieve.

Answers

A. 1. (d) 2. (a) 3. (c) 4. (a) 5. (a) 6. (b) 7. (a) 8. (b) 9. (c) 10. (b)

B. 1. facts; feelings   2. three-tier   3. physical; psychological
4. action   5. body language
6. levelling; sharpening; assimilation   7. confirmatory; corrective
8. give; seek   9. paraphrase; respond
10. entering into question/answer session; seeking advice.

C. 1. False   2. True   3. False   4. False   5. False
6. False   7. False   8. True   9. False   10. False

QUESTIONS FOR DISCUSSION

1. How do you determine whether the sender and the receiver share the same referent for a word?
2. What are the methods that are most effective in listening? Compare and contrast them with methods you normally use for effective listening.
3. What problems arise when a communicator misinterprets feedback?
4. What is the loss to an organisation, in terms of time and energy, when an important message is either sent or received incorrectly?
5. How can some of the sender-oriented barriers be overcome?
6. What factors play an important role in honing listening skills?
7. Discuss some of the receiver-oriented barriers.
8. Feedback is rapidly gaining importance in almost all walks of life. Discuss strategies of giving feedback.
9. How would you plan for an important call that you need to make? What must you keep in mind if you are receiving a call?
10. What are the similarities and dissimilarities between face to face communication and telephonic talk?

EXERCISES

1. Observe carefully the listening habits of five members of a class during different lectures. Make a list of good and bad listening habits that you observe. Suggest ways through which good listening habits can be further developed.
2. Conduct a study to determine the causes for difference in listening in different fields of work. If significant differences occur, try explaining the cause for the same.
3. Attend a symposium/lecture in which you are not interested. Try to identify the level of responsibility on yourself and the speaker in helping you to listen.
4. Identify a situation where you have evidenced a communication breakdown and try to list the reasons for the same.
5. At the end of any one day, list down personal encounters that you have had. What is the role of communication in making them successful or unsuccessful?
6. In an important discussion to take place identify an observer and ask him to note down cues and signals that both the sender and the receiver send forth. Discuss the extent to which these signals are understood by the participants in producing the expected response.

7. List ten factors that have mentally disturbed you in the last six months. In retrospect try to identify situations in which there has been a breakdown in communication because of the element of psychological noise.

8. Attend all business and non-business calls for a day in any administrative set-up. What were the statements you made to make a positive impact on the sender? What strategies did you adopt to ensure listening is correct?

9. Prepare a speech with main and sub-points and deliver it to a class of ten. Ask them to also jot down the main and the sub-points of the speech. Compare your points with those of the class. Are there any disparities? If yes, try to identify the causes for the same.

10. List ten areas of communication that can erect barriers in the mind of either the sender or the receiver.

3

Mechanics of Writing

CONTENTS

- Introduction
- Stages of Writing
- Preparing Notes
- How to Compose Business Messages
- Style and Tone
- Dictionary and Thesaurus Usage
- Punctuation Marks
- Deleting Redundancies/Using Simple Words
- Proofreading

LEARNINGS

After reading this chapter you should be able to:

➢ Understand the steps prior to writing and the stages in the writing process

➢ Learn to compose short, simple, well-constructed business messages

➢ Use appropriate tone, style and punctuation

➢ Distinguish between using the dictionary and thesaurus

➢ Use effective writing strategies to get your reader to take the desired action

➢ Learn to use proof reading marks

KEYWORDS

Predrafting, Drafting, Postdrafting, Reader Participation, Topical Sentence, KISS Principle, SVO Ordering, Connotation, Denotation, You-viewpoint, Style, Tone, Dictionary and Thesaurus, Punctuation, Redundancies, Proofreading Marks,

INTRODUCTION

"In your business writing, you must choose among boredom, shouting and seduction. Which do you choose?"
—The Wizard of Ads, Roy H. Williams

Writing can be a joy provided the basic purpose is clear. It proves to be tedious when the very motive is hazy. In simple terms, *effective business writing* means getting things done. This simple target can be achieved if we write with the following two-fold purpose in mind: to inform the reader and request for action. In written business communication the expectations from the reader are high with respect to involvement. The effectiveness of the business message can be measured in terms of the speed with which the desired action is initiated and subsequent results produced.

Suppose on completion of the writing project a simple question is asked: "So What?" In other words, the writer mulls over the question that if this business message was drafted and sent to the receiver, what will be its impact? What does it hope to achieve? Will the receiver be convinced to take prompt action? Answers to such queries will make the writing coherent and meaningful.

STAGES OF WRITING

TOPIC OBJECTIVES
Learn to plan the three stages of the writing process. Understand the importance of pre-drafting and revision. Identify the steps prior to writing from the point of view of the intended reader/user

"Writing is like a horseback ride into heaven and hell and back. I'm grateful if I can crawl back alive."
—Thomas Sanchez

Acquiring the ability to write in a logical, coherent manner requires a lot in terms of preparation. It can almost be compared to making a presentation where the key mantra is *rehearse, rehearse* and *rehearse*, prior to the final appearance before the audience. Similarly, the amount of time consumed in preparing the written message should far exceed the actual writing process.

The three stages in the writing process are: (a) pre-drafting, (b) drafting, and (c) post-drafting. On most occasions, problems arise because of the improper assignment of time for the three stages of business writing. Maximum amount of time is spent on writing the draft and minimum time on either preparing for the material to be drafted or in revising. The schematic pattern observed for writing is mostly as follows:

Predrafting → Drafting → Post-drafting

Exhibit 3.1   Stages of writing—I.

The amount of time that goes into revising occasionally equals that of preparing for the draft. Contrast this with the situation in which maximum amount of time is spent in preparing the first draft, followed by post-drafting and then, finally, writing. The output is definitely better, well-thought of and clearer. Take a look at the diagram for the various stages of writing.

> Maximum time should be spent in revising the text

Exhibit 3.2   Stages of writing—II.

If the process of writing were to be understood in terms of, say, a twelve-hour time frame, the writer can safely assign one hour for the incubation of the idea, approximately five hours for planning the script, one hour for writing, and four hours for revising. The one-hour that is surplus and not accounted for is needed as time spent in taking a short break after writing. It is a well-known fact that the writer, after completion of the first draft will be able to detect errors if the text is re-read. Hence, it is important that for an unprejudiced correction of the errors we go back to the original text after a short break.

Within the framework suggested, the task of the writer gets simplified if there is identification of the following steps prior to commencing work:

1. Define the problem
2. Gather material
3. Organise material
4. Revise
5. Complete the task

1. **Define the problem.** A proper definition of the problem and clarity of purpose makes writing meaningful. The purpose can be to inform, to persuade, to regulate or to collaborate. A change in this will also result in a change in the style of writing as the level of participation from the reader either increases, decreases or remains stagnant. The style of writing can be passive, if the purpose of writing is to inform, as minimum involvement from the recipient is expected. Persuasion will necessarily require a high level of involvement on the part of the reader. Unless and until the content is robust and the tone convincing, the purpose of the writer will be defeated. Finally, when it comes to either regulation or collaboration, the participation from the receiver is the highest. With the above specified purpose, the style and the tone should, as far as possible, be active so that the receiver is forced to take cognisance of the material provided.

> Purpose could be to inform, persuade, regulate or collaborate

Writing becomes more focussed when similarities and dissimilarities between the existing systems and proposed ones are studied and suitably explained. Similarly, the relevance of the issue within the existing time-frame is also important. If business writing can reflect concerns of the above specified nature, it will be easier to arrive at an effective definition of the work problem.

JAM: Have you identified the purpose of writing? Check to see if you have left your reader behind!

2. **Gather material.** After the problem has been defined, the stage of gathering the material begins. What are the sources that can be tapped for procuring information? Is the material to

> *Material could be internal or external*

be collected internal, that is, it belongs to the organisation where the individual is working or is it external, that is, it is to be collected from sources outside the organisation? Browsing through the library, the previous reports and other written communication pertaining to the problem can also provide sufficient information. Most of the above-mentioned sources will be there in the library.

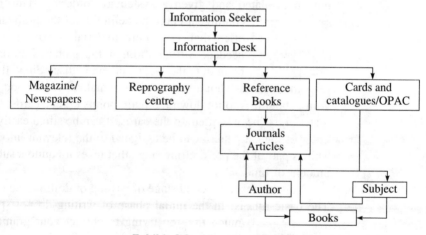

Exhibit 3.3   Library usage chart.

External material, not available in the library, can be collected through interviews for which preparation is critical. People are almost always reluctant to part with information. The first step for preparation of such interviews is rehearsal of techniques for breaking the ice. One of the strategies can be to start with "empty conversation", that is, interaction which really does not have any bearing on the aim of the communication. It is almost always inane, but important from the point of view of building relationships or breaking the ice. Interviewees can be of two types: acquaintances and non-acquaintances. Interaction with the former can begin with almost any topic—the family, weather, work at office, colleagues, etc. Communication with a non-acquaintance can begin with the mention of a friend, or a colleague who had referred the interviewee to the interviewer. Almost always there should be a pause before you plunge straight into business talk. Instead, start with the basic, the most elementary questions revolving round the five W's: What, Why, Who, Where, When, and the one H: How. Let the interviewee take on the lead. As an interviewer, the most important task ahead of you is to listen carefully. Do not disturb with too many ifs and buts. Let the person speak. To ensure that your understanding of what is being said is correct and there are no errors follow a four-tier process of listening, paraphrasing, responding and taking down notes. Together with this also ask follow-up questions to clarify the issues at hand.

> *Start with questions revolving round the five W's & one H*

> *Listen, paraphrase and then respond*

Note: To ensure there is no listening error, listen, paraphrase, respond and take down notes.

3. **Organise the material.** The material gathered through research can now be collated and given a systematic ordering. This again is contingent upon the definition of the problem. More often than not, more material is collected than is needed. Sifting through the gathered information, retaining the relevant and discarding the non-relevant material should be done systematically. A good way of going about it is to jot down the main points on cue cards. Once all material has been written on the cards, it can be sifted easily and an order or logical pattern can be assigned to the relevant information. This is part of the pre-drafting stage that takes up quite a substantial amount of time.

> *Sift through the material*

Now begins the second stage of writing or drafting the message. The basic rule is: In the initial phase of writing do not spend too much time on trying to correct your grammar and language. Just let the content unravel as you move through the points. There is a reason behind not spending too much time at the drafting stage. The mind cannot perform two activities at the same time. If we are very particular of the style and attempt putting all the points in an aesthetically appealing manner, we will end up with either unsatisfactory results or spending more time than is required. Therefore, it is essential that the correction of the written communication be left for the final stage of revision in which the piece of writing can be given an aesthetic appeal.

> *Plan, write and then spend sufficient time in revising*

JAM: Have you allotted adequate time to organise and order your material?

4. **Revise the text.** A lot of time should be spent in revising the piece of written communication. This is the stage when all kinds of errors

> Revise after a short break

in writing and of logic crop up as we attempt to give the entire writing a coherent picture. However, before we come to this stage of revision, there is a "no man's stage" when we take a brief break from the usual work. When we get back to our writing after the short interlude, we view it from a fresh perspective and are able to notice errors, if any. The writer should never be in a rush to send forth the written message. If possible, it should be withheld by the writer for as long as time permits, so that perusal, revision and correction can be systematically carried out.

5. **Finish the text.** Revision does not bring the written piece of information to a close. The text now needs to be carefully pruned to

> Ensure that formatting of text is complete and correct

ensure all formatting, and incorporating of structural details is complete. This is the final stage, and though not time consuming, definitely requires careful reading.

Warning! You will waste time or produce unsatisfactory results if you spend too much time correcting your draft in the initial phase of writing.

PREPARING NOTES

> **TOPIC OBJECTIVES**
> Learn how to prepare notes
> Distinguish between jotting down points and preparing notes

"When a man is in doubt about this or that in his writing, it will often guide him if he asks himself how it will tell a hundred years hence." —Samuel Butler

Preparing notes is a tedious process and requires a high level of concentration. A systematic preparation of notes will comprise the following five stages:

1. Read the text carefully.

2. Select the keywords in the passage or words that communicate the main idea.

3. Construct a sentence that captures the essence of the paragraph or state it in brief, that is, without verbs or conjunctions. The process can be expedited if the first line of the paragraph is carefully studied

> First line of the paragraph contains the key idea

and key words searched for. If the statement needs to be copied as it exists in the original, care should be exercised to avoid punctuation and/or spelling errors, e.g., the writer may be using the American spelling "behavior" instead of the British spelling "behaviour". If you are not careful, you may jot down the British spelling, which would lead to presentation of an erroneous quotation.

4. Note down the page number.

5. Note down the bibliographical details.

Points (4) and (5) are essential because the reader may wish to refer to the original for cross-verification.

Notes can be prepared in the following manner:

Name of Author: Page No.	Name of Book Publishers: Place of Publication:
1. Goal-oriented communication	Goal oriented communication is also referred to as being transaction centric
2. Relationship oriented communication	Furthering and cementing of social relationships

Exhibit 3.4   Preparing notes.

If notes for letters or reports are being prepared, reference numbers are used instead of bibliographical details so that it is easy to retrieve the information when the need arises.

Warning! Check your notes to see if the punctuation and spelling are as in the original text to avoid an erroneous quotation.

HOW TO COMPOSE BUSINESS MESSAGES

TOPIC OBJECTIVES

Learn to put the KISS principle into practice

Apply the tenets of good business writing to sentence and paragraph construction

"I hate writing. I love having written."   —Dorothy Parker

Do you want to compose a business message? It sounds rather simple. Let us consider a hypothetical situation:

Asha and Neha have been working in the HR department of a BPO for quite some time and know each other very well. Asha had been out of town and needed to extend her leave to attend to some family problem. She e-mailed Neha asking her to notify the boss that she would be back only the day after tomorrow.

Dear Neha,

Right now I am in Jabalpur with my mother and have been on leave for the last three days. Mom is not well and I will need to extend my leave.

Please inform boss that I will be back only the day after tomorrow.

Thanks

Asha

The assumption is that there can be no misinterpretation of the message. Neha checks her mail a day after Asha had sent the message and overlooks to calculate "the day after tomorrow" as Asha had meant it. Asha makes the mistake of composing her message in a vague fashion and omits to specify by which date she would return. Neha conveys the misinterpreted information to the boss and Asha is in a soup!

You can see how wrong both are when they assume that they understand each other well.

Errors of judgment and interpretation do arise if a written message is not properly formulated. Some of the basic tenets to be kept in mind are as follows:

1. **Short and simple.** As far as possible, keep the business message short and simple. Adhere to the KISS principle— Keep It Short and Simple—to maintain a good and comprehensible writing style.

> Verbose language to be avoided

Unnecessary facts which may cloud the thinking of the reader should be avoided. Further, care should also be taken to ensure that the material being composed is what the reader requires. Neither should it be too much nor too scanty. Verbose language can be avoided in favour of the short and the simple. Technical language should only be used when the writer feels that the reader belongs to the same discipline, and the impact of the original message will be lost if any other approach is observed.

2. **Choosing correct words.** In order that the message adhere to the "KISS" principle, select appropriate words. Vocabulary used should be such that both the sender and the receiver are conversant with it. In communication it is said that words in themselves mean nothing. It is the intention behind the words which denotes a particular meaning

> Use words with which the reader is familiar

to the spoken or written statement, e.g. if five people were asked to respond to the word "red", probably all will come up with a different answer which may well be as follows: blood, colour, passion, rose and communists. Similarly, the case is for the written word. Each word has a particular *denotation*, that is, the dictionary meaning and a *connotation* or the meaning related to the intention of the sender. If the words are chosen with care the connotation is also correctly understood.

Warning! Do not include unnecessary facts and avoid distracting your reader.

For this it becomes imperative that we adhere to the following principles pertaining to the choice of words:

(a) *Understandable and simple words.* Suppose we were to make a statement of the following nature:

> "Singular specimen of the scientific class of avis contained within the boundaries of the upper prehensile, is equivalently valuable as a doubled inventory of that item located in a low-spreading thicket."

A statement of this nature, though grammatically correct, is bound to give rise to the following queries in the mind of the reader—"What does the writer intend?" "What does the statement exactly mean?" Contrast this with the simple literal paraphrase of the above statement: "A bird in hand is better than two in the bush". How much simpler and meaningful is the statement when expressed in this manner.

(b) *Appropriate technical words.* Often a piece of technical writing necessitates that jargon be used. This does not mean that the text be inundated with all kinds of information that the reader might find difficult to comprehend. Keeping the receiver in mind, draft the message so that it does not get too heavy. To doubly ensure that there are no errors in comprehension on the part of the reader, provide a list of technical words used with their correlates or meaning. This strategy, however, can only be used if the piece of written communication is of a long nature, e.g. a report.

> Provide a list of technical words

(c) *Concrete words.* Abstract messages should be avoided in favour of concrete messages. Words such as tomorrow, day after tomorrow, soon, etc. should, to a great extent, not be used at all. Replace these words by specific dates. Through this process, the use of those words can be avoided that lack objectivity and decisiveness. They can be replaced with a specific time plan that enables the writer and the reader to meet the deadline.

> Avoid abstract words

Note: In the case of a report, a list of the meanings of technical words may be provided.

(d) *Verbs and nouns.* In written communication verbs and nouns should be used as they spell out a positive and concrete rendering of the statement. The simplest pattern of making a statement should be in the order of subject-verb-object ordering (or SVO) which takes into account both the verb and the noun. Adjectives and adverbs should be totally done away with at the time of composing business messages unless, of course, one wishes to be extremely creative. Analyse the following statements:

> Follow a subject-verb-object ordering

1. Your project was extraordinary brilliant!
2. It's hard these days to find competent workers like you.
3. You really have made us happy with your performance.

Statements like these are too flamboyant. Restrict the flow of emotions by being specific and concrete and specify the content rather than the pleasure that one obtains as a result of one's accomplishment. Suppose we were to rephrase the statements and write them as:

1. Your project excelled in the areas of ...
2. Despite difficult circumstances you were able to meet the target.
3. Your dedication and sincerity are appreciated.

In all the three statements there is an objective assessment of the situation and the individual. This is brought about by a choice of well-thought out words that neither express too much nor too little gratitude or appreciation for the task accomplished.

(e) *Positive words*. At the time of writing, negative words should be totally eliminated from the text. The writing should be both positive and polite. As the basic purpose of any writing revolves round involvement of the reader, negative words can be avoided. Ensure that words and statements made and used gently persuade the reader to take action. The emphasis should not be on what you have not done or what you cannot do. On the contrary, it should focus on the person.

Let us take a look at the following statement:

Use positive words and a polite tone	"It is next to impossible to complete the assignment today."

It is surely going to put off the reader. Suppose we change the sentence and, while retaining the original meaning, re-write it in the following manner:

"The assignment would be completed by tomorrow 28 June by 9 a.m."

The receiver cannot miss the positive overtones. The basic issue remains the same, that is, the assignment cannot be completed today. However, the manner in which it is stated spells a level of confidence and even hints at an unspoken promise of not failing to deliver as per the timelines.

To take a look at another example:

"You surely did mess up things last week. Now, you'll have to face the music."

Suppose we were to change the tenor of the statement and rephrase it in the following manner:

"I believe things went amiss last week. Let us discuss and sort out issues. "

The writer has put the reader in a receptive frame of mind. As a technique, politeness, is the best to be adopted in a difficult situation.

JAM: Does your writing gently persuade your reader?

(f) *Correct words.* What we wish to communicate should be absolutely clear in our mind prior to commencing work. Quite often we think in our native language and then try to translate the same idea in English or any other foreign language. Read the ideas in the text carefully for clarity in communication. For example,

> *Read the text carefully to ensure that the choice of words is correct*

> The presenter has but little time to convey himself/herself.

In such a sentence construct, the choice of the word "himself/herself" is inappropriate. If each word was to be weighed in the sentence, the writer will realise that an individual does not convey "himself/herself" rather it is the idea that gets conveyed. Suppose we were to restructure it to read:

> The presenter has but little time to convey his/her ideas.

In a construct of this kind the message is absolutely clear. The sentence contains a few words, and the writer has taken pains to ensure that the language is simple with subject-verb-object ordering. For example, in some cases, the steps or techniques need to be demonstrated by performing them in front of the audience. If one were to analyse this statement, one will find that steps and techniques are not 'performed' but 'demonstrated'. The writer falls in a double trap: one of making an error of logic and, two, of making use of redundant words that we normally refer to as "dead wood" which need to be immediately eliminated from the sentence.

3. **Sentence structure.** Words alone are insufficient to express the meaning intended by the sender. The manner in which they are arranged in a sentence give coherence to the idea. As far as possible, the sentence construction should also be simple. Unnecessary words or "dead wood" can and should be done away with. Occasionally, redundant words creep into the composition of the sentence. If we were to make a conscious effort to read and re-read the text, we will find repetitions embedded in the connotative impact of the sentence. For example: "New Innovations". Innovation itself means new, hence the usage of "new" is redundant.

> *Delete redundancies*

4. **Paragraph construction.** The next level of construction in written communication is the paragraph. Only one or two ideas should be stated in a paragraph. As all the paragraphs form a link to provide the final meaning, there should be a topical sentence at the head of the paragraph. This

> *State one or two ideas*

prepares the reader for what is to follow in the rest of the paragraph.

| First line—Topical sentence |

The last line should provide a link to the topical sentence in the new paragraph. In other words, the beginning and end emphasise the link that leads to an understanding of the main idea.

Often writers use a one-sentence paragraph. It definitely looks

| Link clauses, words and statements |

clumsy if the entire text is not in point form. There has to be further elaboration on the stated point. As a paragraph is a composite of over two sentences, care has to be taken at the time of writing. Clauses have to be linked and all words and statements should show a connection. Examine the following sentence:

> Some of the common obstacles to planning are: that planning takes time, it is interrupted by daily tasks, procrastination, etc.

In a sentence of this kind, the points presented are totally disjointed. It leaves the reader disoriented. Suppose we were to restructure it in the following manner:

> Some of the common obstacles to planning are procrastination and time constraint.

The middle clause, "it is interrupted by daily tasks" is already taken care of in the factor of "time constraint" spelt out in the corrected sentence. We have now succeeded in both eliminating redundancy and presenting clauses in a conjoined manner, which speak of an aesthetically and grammatically correct construction.

The paragraphs should be conjoined to one another in a logical sequence. The main idea is always presented in the beginning and

| Conjoin paragraphs |

is followed by ancillary points. The points in the various paragraphs should not be presented randomly. Instead, they should flow from one another.

JAM: Are there too many ideas in your paragraph?

5. **"You"-viewpoint.** In all types of communication the emphasis should be on "you" instead of "I". If the reader is able to appreciate the viewpoint presented in the written communication as pertaining

| Concentrate on "You" instead of "I" |

specifically to him/her, there will be promptness in taking action. Contrast the two statements for two letters wishing to congratulate a subordinate on successful completion of an internal examination.

> (a) I was very happy to learn that you had cleared your internal examination. Now I can recommend you for a promotion at the earliest.

> (b) Congratulations on your successful completion of the examination. You will be happy to learn that your name can now be recommended for promotion.

The second approach makes the letter sound more positive and solicits the good will of the subordinate. On the other hand, the first example with excessive use of "I" sounds pompous and does not project the desire to share the happiness of the other. It is an objective statement rather than a desire to genuinely reflect happiness at the success of the other.

One must, however, be very careful with the usage of the pronoun "you". If used in excess it can have damaging results. It

| *Assess the situation when "You-Attitude" should be used* |

could even sound like a directive. For example, "You must settle the dispute at once as you were part of the controversy that began in your room". Further, it is not always necessary to use "you" to indicate a "You-attitude". Many a time it is implicit and built in the statement made. The usage also depends on the organisational culture. Does the writer wish to adhere to a formal style or does he/she wish to make written communication informal in nature? The answer to this query would sort out the underlying problem.

Note: Adopt a "You"-viewpoint for your reader to be able to appreciate your concerns and take swift action.

STYLE AND TONE

TOPIC OBJECTIVES

Identify the factors that determine the tone of the business message
Learn to choose the appropriate style to reflect the mood of the message

"The greatest possible merit of style is, of course, to make the words absolutely disappear into the thought."
—Nathaniel Hawthorne

The tone and the style of writing changes with a change in readership. Different types of styles and tones can be adopted for different occasions. Style of writing can be formal or informal. While a formal business style is appropriate, an informal style tends to make the writing colloquial. Which style to adopt and when? Different occasions

| *The style depends on the writer, reader, occasion and content* |

require a different style of writing. While the highly formal prose is acceptable for reports or documentation, a slightly informal style can be adopted when it comes to business correspondence. Once again this is contingent on the relationship between the sender and the receiver. If styles of writing were viewed on a continuum from extremely formal to extremely informal, almost all business writing falls as a cluster in between the formal and somewhat informal points of reference. This cluster could then be used to understand the tone used for communicating messages that can vary from active to passive, personal to impersonal, colourful to colourless. The choice of the tone for depicting these styles is dependent on the sender (who), reader (to whom), occasion (when and where), and content (what). With a change in any one of these factors, there will be a change in the tone of the message.

Let us consider a few examples of formal and informal words:

Formal	*Informal*
1. Subsequent to	After
2. With respect to the possibility of	Whether we could
3. We trust	I hope
4. Consulted	Checked
5. Undertake	Handle
6. Rearrange	Juggle

In the first three examples, the extremely formal phrases lend gravity to the message. If they can possibly be replaced by the informal words or phrases as suggested in the opposite column, there will be greater conviction and appeal in the message. Contrast this with the last three informal examples: "checked", "handle" and "juggle". All three are colloquial and more suited for spoken messages. They definitely need to be replaced by more suitable words, as suggested in the formal column, viz., "consulted", "undertake" and "rearrange".

Let us take a look at the various styles that can be used to reflect different moods.

1. **Active.** An active tone reflects a desire to get things done at the earliest. There is also a sense of responsibility for what is being communicated. In this style, the simplest of the sentence constructions is used, that is, the Subject-Verb-Object (SVO) ordering. Messages are short, pithy, and normally directives are used. The tone is commanding and is used by people at the helm of affairs who are in the habit of issuing directives.

> Messages are short and pithy, active voice and SVO ordering for sentences

Direct statements are used and no efforts are made to camouflage the impact of a direct utterance that could have a negative impact. For example:

> The Project Report should be completed by 12 November 1999.

Look at the above statement carefully and listen to the tone that the combination of words produce. Such a statement uses the active tone which reflects a desire to get things done. There is also a sense of responsibility for what is being communicated. In this style, the simplest of the sentence constructions is used, that is, the SVO ordering.

2. **Passive.** This is a rather soft style and is used in situations when some negative message is to be communicated and the sender does

> *Passive voice, long sentences cushioned in suppositions*

not wish to sound imposing. This style is also used in reports where the statements are not universal truths but need to be studied and critically examined. Hence, words such as, "maybe", "perhaps" and "possibly" are used. Nothing is stated that would communicate a feeling that this is the ultimate truth. Compared to the active style, the sentences are longer and cushioned in suppositions. Even the sentence ordering is reversed. It follows a object-verb-subject patterning. For example:

The date for completion of the Project Report is 12 November 2014.

Where does the emphasis lie? Yes, on the "date for completion". Does it specify that an urgent action needs to be taken? No! It is a statement/utterance that has been made with little or no impact. If you count the number of words in the same sentence written in the active and passive voice (as exemplified in the examples provided), you will notice that to communicate the same message the active sentence uses 10 words and passive, 12.

3. **Personal.** A personal style is used when an individual wishes to be personal in communication. It is much like the spoken message and

> *Use of "I" and "You"; brief sentences and conversational tone*

part of the personality of the sender gets reflected. Pronouns as "I" and "you" are used, and the receivers are referred to by their first name instead of their surname. Personal references maybe made that show ties between the sender and the receiver. Sentences, in this form of writing, are brief and short and the overall tone is conversational. The active voice for communication of messages is used and on occasions even direct questions can be asked to the reader. Example, I want you to complete the Project Report immediately.

In this example, it is clear that the sender is in a senior position. The directive is made more personal by the use of "I" and "you". The receiver has little choice, but to comply!

4. **Impersonal.** In contrast to the personal style, the impersonal style

> *Use of "We"; passive voice; long complex sentences*

is tedious. It is withdrawn and is more pompous. Personal pronouns such as "I" and "You" are avoided and are replaced by a more corporate word, "we". The names of receivers are not mentioned and the tone is passive. Occasionally the sentences are long and complex, making the written message complex and weighty. Example,

> We would greatly benefit as a result of completion of the Project Report.

The "We" in the sentence lacks clarity, "greatly" is not specified, and what will be the benefit—tangible or intangible—still remains to be answered.

5. **Colourful style.** Normally used for literary purposes, it increases the impact of the written message. Adjectives and adverbs are frequently used to add weight and give colour to the written message. Further, concrete words or those that add to the visual impact of the written message, like metaphors, similes and other figures of speech are used. In the colourful style of writing, the choice of words is extremely important. As the impact of the message being transmitted is contingent upon these, appropriate words should be juxtaposed to provide the statement the desired impact. Example,

Use of adjectives and adverbs, metaphors, similes

> Preparing the Project Report can be a challenging task. If it is completed by November 12, 2014, it will be a tremendous feat accomplished.

In the example above, the reader can visualise the challenge and equate the writing and completion of the report to a "feat". Definitely this style uses more words as the message is garbed to provide the desired emotional connect with the reader

6. **Colourless style.** A colourless style is a composite of an impersonal and passive style. This is a dull and monotonous way of communicating the message. It avoids concrete in favour of the abstract. The message is absolutely colourless without any similes, metaphors or figures of speech. In fact, it is one of the most depressing styles as there is neither intellectual nor emotional vigour and appeal in the writing. For example:

Impersonal passive style

> The completion of the Project Report at the earliest will be appreciated.

Sure it would! Some questions that crop up: What could "earliest" mean? Today, tomorrow or a week later? Who will appreciate? What will be appreciated—the report or the completion of the task? Questions of this nature rob the writing of authenticity and credibility.

DICTIONARY AND THESAURUS USAGE

TOPIC OBJECTIVES

Learn how to use the dictionary
Distinguish between the uses
of the dictionary and
thesaurus

"I was reading the dictionary. I thought it was a poem about everything."   —Steven Wright

Looking for the meaning of a word, usage or its spelling in a dictionary begins by a search for the word in the alphabetical order. The dictionary proceeds on one of the basic lexicographic facts that the definition is always written in a simpler manner than the words they describe. The coverage comprises words used in different national varieties of English, specifically British and American. A dictionary provides guidance along the following lines:

1. The words that are accompanied by either *BrE* (British English) or *AmE* (American English) indicate English as used in that country. However, there are certain words that are not labelled at all. This indicates that their usage is universal or they are acceptable throughout the world. Let us consider an example: Au-tumn*AmE* also fall-*n* the season between summer and winter when leaves turn gold and fruits become ripe. In this example, a different word is provided, namely, fall that means the same as autumn, but is used in American English.

2. The part of speech which the word represents is also mentioned. In the example cited above, "n" stands for a noun.

3. Information about the use of a grammatical word is given either before the meaning or instead of a meaning. e.g. if (not usually followed by the future tense) supposing that; on condition that, and so on.

4. There is further explanation on how words are formed by adding a prefix or a suffix, e.g. unending (prefix, un) or stupidity (suffix, ity). Verbs that are used with prepositions like "go on", are always shown as a separate entry. Opposites are also indicated in the dictionary. e.g. for the word "aft" the opposite "fore" is also mentioned.

5. Irregular plural words and their pronunciations are also provided, e.g. cranium-niums or -nia.

6. A different spelling that is not so common, e.g. lakh, lac.

7. Information about possible other forms of the word, e.g. fault 1. A mistake or imperfection. 2. a bad point, but not of a serious moral kind, in someone's character.

8. List of related compound words, e.g. rain. *See also* Rain down, Rain off, Rain on, Rain out.

9. Places at which the word should be broken, as at the end of a line, e.g. ree-fer?

Many dictionaries, e.g. Longman Dictionary of Contemporary English, provide the usage of the word together with its meaning.

Using a thesaurus is slightly different from using a dictionary. In the former, we begin with the idea and find the synonym closest to it. The numbered section is provided at the end of the text with synonyms and closely associated words. For instance, if we were looking for a word meaning for "to protect from sunlight", we need to look for a synonym for the verb "protect". The two synonyms provided in the thesaurus are "shield" and "defend". The former meaning clearly expresses the idea in the phrase. Next begins the search for the appropriate word under the category of "shield". A number of synonyms would be provided in the noun, verb and the adjective forms. The choice is then with the writer to select the right word to convey the meaning.

Note: When certain words are not labelled to indicate country of usage, it means they are universally used.

PUNCTUATION MARKS

TOPIC OBJECTIVES

Know the function of punctuation marks

Use punctuation where required

Cut out all these exclamation points. An exclamation point is like laughing at your own joke
—F. Scott Fitzgerald

Begin a writing exercise without paying heed to the use of punctuations. After having written the passage, you will not be able to make much sense of what you have written. For instance,

Bolster Electronics located in Waterloo Ontario is among the four largest suppliers of industrial video equipment for harsh environments like other companies it sells its products through national distributors who held products from more than one supplier's product line.

Correct and appropriate use of punctuations adds much to the meaning of the sentence or the paragraph.

The example cited above can be corrected to read as follows:

Bolster Electronics located in Waterloo, Ontario is among the four largest suppliers of industrial video equipment for harsh environments. Like other companies, it sells its products through national distributors who held products from more than one supplier's product line.

Some of the commonly used marks are periods, commas, colons, semicolons, dashes and parentheses.

Period

Period is the end of a sentence

A period is normally understood as a full stop. Its usage indicates the end of a sentence or the end of the postulation of a concept. It is the most major stop sign and is equivalent to the fading of the voice in oral communication. A period is used:

1. At the end of a sentence.
2. After initials and some abbreviations, e.g., Mr. H. Kaul, Ph.D.,
3. While denoting time, i.e., a.m. and p.m.
4. Between rupees and paise when expressed in figures, e.g., ₹ 100.42. However, when the paise is not shown, there is no period, e.g., He gave ₹ 400 to his friend.

Comma

A comma is used in the middle of a sentence to mark a short break or a pause after which the idea being discussed is resumed. In oral communication it can be equated with a pause where the sender breaks off in the sentence to think or give time to the receiver to absorb the message.

Comma is a short break

A comma is used in the following instances:

1. After certain words, e.g., moreover, however, therefore, finally, consequently, perhaps, and so on.
2. After certain clauses, e.g., I think, I believe, I repeat, she states, as you know, etc.
3. After certain phrases, for instance, in fact, of course, in short, in brief, without doubt, if possible, etc.
4. After use of certain adjectives of almost equal rank. If we were to pronounce these adjectives , they would receive equal stress. A good way of testing this strategy is to reverse the order of the adjectives. If there is no fundamental change in the sentence after the adjective reversal, it means that the usage is correct. For example: He is a healthy, wealthy and rich man.
5. After words in direct address, for instances, Mr. Chairman, it is our great pleasure...
6. Comma is also used to set off sentence elements that may be incorrectly read and comprehended. For example: In our library books have gone for binding. Contrast this sentence with, In our library, books have gone for binding. While the first one can be misleading, the second more than makes up for any misunderstanding that leads to a second reading of the text.
7. To separate words or word groups used in a series consisting of more than three units. Example: The products exported to India are bauxite, manganese, and mica.
8. Between independent clauses, such as, I spoke to my father about my problem, and he spoke to my mother.
9. Between a dependent clause at the start of the sentence and an independent clause at the end of the sentence. Example: We may be able to use this product, although it may involve heavy expenditure.

10. Before and after the year when writing month, day, and year. Example: On September 20, 1999, we intend inviting our MD. However, if the manner of stating the time frame is changed, there is no need to use a comma in between, for instance, 20 September 1999.

11. To separate a quotation from the rest of the sentence. Example: The author states, "Business Communication..." However, when the quotation is built into the sentence, no comma is used. Example: He shouted "Watch out!" as he bumped into the lady stenographer.

12. To surround parenthetical phrases or words that can be removed from the sentence without changing the meaning. Example: The new car, *Opel Astra*, is running 15 kilometres in one litre of petrol.

Note: The comma is equivalent to the pause in oral communication, when the sender allows for time for the message to be absorbed.

Colon

Colon is to be used in the following situations:

1. After salutation in a formal business letter, e.g. Dear Mr. X:

2. After a sentence or phrase that introduces a list, quotation or an idea. Example: The three points discussed were as follows: induction, remuneration and promotion. A colon should not be used when the list, quotation or idea is a part of the introductory phrase of the sentence. It is important to notice the absence of a colon in the following sentence: In our class there are 40 chairs, two white boards, and one OHP.

3. When an idea or concept is to be amplified.

4. For subtitles in books, subtitle of a heading, etc.

5. Instead of dash to avoid repetition of the latter.

Semicolon

Semicolons are not used too frequently. The three instances when they can be used are as follows:

1. To separate two closely related independent clauses. Example: The pre-placement talk would be held at the end of the week: the placement by the end of the month.

2. To show separation within a series or list that has commas within it. Example: Companies would be coming for on-campus recruitment on October 12, 1999; November 20, 1999; and December 18, 1999.

3. To show separation between two independent clauses in which the second one begins with words such as however, therefore, nevertheless, and phrases such as: for example, in that case. Example: Company A has not responded so far; however, Company B's response has been rather positive.

JAM: Check if your semicolons have been used only where strictly necessary.

Dash

Dashes are very useful, but should be used with caution. They should not be confused with hyphens that are used to clarify a phrase as "self-regulated system".

1. Whenever a word or a phrase is a sudden turn in the thinking process, a dash is used to exemplify the same. Example: Buying a house in Sushant Lok—though far off—is sure to yield fruitful results at a later date.

2. Dashes are also used to set off phrases in which there are commas used. Example: Details of our offices—in Japan, China, and Italy—can be procured from our New Delhi office.

Warning! Do not confuse the dash with the hyphen.

Parentheses

Parentheses, as far as possible, should be avoided. They are normally used to

1. Surround comments that are purely incidental. Attempts should be made to incorporate these incidental comments in the body of the written message. Example: The consignment we received was viewed favourably by many (I personally felt it was no good.)

2. In legal documents or official correspondence to surround the arabic numeral that follows the same amount written in words, e.g. Rupees fifty thousand, four hundred and two only (₹ 50,402 only).

3. To enclose a sentence, remark or comment that is not part of the main idea (see point 1)

4. In References or Bibliography for denoting the years, e.g. Kotler, Philip (1999).

DELETING REDUNDANCIES/USING SIMPLE WORDS

TOPIC OBJECTIVES
Know how to make messages brief, concise and effective
Learn to re-read the text and delete dead wood

"The more you say, the less people remember. The fewer the words, the greater the profit."
—Francois FeNelon

Written communication, re-read after a short break, reveals errors of numerous kinds. Primary among them is the use of extra or unnecessary words that do not add value to the written text. If these "redundancies" or "dead wood" is deleted, the text gains in terms of brevity and communicates more effectively. Let us take a look at the following examples: Cross out unnecessary words in the following phrases:

Original	Corrected
Consensus of opinion	Consensus
Exact replica	Replica
New innovations	Innovations
Most unique	Unique
True facts	Facts
Surrounded on all sides	Surrounded
The month of May	May
Visible to the eye	Visible
Maximum possible	Maximum
Eight in number	Eight
Important essential	Essential
Red in colour	Red
The state of California	California
My personal opinion	My opinion
Entirely complete	Complete
Just recently	Recently
Refer back	Refer
Whether or not	Whether
Continue on	Continue
Past experience	Experience
Long period of time	Long period
At a distance of 100 feet	At 100 feet
At a price of ₹ 20	At ₹ 20
Remember the fact that	Remember that
I would like to recommend	I recommend

Exhibit 3.5   Deleting redundancies.

Further, a message can also be communicated effectively by making phrases brief and pithy. The following phrases have been restructured to bring about brevity in the written statement.

Original	Corrected
In the near future	shortly
In the event that	in case
In order that	so that
For the purpose of	for
With regard to	Regarding
I am of the opinion that	I think
Please do not hesitate to let me know	Please let me know
I wish to take this occasion to express my thanks	I thank

Exhibit 3.6   (Contd.)

Original	Corrected
In the early part of next week	Early next week
Your cheque for the amount of	Your cheque for ₹
It is quite probable that	Probably
It may be that	Possibly
At an early date	Early
In very few cases	Rarely
With reference to	As per
A large number	Many
At the present time	Currently
There is no doubt that	Undoubtedly
Most of the time	Frequently
In the same way	Similarly

Exhibit 3.6   Restructuring for brevity.

Brevity in writing, if coupled with the right choice of words, adds much to the effectiveness of a written message. Short, simple words should form part of the used business vocabulary. Some examples of simple words are provided below.

Original	Changed
Terminate	End
Utilise	Use
Anticipate	Expect
Assistance	Help
Endeavour	Effort
Ascertain	Confirm
Procure	Get
Consummate	Complete
Advise	Suggest
Alteration	Change
Fabricate	Make
Nevertheless	Even then
Substantial	Quite a lot
Fundamental	Basic
Afford an opportunity	Try
Approximately	Nearly
Accomplished	Completed
Accumulate	Amass
Additionally	Further
Commence	Begin
Compensate	Make up for
Demonstrate	To show
Encounter	Meeting
Expedite	Speed up

Exhibit 3.7   (*Contd.*)

Original	Changed
Facilitate	Make easy
Initiate	Start/begin
Indicate	Point out
Maintain	Sustain
Objectives	Aims
Obligation	Service done for
Participate	Share
Subsequent	Following
Sufficient	Enough
Transmit	Send
Unavailability	Absence
Voluminous	Bulky

Exhibit 3.7   Restructuring for simplicity.

PROOFREADING

TOPIC OBJECTIVES

Learn to proofread to make the text error free
Know techniques of accuracy in proof reading

"I was working on the proof of one of my poems all the morning, and took out a comma."

—Oscar Wilde

After completing the writing process, proofreading is mandatory. There may be typing errors that need to be corrected. Certain proofreading marks can be used that would make it easy to carry out corrections in the final script.

Proofreading marks are enumerated below:

Symbol	Meaning	Usage	Corrected version
=	Align horizontally	right ᵗʰᵉre	right there
||	Align vertically	1.|Name 2.| Address	1. Name 2. Address
(uc)	Capitalise	(uc) Don't touch	DON'T TOUCH
≡	Capitalise	Herbert co	HerbertCo
⌒	Close up	Break even	Breakeven
ℛ	Delete	love and regard	love
(Stet)	Restore to original	by the watch (Stet)	by the watch
∧	Insert	and guns roses	guns and roses
⅄	Insert comma	1,2 and 3	1,2, and 3
⊙	Insert period	rivers etc⊙	rivers etc.
/	Lower case	ALLAHABAD in	Allahabad in

(Contd.)

Symbol	Meaning	Usage	Corrected version
⊏	Move left	copy: ⌐manager	copy: manager
⊐	Move right	yours sincerely⌐	yours sincerely
⊔	Move down	|friends|	friends
⊓	Move up	|see through|	see through
⊐ (	Centre	⊐The Rock (	The Rock
⎘	Start new line	Mario,⁄Newyork	Mario, Newyork
⟲	Run lines together	manager, sales	manager, sales
⤶	Start paragraph	⤶It is a nice way of doing this.	It is a nice way of doing this.
#	Leave space	test⁄drive	test drive
◯	Spell out	⟨FOB⟩	Free on board
⟨sp⟩	Spell out	⟨sp⟩ Ins. of Engg.	Institution of Engineers
↶	Transpose	good,⁄and better, best	good, better, and best
⟍	Delete punctuation mark	on November 3⟍ it	on November 3 it
5	Indent 5 spaces	5⌉In January	In January

SUMMARY

Effective business writing means getting things done. This can be achieved by keeping in mind a two-fold purpose: to inform the reader and to request for action.

The three stages in the writing process are (a) pre-drafting, (b) drafting, and (c) postdrafting. Maximum amount of time must be allocated to pre-drafting. It is simpler if prior to commencing work, the writer defines the problem, gathers the material, organises it, revises and then completes the task.

To prepare notes, read the text carefully, select the keywords and construct a sentence without conjunctions and verbs to capture the essence of the idea. Note down the page number and biographical details as well.

An effective business message is composed in as short and simple a manner as possible. The correct words are used. Paragraphs and sentence constructions are kept simple, each dealing with a single idea to make for easy readability.

The tone and the style of writing changes with a change in readership. Different types of styles and tones can be adopted for different occasions and to reflect different moods.

The meaning of a word, usage or its spelling can be looked up in a dictionary which is arranged in the alphabetical order. The definition is always written in a simpler manner than the words they describe.

Correct and appropriate use of punctuations adds much to the meaning of the sentence. Some of the commonly used marks are periods, commas, colons, semicolons, dashes and parentheses.

After completing the writing process, proofreading is mandatory. Proofreading marks can be used that will make it easy to carry out corrections in the final script.

CHECKLIST

Do's	Don'ts
Follow the necessary preparatory steps prior to writing.	Cease the writing exercise after revision. Ensure that the text is properly formatted and structured.
Take a break after writing to clear the mind of prejudices.	Spend the maximum amount of time writing the text.
Ask your interviewee follow up questions for clarifications.	Interrupt your interviewee with too many ifs and buts.
Note down page number, bibliographical details or reference details for easy reference later.	Take care with punctuation and spelling when the original text needs to be quoted in the notes.
Compose concrete, short and simple messages without redundancies.	Use jargon when not required.
Choose your style and tone keeping in mind the sender (who), reader (to whom), the occasion (when and where), and the content (what).	Be quick and impulsive in writing.
Use commas to set off sentence elements that may be incorrectly read and comprehended.	Use commas intuitively.
Use colons after a formal salutation, and after an introductory phrase.	Use colons when the list, quotation or idea is part of the introductory phrase.
Use parenthesis to enclose a sentence, remark or comment that is not part of the main idea.	Use parenthesis often.
Delete redundancies for the sake of brevity.	Be long and winding.

Read the passage carefully and rewrite to make it short and pithy

Mike Valenti, owner of Michael's Homestyle Pasta—company with sales of $17 million, is a fair, innovative and people oriented entrepreneur. His style of management is very interactive and hands on. He mingles well with employees and ensures the results are achieved. This has made him favourite of employees.

Michael's specializes in gourmet stuffed pasta shells and has managed to keep it distinct from machine made pasta. Apart from them, only one other company, Southern Pasta, can produce similar product. Southern has managed good market share; and it has a chain of 200 restaurants on clientele which values about half the revenue. This is why Mike took over Southern in December 2001. Though Michael's did not have enough information about Southern, due to fear of someone else snatching the opportunity Mike closed the deal.

Southern had a problem of salmonella contamination in seafood stuffed shells in May 2001 and had to recall all shipments. After this, plant had to be thoroughly cleaned and was inspected by both FDA and client. A new system of tracking individual lot and approved cooking procedures were put in place with help of customer. All these cost around half a million dollars. Restaurant too invested its resources for better systems and adopted new protocols, which shows the nature of business relationship they have with Southern. Contrary to this, Michael's has a good image in market and new management will bring similar values to Southern also.

There is perceptible difference between cultures of two companies. Employees at Southern are not satisfied with top down approach of top management which is exactly opposite to that of Mike's. But after acquisition, Mike was not able to spend enough time with new team at Southern as his wife was pregnant. But this very fact has kept employees of Southern away from Mike's open leadership. Due to this trench of culture and distance maintained by Mike, a very serious problem has not come to notice.

On morning of New Year's Eve, quality assurance manger of Southern, Fred, informed about the contaminated shells supplied to customer. He too confessed that he used to doctor the lab sample under pressure of ex vice-president of Southern. In the month before takeover, each lot of seafood stuffed shells was contaminated. This was because of low standards of cleanliness. And product is heated only up to 140 Fahrenheit compared to 158 which is required to kill bacteria. Product has already been shipped to restaurant chain and within few hours is to be served. Restaurants are supposed to heat it up to 160 Fahrenheit before serving. So if they follow protocols there will not be a problem but they have to take this responsibility. Otherwise both Southern as well as customer will have to bear losses: both monetary as well as intangible.

RAPID REVIEW

A. Pick Your Choice

1. Maximum amount of time should be spent in
   - (a) pre-drafting
   - (b) drafting
   - (c) post-drafting
2. The "You attitude" can on occasions be done away with as it
   - (a) is implicit
   - (b) creates barriers
   - (c) is impolite

3. The most important task ahead of the interviewer is to
   (a) listen carefully   (b) formulate effective questions
   (c) make the interviewee comfortable
4. The quantum of information in the written text should be
   (a) in excess   (b) very brief
   (c) neither too much nor too little
5. Simplest pattern of writing is the
   (a) subject verb object ordering
   (b) subject adjective object ordering
   (c) none of the earlier stated
6. The writing stands to gain much in terms of acceptability if the tone is
   (a) polite   (b) positive   (c) both
7. In all types of written communication the emphasis should be on
   (a) I   (b) You   (c) We
8. For a persuasive text the tone of the writing needs to be
   (a) pleading   (b) commanding   (c) convincing
9. At the time of writing a text for the purpose of reflection or collaboration, the style and the tone should be
   (a) active   (b) convincing   (c) commanding
10. The main points of the gathered information can be collated on
   (a) separate sheets of paper
   (b) cue cards
   (c) foolscap sheet

B. True or False

1. Defining the problem right in the beginning leads to confusion.
2. No preparation is needed at the time of interviewing people.
3. The collation of the material is very important.
4. At the time of preparing the first draft we should be very particular of the style of writing.
5. Always take a break after preparing the first draft.
6. The KISS Principle states—Keep it short, silly.
7. Using simple words creates a negative impact in the mind of the reader.
8. To impress the reader abstract words should be used.
9. For technical writing a list of technical words should be provided for ease in comprehension.
10. The arrangement of words in a sentence contributes much to giving the message a particular structure.

C. **Fill in the Blanks**

1. The two-fold purpose at the time of writing should be _____ and _____.

2. At the time of composing a business message the most positive way of reaching a positive conclusion is to ask yourself the question _____?

3. A logical and coherent piece of writing requires a lot of time for _____.

4. If sufficient time is spent in the pre-drafting stage the _____ is definitely going to be better.

5. The four types of purpose around which the author prepares the draft are: _____, _____, _____, and _____.

6. Errors of _____ should be avoided.

7. The _____ should be conjoined logically.

8. _____ and _____ a text helps us to identify errors, if any.

9. Writing can be tedious if the _____ for writing is not clear.

10. Much of the secondary information can be gathered from the _____.

Answers

A. 1. (a) 2. (a) 3. (b) 4. (c) 5. (a) 6. (c) 7. (b) 8. (c) 9. (a) 10. (c)

B. 1. False   2. False   3. True   4. False   5. True
        6. False   7. False   8. False   9. True   10. True.

C. 1. To tell you; to ask you   2. so what   3. preparation
        4. output   5. To inform; to persuade; to regulate; to collaborate
        6. logic   7. sentences/paragraphs   8. Reading; re-reading
        9. Motive   10. library.

QUESTIONS FOR DISCUSSION

1. Discuss the advantages of spending extra time in the pre-drafting and post-drafting stages instead of the drafting stage.

2. What are the five steps a report writer should identify to write an effective report?

3. How should business messages be composed? What factors should be kept in mind?

4. You are writing an important message and have got stuck on the usage of a particular word. What would you refer to—dictionary or thesaurus and why?

5. When should a dictionary be consulted?

6. How is a thesaurus used?

7. Discuss the importance of the Principles of writing.

8. Discuss the strategies through which you can turn an expected tough interview situation to your advantage.

9. When can a colon be used?

10. What are the instances when a comma can be used?

EXERCISES

1. You are expected to write a report on Quality Circles. Visit your library and identify sources from which you can gather material for your report.

2. Select a friend who has a terse style of writing. Browse through five pages of any of the friend's written assignment and try to identify common errors in sentences. Correct and rewrite.

3. Write a letter of application of leave to the Director of your Institute. Assess the time that you took in pre-drafting, drafting and post-drafting.

4. Leaf through any of your earlier written assignments. Pick out any one of them. Re-read the entire text. Do you think any changes can be brought about? Would it improve the style and tone and make it more forceful?

5. Rewrite the following sentences so that they are short, simple and aesthetically sound:

    (a) These customers want the convenience of buying everything at one place.

    (b) The shopping complex had been doing good business for the past seventeen years.

    (c) There is a great perceived demand for them over here.

    (d) The thing that can make an impact for Shipyard is improvement in its facilities.

    (e) Our manner of discussion had been achieving the right impact.

6. You need to collect data from a tough client. Write the stages of preparation you will undertake to ensure that the client responds favourably to you.

7. Visit your library and prepare a library usage chart to be put up on the notice board.

8. Draft a page of technical information that you need to send to your boss who is a non-technical person. Was the composition of the message easy or difficult?

9. Pick up an article from a business journal and try to make a brief of it. Show it to your teacher or friend and ascertain whether your article has been able to retain the essence of the topic. Discuss with your friends the techniques that you used in simplifying and shortening the article.

10. Prepare a list of ten items of often used phraseology. Discuss errors, if any and how can they be modified so that this phraseology can be included in formal business writing.

CONTENTS

LEARNINGS

After reading this chapter you should be able to:

- Learn to distinguish between an informative and an analytical approach
- Acquire clarity about the purpose and function of the report
- Understand that a plan for a report is essential
- Use an outline to segregate, collate and arrange ideas
- Comprehend methods of organising issues or topics
- Select the appropriate visual aid

KEYWORDS

5 Ws and 1 H, Informational Report, Analytical Report, Structural Organisation, Deductive Approach, Inductive Approach, Informative Headings, Descriptive Headings, Parallel Ordering, Group Based Ordering, Logical Sequencing, Numbering Systems, Graphic Representation, Floating Wedge

INTRODUCTION

"And so while the great ones depart to their dinner, the secretary stays, growing thinner and thinner, racking his brain to record and report what he thinks that they think that they ought to have thought."

—Arthur Bryan

A report is a presentation and summation of facts and figures either collated or derived. It is a logical and coherent structuring of information, ideas and concepts. As a neatly structured piece of work, the report, for greater ease in comprehension, is segregated into various sections. Understanding the import of these sections, and connecting them logically is the first requirement of a well written report.

FIVE Ws AND ONE H

TOPIC OBJECTIVES
Learn to ask and answer the right questions for a focussed report
Outline the stages in report planning

"Instead of following the rules without regard for whether they're making our writing effective or not, we often need to question the rules. To write with style, we need at times to break the rules."

—Donna Gorrell

Prior to commencing work on a report, a few queries should be raised by the reportwriter to facilitate the writing process. The queries centre on the five Ws and the one H. *What* is the problem? What is it that needs to be ascertained? Clarity along these lines helps in eliminating any redundancies that might crop up. Identification of the genesis of the problem helps in streamlining the approach. The problem could, for instance, be one that has to determine the cause for the decrease in sales.

What

Why is the issue important? What is its relevance and significance to the department in specific, and organisation in general? The issue is important because a decrease in sales is a cause for concern to the entire organisation. Strategies need to be chalked-out for redemption of the situation. *Why* (purpose) should the problem be analysed? What are the benefits that will accrue from this particular report—to the department, the organisation, and the self? The report would probably lead to suggestion of multiple action points that could be implemented. This, in turn, would, as suggested in the report, lead to increase in sales.

Why

Who is involved in the situation? This could take into account both the reader(s) and the writer. In case there is a third party involved, it would also account for that. *Who* is going to be my reader? With a change in the reader, approach in the report also undergoes a change. The marketing and the production department people would probably be the readers in this particular case.

Who

Further, *when* did the trouble begin? In case it is an analytical report, one would also need to address the source and time of the problem before reaching any conclusion. This would entail, tracing in brief, the downward curve of the sales graph. It may be asked: *When* am I going to write the report? The time factor is critical. Chalking out or revising strategies should be done prior to the marketing season or entrance of new players in the market.

> When

From where did the problem begin? Assessment of the situation and the problem location will help place the report in the right perspective. The approach and recommendations then can be generic or specific.

> Where

Finally, *how* would the report be written? What information is to be included and what to be excluded/which graphs and charts would be used/ avoided? All these queries need to be satisfied before beginning a report. They give the report a particular direction, and help the writer to concentrate on the acceptability of the report by the audience to which it is aimed.

> How

Let us take a look at a project report to be prepared by a financial institution.

Why—Why should project A be supported?

What—What is the justification of a loan for project A?

Who—Who would read the report? Would it act as precedence for further similar loans to be sanctioned? Or would it remain just one of the usual reports written within a standard format?

When—When was the loan requisitioned and when sanctioned? Is the report being written close to the time of sanctioning of the loan, or is it merely an informative one, providing information on the various factors leading to the sanctioning of the loan?

How—How should the report be written? Should the style be objective or subjective? If the sanctioning of the loan is important, persuasive language can be used to get the ideas and message across. All details should be provided and meticulous care should be taken to ensure that nothing unwarranted is included.

Answers to these queries would also bring about a change in the writing style.

REPORT PLANNING

TOPIC OBJECTIVES

Learn to present information which is true, and make the report useful by logically and coherently structuring the information and ideas

Outline the steps involved in report planning

"Writing is like a lump of coal. Put it under enough pressure and polish it enough and you might just end up with a diamond. Otherwise, you can burn it to keep warm."
—A.J. Dalton

We already know that a report must present and sum up facts and figures either collated or derived. We know that we must ask ourselves some important questions about the purpose and scope of the report, much like Socrates' filters, to present that which is true and good. But to make it useful, it must be logically and coherently structured so that the information, ideas and concepts are absorbed by the reader.

One day Socrates, the Greek philosopher came upon an acquaintance who ran up to him excitedly and said, "Socrates, do you know what I just heard about one of your students?" Wait a moment," Socrates replied. "Before you tell me I'd like you to pass a little test. It's called the Triple Filter Test." "Triple filter?" "That's right," Socrates continued. "Before you talk to me about my student let's take a moment to filter what you're going to say. The first filter is Truth. Have you made absolutely sure that what you are about to tell me is true?" "No," the man said, "actually I just heard about it and..." "All right," said Socrates. "So you don't really know if it's true or not. Now let's try the second filter, the filter of Goodness. Is what you are about to tell me about my student something good?" "No, on the contrary..." "So," Socrates continued, "you want to tell me something bad about him, even though you're not certain it's true?" The man shrugged, a little embarrassed. Socrates continued. "You may still pass the test though, because there is a third filter—the filter of Usefulness. Is what you want to tell me about my student going to be useful to me?" "No, not really..." "Well," concluded Socrates, "if what you want to tell me is neither True nor Good nor even Useful, why tell it to me at all?"
Retrieved on December 14, 2013 from http://anecdotes2008.blogspot.com/search/label/Triple%20Filter%20Test

The planning stage is the most crucial one. Spend as much time as possible in collecting material, synchronising details, and ensuring that nothing has been left out. If a detailed planning is done in the initial phase there are very few chances of missing out on important details or errors at the final stage. In fact, planning for a report is as important as the process of writing itself. The various steps involved in report planning are as follows:

1. **Define the problem and the purpose.** The problem and purpose had already been identified at the stage when the answers to the question *what* and *why* were attempted. It is essential at this stage to understand the nature of the report— | Defining problem and purpose | whether it is informational or analytical. In an informational report the writer will lay stress on facts and figures and their positioning. On the other hand, in an analytical report the writer will need to define the problem, generate criteria and options and then evaluate the feasibility of the proposed option. With a variance in the type of the report, there is sure to be a difference in the problem definition and statement of purpose.

2. **Outline issues for investigation.** In a problem solving or analytical report, all issues pertaining to the problem need to be highlighted in | Outlining issues | the initial stage. None of the alternatives or variables should be ignored or side-tracked. Once the issues have been clarified, delineation of the points

becomes easier. Further, if the report is of an informational nature, all issues that need to be exemplified should be outlined. Even the methodology adopted for this process has to be understood. There is a basic pattern that has to be observed and it should be clearly identified and followed in shaping content.

JAM: Have you considered all your variables or alternatives?

3. **Prepare a work-plan.** What is the best procedure to collect the data? How should the writer proceed? What are the techniques that need to be observed? These are a few of the questions that need to be well-answered before taking the final plunge into conducting research on the topic.

> *Preparing a work-plan*

4. **Conduct research, analyse and interpret.** The modus operandi at the time of conducting research should be examined. This should, however, be taken care of at the stage of preparing a work-plan. The manner in which research is conducted is contingent upon the problem defined in the initial phase of report writing. Once the research has been conducted, begins the process of analysis and the subsequent interpretation, which happen to be the toughest parts in report making. As far as possible, an attempt should be made to bring about accuracy in the analysis and make the interpretation objective and unbiased.

> *Conducting research, analyzing and interpreting*

5. **Draw conclusions.** Subsequent to the stage of interpretation of data, certain conclusions need to be drawn and recommendations or suggestions made. This comprises the last stage of the report and the tone of it is determined by the position held by the report writer. For instance, if it is a report being written by a subordinate, only suggestions can be made. However, if it is one being written by a team leader, it will, in the concluding section, have a rather well-developed recommendation section.

Note: The manner of defining the problem determines the type of report to be written.

TYPES OF REPORTS

"I don't make jokes. I just watch the government and report the facts."
—Will Rogers

The most commonly used reports fall under the following two categories:

1. Informational report
2. Analytical report

TOPIC OBJECTIVES

Differentiate between the structural organisation of informational and analytical reports

Distinguish the deductive approach from the inductive approach

Broadly speaking, both types of reports contain similar components in terms of structure or organisation. The three major sections in a report are:

1. Introduction
2. Text
3. Terminal section

However, there is a major difference in the structuring of these three sections in informational and analytical reports. This stems primarily from the nature of the task attempted in the two different types of reports.

Informational Report

An informational report, as the name suggests, entails provision of all details and facts pertaining to the problem. For instance, it can be a report that attempts to trace the growth of Company X in the automobile industry. In a report of this kind, the presentation of all details that led to the growth of Company X should be listed in a chronological order.

The sequential arrangement of issues or topics in an informational report could observe any one of the following ways of presentation.

- Chronology
- Importance
- Sequence/procedure
- Category
- Alphabetisation or
- Familiarity

Structural organisation

As the presentation of information is the basic purpose of the report, details are worked out in a systematic and coherent manner. The structural orientation in an informational report should be clearly evident to the reader and its significance also grasped.

In a report of this kind, the various sections are simple and self-explanatory. The introduction is followed by a presentation of information or facts and a summary thereafter where all the details are collated in brief for a recall or recap of earlier sections.

Types	Structure
Informational	Introduction
	Text
	Terminal section
Analytical	Terminal section
	Introduction
	Text

Exhibit 4.1   Types of reports and their structure.

Analytical Report

The analytical report comprises stages in which there is a proper identification of the problem, analysis and subsequent interpretation. Recommendations or suggestions are then incorporated in the report, depending on the requirement of the audience/readers. Thus, in a problem-solving method, the steps observed are as follows:

1. Draft problem statement
2. Evolve criteria
3. Suggest alternatives and evaluation
4. Draw conclusion(s) and make recommendations

The structure of an analytical report can follow any of the two patterns—deductive or inductive. An inductive ordering follows a simple, logical arrangement in which you proceed from the known to the unknown. There are two premises or syllogisms that conjoin to yield a final conclusion, e.g.

Syllogism 1	Ram is a man and mortal.
Syllogism 2	Shyam is a man and mortal.
Syllogism 3	....
Syllogism n	....
Conclusion	Therefore, all men are mortal.

One can formulate umpteen number of syllogisms to reach a final conclusion which is always based on the number of experiments conducted or factors observed. Certain disciplines, in which experiments have to be done and surveys conducted, naturally follow this pattern. Here the progression is always a move from the known to the unknown conclusion.

However, inductive patterning, while normally followed for organisation based studies and experiments, suffers from a major drawback. As it is not based on any universal truth, it holds valid only up to the point when a discovery is made that is contrary to the findings in the report. It is by nature only relevant in the present and no universal claims to the same can be made.

On the other hand, a deductive ordering observes a reverse patterning where it proceeds from the unknown to the known. Universal truths are taken as the formulation point for the problem. The various alternatives are suggested, evaluated and conclusions drawn, keeping in mind the original stated problem. To take a look at the manner of approach in deductive methodology, let us take an example.

Conclusion	All men are mortal.
Syllogism 1	Ram is a man and mortal.
Syllogism 2	Shyam is a man and mortal.
Syllogism 3	....
Syllogism n	....

While in an inductive method the pattern of the report would normally follow the sequence of introduction, text and terminal section, in deductive method the structure can also be altered. It can begin with the terminal section in which conclusion and recommendations are stated at the beginning followed by an introduction and the text section. This pattern will be observed if the report is of high importance and the receiver does not have the time to browse through the entire report. Merely a glance at the initial pages will help the reader get the import of the content. Such readership will only be concerned with the conclusions and recommendations/suggestions or plan of action.

JAM: Remember to begin with conclusions and recommendations, if you want your reader to grasp the topic quickly.

Inductive approach	Deductive approach
The automobile sector in India seems to have made tremendous headway in the last ten years. Company X has produced three models of cars. However, with the entry of new players in the market the company is facing stiff competition. There is also a slump in the market with excessive production and insufficient demand. The current study analyses the growth prospects of Company X vis-á-vis its competitors. The study focusses attention on the following three questions: 1. Who are the competitors? 2. Will Company X be able to face stiff competition from other companies? 3. What are the prospects of growth? The report attempts to analyse...	The automobile sector in India seems to have made tremendous headway in the last ten years. Company X has produced three models of cars. However, with the entry of new players in the market, Company X is facing stiff competition. There is also a slump in the market with excessive production and insufficient demand. The current study analyses the growth prospects of Company X vis-á-vis its competitors. It can easily be concluded that: 1. Company X is facing severe competition from Companies Y and Z. 2. Unless Company X brings down its price to match that of the competitors, it will not be able to cover a substantial market share. It is recommended that an additional feature such as power steering be introduced as an extra facility or a reasonable reduction in price be carried out. Further, it is recommended that Company X target students pursuing professional courses with a lowered price and basic strip down model so that it appeals to their taste and fits their pocket. The conclusions arrived at and recommendations made are based on the following study. Five sample automobile companies were taken...

Exhibit 4.2   Different styles of opening a report.

DEVELOPING AN OUTLINE

TOPIC OBJECTIVES

Identify consistency in grammar and logic in the organisation of ideas
Understand the logic and system of divisions and numbering

"I try to leave out the parts that people skip."
—Elmore Leonard.

It is extremely important to develop an outline of the report prior to commencing work on the report. The formatting of the report should be carried out only after completion of the outline. As stated earlier, questions revolving round the five Ws and one H should be answered or kept in mind at the time of preparing an outline.

Sir Charles Chaplin

The playwright Charles MacArthur had been brought to Hollywood to do a screenplay, but was finding it difficult to write visual jokes.

"What's the problem?" asked Chaplin.

"How, for example, could I make a fat lady, walking down Fifth Avenue, slip on a banana peel and still get a laugh? It's been done a million times," said MacArthur. "What's the best way to GET the laugh? Do I show first the banana peel, then the fat lady approaching, then she slips? Or do I show the fat lady first, then the banana peel, and THEN she slips?"

"Neither," said Chaplin without a moment's hesitation. "You show the fat lady approaching; then you show the banana peel; then you show the fat lady and the banana peel together; then she steps OVER the banana peel and disappears down a manhole."

Retrieved on June 16, 2014 from http://www.batchmates.com/bmtimes/content.aspx?contentid=1940

Once these questions have been satisfactorily tackled should begin the process of brainstorming. All ideas that come to the mind should be written on small pieces of cue cards so that at a later stage it is easier to arrange them in a sequential order. Brainstorming will generate a host of ideas, some of which form main points and others ancillary points. Now comes the tedious task of assigning an order to the cues. This can be done to ensure that the following points are considered:

1. A logical, general description
2. A schematic summary
3. An organisational pattern
4. A visual, conceptual design of writing

Once this is completed begins a three-stage process:

1. All group-related ideas are clubbed together.
2. Points are organised in the form of sections and sub-sections. The expected progression is from the general to the specific or abstract to the concrete.

3. Main and sub-headings are created keeping in mind the fact that all follow a similar grammatical pattern.

Note: Ideas may be segregated on cue cards and later developed into main points and ancillary points.

NATURE OF HEADINGS

TOPIC OBJECTIVES
Understand the nature of heading required for the document
Learn to consistently use either informative or descriptive headings

"Headlines are so great in a sense that they can take a little bit from an article completely out of context and blow it into something it's not. Some people really only read headlines."   —Kristin Cavallari

Headings can be of two types: *informative* and *descriptive*, depending on the nature of the report which is being written. An informative heading should present information in the direct order and be geared towards a more receptive audience. For example, in discussing the various alternatives, a heading can be of the following nature.

1. Change the size of tins

If the same were to be converted into a descriptive heading, it would be written as:

2. Size of tins

A descriptive heading presents the point indirectly. It fails to draw the attention of the readers who are less receptive to content than in the case of informative headings.

JAM: IS your informative heading written in a direct fashion?

POINT FORMULATION

TOPIC OBJECTIVES
Understand the significance of point formulation
Learn to be consistent in ordering of points and headings

"You can have brilliant ideas, but if you can't get them across, your ideas won't get you anywhere."
—Lee Iacocca

Look at the following excerpt from a business report written by a management student and study it carefully.

1. Increase promotional efforts.
2. Changing the size of tins.
3. Installing more capacity.

You will realise that the writer has followed a visually appealing pattern of ordering points in parallel form. You also notice, that the writer has been inconsistent with the use of verb+ing in all points.

To make this better and more logical, let us rearrange the points:

> 1. Increase promotional efforts
> 2. Change the size of tins
> 3. Install more capacity

You can change it even further if you so wish by using a similar verb+ing form in the first point as has been used in the second and third points:

> 1. Increasing promotional efforts
> 2. Changing the size of tins
> 3. Installing more capacity

Note: Put your headings in parallel form to make it easy on the eye.

Organise Group Related Ideas Together

Together with putting all the headings in a grammatically similar pattern, a consistent pattern of clubbing them together should be followed. In other words, the general or specific connotations should be the same.

Incorrect formulation

> 1. Piling inventory
> 2. Promotional aspects
> 3. Distribution networks

The above formulation is incorrect as it does not place items of the same specificity in the same category. While in the first the writer talks about the piling up of the inventory because of disuse; in the second, a number of promotional strategies are hinted which can be in the nature of advertisements, hoardings, etc. The third category again presupposes a number of networks through which the distribution is done.

Correction

> 1. Piling inventory
>   - Disuse
> 2. Promotional aspects
>   - Advertisements
>   - Hoardings
> 3. Distribution networks
>   - Institutional markets
>   - Shelf display

Warning! Do not include items with different specificity within the same category.

Logical Sequencing of Points

Finally, a logical sequence should be followed in the arrangement or the connection between the sub-sections and the main section. The relationship between the main heading and its sub-sections should be the same and the progression, as far as possible, be from the abstract to the concrete and from the general to the specific.

Correct arrangement

A. Tact maxim
  1. Minimise cost to other
  2. Maximise benefit to other
B. Generosity maxim
  1. Minimise benefit to self
  2. Maximise cost to self

Incorrect arrangement

A. Tact maxim
  1. Minimise cost to other
  2. Strategies
  3. Usefulness

The problem with a formulation of this kind is that the example uses the alphabet A without a B. Further, 1, 2 and 3 are not of the same specificity. The first falls in the nature of issuing a directive, the second is a noun and the third is a quality that may be applicable or non-applicable according to the prevailing conditions.

Correction

A. Cost strategy
  1. Minimise cost to other
  2. Maximise cost to self
B. Benefit strategy
  1. Minimise benefit to self
  2. Maximise benefit to other

Warning! Make sure the connections between the main heading and its sub-sections are the same.

DIVISIONS

TOPIC OBJECTIVES

Learn to posit the ideas correctly under textual divisions

Understand the techniques of breaking up the text into appropriate divisions and sub-divisions

"Examine every word you put on paper. You'll find a surprising number that don't serve any purpose."
—William Knowlton Zinsser

In order to carry on with divisions the writer needs to document at least two parts. There cannot be a 1 without a 2, an 'A' without a 'B' and so on and so forth. Care should be exercised at the time of dividing the headings into sub-sections as the basis of division should be similar.

Incorrect division

A. Opening section
   1. Introduction
   2. Greeting
   3. Main topic and sub-topic repetitions
   4. Action-related exchange leading to digressions
B. Concluding section
   1. Summary of main topic and sub-topics
   2. Justification
   3. Repetitions in leave-taking and well-wishing
   4. Contact-termination

The incorrect division on many occasions takes more than one category into account, for example, main-topic and sub-topic repetitions and similarly for B. In two headings we have a sub-division within a sub-section: Summary of main topics and sub-topics and repetition in leave-taking and well-wishing.

Correction

A. Opening section
   1. Introduction
   2. Greetings
   3. Repetitions
      (a) Main topic
      (b) Sub-topics
   4. Digressions
      (a) Action-related exchange
      (b) Anecdote narrations
B. Closing section
   1. Summary
      (a) Main topic
      (b) Sub-topics

2. Justifications
3. Repetitions
   (a) Leave-taking
   (b) Well-wishing
4. Contact termination

JAM: Have you checked if in positing your ideas in the point format you have taken more than one category into account?

Numbering

The report can follow any one of the numbering systems: the Roman numerals and letters or the arabic numerals and the decimal.

Roman Numeral and letters

I.
    A.
    B.
        1.
        2.
II.
    A.
    B.
        1.
        2.

Further subdivisions may be done by capitalisation and different typography (as computer setting facility is available today)

Arabic Numeral and Decimal

1.0
    1.1
    1.2
        1.2.1
        1.2.2
2.0
    2.1
    2.2
        2.2.1
        2.2.2

It should be kept in mind that with introduction of sub-sections the lines keep getting indented. Further, it is essential to note that in the Roman numerals and letters, there is always a period or a full-stop after indication of the letter or numeral, for instance, I., A. However, the same pattern is not followed in the decimal system. There is no stop or period at the end of the numeral, e.g. 1.0, 1.1, 1.1.1, etc.

Further subdivisions may be done by different typography using the computer setting facility.

Note: Sub-sections are differentiated by indenting them.

VISUAL AIDS

TOPIC OBJECTIVES

Analyse the need for and function of visual aids. Map the methods of graphic presentation.

"It's much easier to consume the visual image than to read something."   —Lawrence Ferlinghetti

Translating words and ideas in a visual form requires a lot of ingenuity on the part of the writer. Visual aids by way of charts and graphs cannot be included at any juncture. There has to be a systematic ordering by which the writer decides which part of the information is to be incorporated in the form of words and which, in the form of charts and tables.

The raw material or data that the individual possesses has to be given a structured ordering. The steps that enable the writer to proceed at an easy pace are:

1. **Confirm reader's needs and thought pattern.** This is the first stage for the writer to be cognisant of before conceptualising the use of visual aids. The reader may be looking for the entire report as a visual presentation or a verbal one or maybe a combination of the two. Depending on the requirement of the reader, the verbal and visual can be balanced.

2. **Clarify which ideas would be best represented in visual form.** It is difficult to present all ideas through graphics. Some ideas can communicate with greater impact if presented through charts or tables, e.g. comparison between the sales figures of two consecutive years. It is the discretion of the report writer and understanding of the reader requirements that determine the graphic or verbal representation of points.

3. **Visualise the presentation of the same points in graphic form.** Once the sorting of the points or ideas is complete, the next stage begins, that is, the imaginary conceptualising of the same points. For example, which of the charts or table would be most-suited to represent a point. If one was to take up the comparison between the sales figures of two consecutive years, one could use both the tabular form and the comparative bar diagram. It is now for the report writer to decide which format should be adopted.

4. **Establish balance between the verbal and the visual.** Too much of visual and too little of verbal or the other way round adds to the

monotony of the text. There should be a good mix between the two so that report reading process is not tedious.

While it may seem rather exciting entering the domain of visuals, care should be exercised from the point of view of presentation. A badly presented visual can have a negative impact. Probably the following points, if kept in mind, can improve the quality of presentation.

1. Thick line implies more power
2. More mass indicates solidity
3. Bold colour implies emphasis

JAM: Have your exercised your discretion in choosing which ideas need to be represented in visual form?

One could make use of these techniques effectively at the time of indicating contrast or showing comparison.

There are a number of ways through which graphic presentations can be done:

1. Tables
2. Bar graphs
   (a) Vertical bar graphs
   (b) Stacked vertical bar graphs
   (c) Horizontal bar graphs
   (d) Multiple bar graphs
3. Pie-charts
4. Line graphs
5. Pictograms/Pictorial graph
6. Flow charts and organisation charts
7. Drawings, diagrams and maps

Tables

These are the simplest of the visual presentations and require a form in which there are both horizontal rows as well as vertical columns. These tables are mostly numerical, but word tables are also used. In a survey concerning TV viewing habits of men, women and children the results can be presented in Table 4.3.

Category	Percentage of viewers	Percentage of non-viewers
Men	44	56
Women	70	30
Children	80	20

Exhibit 4.3   TV viewing habits.

The tabular form of presentation, while simple for the report writer, has both advantages and disadvantages. A lot of figures can be depicted. A

Advantages and disadvantages of tables

number of combinations are possible in this tabular form, for example, numeric and non-numeric data can be presented simultaneously. However, it also has certain disadvantages: While it is part of the visual depiction yet, visually the details are not evident at a glance. Occasionally, the writer may clutter the table with too much data, making it complicated and robbing it of visual appeal.

Multiple Bar Graph

These are the simplest to construct and make for easy comprehension by the reader. They can be of various types: Vertical with singular or multiple bars

Advantages and disadvantages of bar graphs

(Exhibit 4.4), stacked or comparative and horizontal (Exhibit 4.5). If these graphs depict more than one variable, two colours or designs are used so as to highlight the difference between the two variables. These graphs are comparative and if more than two variables in terms of the same time frame are used a stacked vertical or horizontal bar chart is used. The greatest advantage of these bar diagrams is that they can also be used with a three-dimensional effect.

Presentations in this form are advantageous as they have a compelling impact and two or more variables can be stacked without leading to difficulties in grasping the details. The colour and schematic designs added to the bars lend visual appeal to these charts. However, there can be lack of precision in presentation of details as the variables may become too cluttered and the lettering too small.

Note: Since bar graphs can be used with a three-dimensional effect, they make for greater visual appeal and easy comprehension.

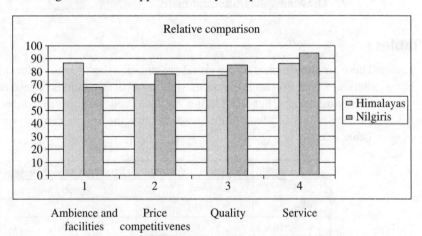

Exhibit 4.4   Multiple bar graphs.

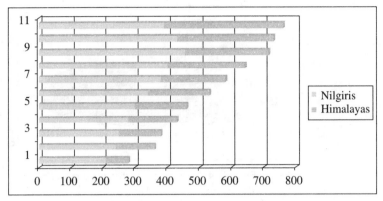

Exhibit 4.5   Horizontal stacked bar graph.

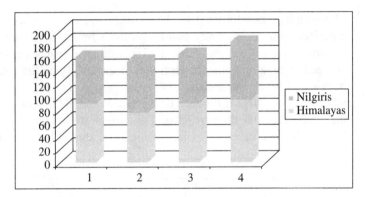

Exhibit 4.6   Three-dimensional stacked vertical bar diagram.

Pie-Chart

This is one of the most popular forms to depict the share of the various categories and their correlation to the whole as a percentage. If there is a need to emphasise a particular segment it is detached from the pie and referred to as the floating wedge. The other segments are demarcated by lines or differing colours in a circular form.

The pie chart captures the attention of the reader at a much faster pace than probably any other graphic presentation. Within one chart segments can be highlighted. In addition to the colour pattern used, the categorisation of the segments can be within, outside or alongside the chart. However, there can be occasions when the difference is small and may not show up effectively. For example, a 0.5 per cent may be too small to draw attention. Further, if the patterning of the segments has not been done imaginatively they may merge and lead to a confused reading of the graph.

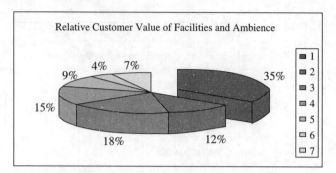

Exhibit 4.7   Pie-chart with a floating wedge.

Line Graph

This graph is usually used to depict time and the variations in time over a period. Time is normally plotted on the *x* or the horizontal axis and the variable on the *y* or the vertical axis. Both the scales begin at zero and proceed in equal increments. However, occasionally on the *y*-axis there may be a small break immediately after the zero point. This is normally done when there is a large difference between zero and the first quantity to indicate that some data has no bearing on the current study and has therefore been left out. In such cases, all points of omission should be carefully indicated.

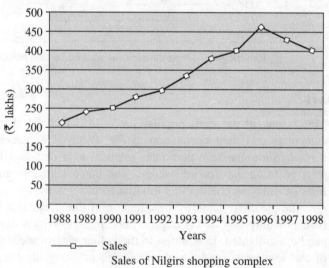

Exhibit 4.8   Line graph.

A lot of trends over a specific period can be depicted by the line graph. A little caution should be exercised if the lines cross each other at certain points. In line diagrams, if there is an overlap among variables be restrictive and present only three variables to avoid loss of information.

This form of representation, though does allow the writer to present multiple non-overlapping variables that indicate trends over time allowing easy comparisons. However, as stated above, problems can arise if too many variables are plotted preventing fine distinctions from being evidenced or noticed.

> Advantages and disadvantages of line graphs

Note: Trends over a specific period can be depicted by the line graph.

Pictograms/Pictorial Graph

> Advantages and disadvantages of pictograms

These are more in the nature of bar charts with figures or small pictures plotted instead of lines. The pictures are chosen in accordance with the topic or the subject matter. This chart is self-explanatory, e.g. if a chart were to be prepared indicating the population boom in the last five years, human figures can be used to exemplify the point made by the report writer. In this example, a cluster of the figures or pictures at a certain point will be self-explanatory. This chart is not used extensively for business reports.

Year		Population (millions)
1000	☺☺☺☺☺☺☺	700
1500	☺☺☺☺☺☺☺☺	800
1800	☺☺☺☺☺☺☺☺☺	900
1900	☺☺☺☺☺☺☺☺☺☺	1100
1950	☺☺☺☺☺☺☺☺☺☺☺	1300
1960	☺☺☺☺☺☺☺☺☺☺☺☺	1600
1970	☺☺☺☺☺☺☺☺☺☺☺☺☺	1700
1980	☺☺☺☺☺☺☺☺☺☺☺☺☺☺	2000
1990	☺☺☺☺☺☺☺☺☺☺☺☺☺☺☺	2200

☺ = 100 millions of population

Exhibit 4.9   Pictorial graph showing European population from 1000 AD to 1990 AD.

The advantage of this chart is that large numbers can be presented by a single cluster of figures. Much time and effort goes into the designing of this chart so as to make it truly representative of the problem that it seeks to address. However, it is not very useful for business reports as they are more concrete and not based on pictorial depiction of the problem.

Flow Charts and Organisation Charts

Flow charts present a sequence of activities from start to finish. They are used to illustrate processes, procedures and relationships. The various elements in the chart can also be depicted either with figures or geometrical designs.

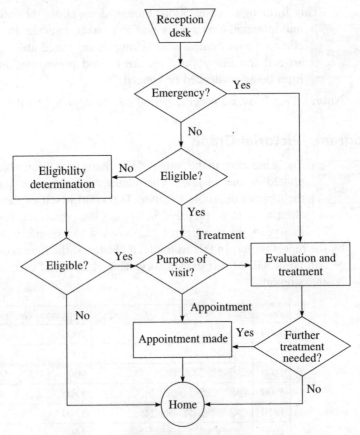

Exhibit 4.10 Flowchart.

Organisation charts illustrate the various positions or functions within the organisation. Most of the communication channels in an organisation are described with the usage of these kinds of charts.

JAM: Have you kept the reader's need in mind while determining your visual aid?

Drawings, Diagrams and Maps

Various drawings and diagrams can be used in business reports, though their usage is definitely limited. Most of these are added to make the report colourful and decorative. However, they should be used sparingly so that the reader does not get swayed and lose track of the import of the message.

Maps are rather appropriate for use when the writer wishes to present statistical data through geographical indicators or so wishes to express locational relationships.

SUMMARY

A report is a presentation and summation of facts and figures either collated or derived. It is a logical and coherent structuring of information, ideas and concepts.

Prior to commencing work on a report, queries should be raised and satisfactorily answered on the five W's and the one H.

Planning for a report involves defining the problem and the purpose, outlining the issues for investigation, preparing a work-plan, conducting research, analysing and interpreting, and drawing conclusions.

An informational report entails provision of all details and facts pertaining to the problem. The introduction is followed by a presentation of information or facts and a summary thereafter.

The analytical report comprises the problem, analysis, interpretation, and in some cases, recommendation. The structure of an analytical report could follow any of the two patterns— deductive or inductive.

Ideas for the content of the report could be structured in a logical manner, given an organisational pattern with visual appeal.

Headings can be of two types: informative and descriptive. Headings should be expressed in a parallel form and in a grammatically similar pattern. There should be a consistent pattern of clubbing them together. In other words, the general or specific connotations should be the same.

Division and numbering of content must clearly follow the system of indentation to differentiate various sub-sections. The connection between the sub-sections and the main section should follow a logical sequence.

Graphic presentations can be done with the means of tables, bar graphs, pie-charts, line graphs, pictograms/pictorial graph, flow charts and organisation charts, drawings, diagrams and maps. They should be used judiciously, keeping in mind the requirements of the reader, the report and the balance between the verbal and the visual.

CHECKLIST

Do's	Don'ts
Ask yourself questions focussing on the 5 Ws and 1 H	Forget the 5 Ws and 1 H
Identify if the report has to be informational or analytical	Interchange the required structure for informational and analytical reports
Write out the ideas on cue cards to enable easy sequencing of ideas	Omit to develop an outline prior to commencing work on the report
Express headings in a parallel form	Be grammatically and logically inconsistent in your headings

Do's	Don'ts
Organise your points in the form of sections and sub-sections	Use the wrong progression, from specific to general, while organising your points
Use a period or a full stop when using Roman numerals and letters	Use a stop or period at the end of the numeral in the decimal system
Use thick and solid lines with more colour in your visuals to make it more powerful	Include visual aids at each and any juncture
Use a stacked vertical or horizontal bar chart if more than two variables are used within the same time frame	Use the same colour and design for all the bars depicting different variables
Use pictograms to represent large numbers through pictorial cluster figures	Use pictograms for business reports that require concrete information
Use maps to discuss or present statistical data through geographical indicators, or locational relationships	Use drawings, diagrams and maps to only make the report more colourful

RAPID REVIEW

A. Pick Your Choice

1. A descriptive heading
   (a) describes   (b) informs
   (c) reports in an indirect order
2. Questions pertaining to the five Ws and the one H
   (a) help in streamlining the report outline
   (b) add unnecessary length   (c) neither (a) or (b)
3. Interpretation of data is followed by
   (a) recommendations   (b) suggestions   (c) conclusions
4. In an analytical report there is
   (a) identification of the problem   (b) analysis
   (c) interpretation   (d) all of these
5. Visual aids
   (a) break monotony   (b) can be added at any stage
   (c) should be used prudently
6. Thick line implies
   (a) power   (b) leaking pen   (c) aesthetic outburst
7. Visual aids by way of charts and graphs
   (a) can be included at will
   (b) have to be carefully planned and strategically placed
   (c) cannot be used without the reader's consent

8. (a) Confirm reader's level   (b) Cross check with reader

   (c) Establish balance between verbal and visual

is the first stage that should be adhered to before conceptualising the use of visual aids.

9. Bold colour implies

   (a) emphasis   (b) attention   (c) power

10. The tables lack

   (a) accuracy in presentation

   (b) visual appeal

   (c) three-dimensional effect

B. True or False

1. There is a difference between informational and analytical reports.
2. In an informational report the structure is always in the form of introduction, text, and conclusion.
3. In a deductive report the structure is almost always in the form of introduction, text and conclusion.
4. In a problem-solving report there are three steps.
5. Inductive reasoning proceeds from the known to the unknown.
6. There are six crucial steps in designing the outline of a report.
7. All group related ideas are clubbed together.
8. The progression of the points is in the form of general to abstract and specific to the concrete.
9. An informative heading is interesting and captivating.
10. A line graph shows a particular trend over a period of time.

C. Fill in the Blanks

1. A report is a presentation and summation of facts and figures either _____ or _____.
2. The manner in which research is conducted is contingent upon the _____ defined in the initial phase of report writing.
3. An analytical report could be written in either of the two patterns _____ or _____.
4. Tables require both _____ rows and _____ columns.
5. Tables can present both _____ and _____ data.
6. In bar graphs _____ or _____ colours or designs are used to highlight the difference between the two variables.
7. If there is a need to emphasise a particular segment it is detached from the pie and referred to as a _____.

8. In a line graph _____ is plotted on the x-axis and the _____ on the y-axis.

9. In a line graph it is always preferable to plot only _____ variables for ease of comprehension of visuals.

10. The usage of various drawings and diagrams in business reports is _____.

Answers

A. 1. (c) 2. (a) 3. (c) 4. (d) 5. (c) 6. (a) 7. (b) 8. (a) 9. (a) 10. (b)

B. 1. True   2. True   3. False   4. False   5. True
     6. False   7. True   8. False   9. True   10. True

C. 1. collated; derived   2. problem   3. deductive; inductive
     4. horizontal; vertical 5. Numeric; non-numeric   6. Two; more
     7. Floating wedge   8. Time; variable   9. Three   10. Limited.

QUESTIONS FOR DISCUSSION

1. What are the goals of an analytical report?
2. What is the difference between an informational and analytical report?
3. Elucidate the five steps in report planning. How does preplanning help in writing the report.
4. What steps are followed in an analytical report?
5. What is the difference between an informative and descriptive heading? Cite an example for each.
6. Compare pictograms with diagrams, drawings and maps.
7. When the same message can be transmitted through words what is the necessity of visual aids in a report?
8. How should a report writer number the sub-sections in the report?
9. What steps should a report writer consider before using visual aids?
10. What techniques can you use in a chart/graph to accentuate high focal points?

EXERCISES

1. Prepare the outline of a report discussing the marketing strategies for the launch of a new product. Answer the questions pertaining to the 5 Ws and the 1 H.
2. Write the introduction for a deductive and an inductive report. Compare and contrast the two.

3. You have to write an informational report on ISO 9000. Prepare a draft in point format. Specify the headings and the sub-headings of the report.

4. In a management institute the percentage of students from different disciplines is as follows:

38%	Engineers
10%	Science Graduates
12%	Arts Graduates
25%	Commerce Graduates
15%	Others

Draw a pie chart to show the relationships among the provided data points.

5. Prepare a chart to show the escalation in sales of a detergent soap over the last three years. You can assume certain numbers to project the growth.

6. Prepare the draft of an informational report on JIT in point format and arrange the points in order of

(a) importance

(b) sequence/procedure

7. Draw a pictogram presenting the growth of the automobile sector in the last ten years.

8. Write five point headings in parallel form for a report on the launch of a new product.

9. Two students should independently work on the following assignment.

Design graphics for a report on the sale of antibiotics by four different companies in six months.

Mahagony 50,000; Stanley 80,000; Milieu 65,000; Finesse 30,000.

Once the assignment is over, compare notes. Which graph best presents the data specified?

10. Five of your friends are going mountaineering with you. Prepare a flow chart of the travel plan to be circulated to all friends.

5

Sections of the Report

CONTENTS	LEARNINGS
• Introduction • Prefactory Parts • Abstract • Main Parts of the Reports • Terminal Section • Supplemental Parts • Sample Copy of a Report	After reading this chapter you should be able to: ➢ Understand the various components in a report ➢ Comprehend the process of composing a logical report ➢ Develop ability to identify and analyse patterns in report structuring and writing ➢ Manage neat segregation of the report into small sections and sub-sections ➢ Learn to write an aesthetically well-structured report

KEYWORDS

Title, Acknowledgement, Authorisation, Letter of Transmittal, Table of Contents, Informational Abstract, Descriptive Abstract, Background History, Scope, Conclusions, Recommendations, Plan of Action, References, Bibliography

INTRODUCTION

"I think I did pretty well, considering I started out with nothing but a bunch of blank paper."
—Steve Martin

A report structurally follows a set pattern that makes it easier for the reader to grasp the content. Understanding the various components in a report and the proper arrangement of the same adds to both, aesthetic and logical appeal. The various parts of a report are as follows:

Prefatory Parts	Cover/Title Page
	Acknowledgements
	Table of Contents
	Executive Summary/Abstract
Main Parts	Introduction
	Text
	(Method—Design and Procedure)
Terminal Section	Conclusions
	Recommendations/Suggestions
	Plan of Action/Future Directions
Supplemental Parts	References
	Bibliography
	Annexures (Optional)

PREFATORY PARTS

TOPIC OBJECTIVES

Learn to structure the title page which has aesthetic appeal
Understand the importance of appropriate formatting of the title page

"I usually get the title for a book first, and I type it up immediately. I sit there and look at it and admire it, and I think to myself, I just need four thousand sentences to go with this and I'll have a book. It is such a pleasurable moment that I type many more title pages than I could ever use."
—Betsy Byars

Cover/Title Page

The title page, being the first in the report, captures the attention of the reader. There is a standard format for designing the title page. Normally, the information provided on the title page is centred. However, for aesthetic purposes there are certain variations that are now being introduced and even accepted. Once again, it is contingent on the writer who, if creative, can apply different strategies. For example, the title and the name of the writer can be "left-justified". Whichever technique is applied, the following information is provided:

Report Title

Prepared for (Name of the reader in full with designation)

Prepared by (Your Full Name)

Name of the Institution/Organisation or Department

Date, Month and Year

Caution should be exercised at the time of deciding on the title of the report. The reader should be stimulated to read the report and should not be put off by the mere title. This means that the title of the report should not be overtly long where the reader loses track of what was the beginning point. Wordiness can be done away with. Beginning a title with words as "A Study of...", "A Survey Conducted to Study...", "An Investigation ..." are all outmoded ways of creating large titles by using up valuable word space. It should, as far as possible, fall within the fifteen word-limit, which anyway is on the higher side. Consider the following title:

Simulated Talk: A Study of Communication in Role-Plays

In a title of this kind, there can be many queries in the mind of the reader. Does the study revolve round the structure or the content? Would communication be studied as a composite of opening, middle and closing with certain subsections interposed? Though the title definitely does not exceed fifteen words, yet it fails to communicate the true import of the report. Suppose we tried to shorten the title and put it as:

Communication in Role-Plays

Though definitely brief, it provides too little information and leaves the reader in an uncertain frame of mind. Once again, the reader is really at a loss with a title of this nature. The quantum of information provided in the title should be just right—neither too much nor too little. Let us take a look at the following title:

Simulated Talk in Role-Plays: A Stylistic Approach
or
A Stylistic Approach to Simulated Talk in Role-Plays
or
Simulated Talk: A Stylistic Approach to Communication in Role-Plays

In all the three suggested titles, the number of words used is fairly reasonable. At the same time, each one of them familiarise the reader with what to expect in the report.

The normal and universally accepted formatting of the title page is as shown in Exhibit 5.1.

In case the report is general and is meant for all people working in that department, "Prepared for" is replaced by "Prepared by", and the name of

```
┌──────────────────────────────────────────────────┐
│                SIMULATED TALK                      │
│   A Stylistic Approach to Communication in Role-Plays │
│                                                    │
│                                                    │
│                  Prepared for                      │
│                  S.K. JOHN                         │
│                                                    │
│                                                    │
│                  Prepared by                       │
│                  A.K. VIJAYAN                      │
│                                                    │
│                                                    │
│          Name of Institution/Department            │
│                20 September 1999                   │
└──────────────────────────────────────────────────┘
```

Exhibit 5.1   Title page.

the report writer goes to the centre of the page position. The date, month and the year written at the bottom of the page should be accurate. There are two formats which can be followed for stating the above-mentioned details.

1. 20 September 2014
2. September 20, 2014

In the first kind of formatting, there is no comma between the month and the year. However, in the second manner of presentation, we have the name of the month followed by the date, a comma and then the year.

Note: Your title must stimulate the reader and familiarise him/her with what to expect in the report.

Acknowledgements

"We value virtue, but do not discuss it. The honest bookkeeper, the faithful wife, the earnest scholar get little of our attention compared to the embezzler, the tramp, the cheat."   —John Steinbeck

If it is felt that acknowledgements are due to certain people in the organisation who have helped in the shaping of the report, due credit should be given on the page entitled "Acknowledgements".

Courtesy demands that at least a line or word of gratitude be expressed for even the smallest kind of gesture rendered at the time of writing the report.

Typical statements that can be made for expressing gratitude are as follows:

* I would like to express my gratitude to Mr...
* I am deeply indebted to Mr...
* My sincere thanks to Dr...

> - My thanks are also due to Mrs...
> - Further, without the cooperation and support of friends and colleagues ...
> - Words are insufficient to express my gratitude to...
> - Without the unstinting support of ...
> - Special thanks to ...
> - My gratitude to ...
> - Without the full-hearted support and cooperation of ...

These are just some of the ways which can be used to acknowledge a superior, colleague or friend. As there are a number of ways through which gratitude can be expressed, repetition of statements should be avoided.

The Acknowledgement can be followed by name of the author on the right and place, month and year on the left.

JAM: Do not use the same expression when acknowledging multiple people.

Letter of Authorisation

If the report writer has been authorised to prepare a report by the letter, the same (or memo of authorisation) is affixed to the report. It normally follows the direct-request plan and typically specifies the problem, the scope, restrictions, if any, time specifications and due date.

JAM: Have you affixed your letter of authorisation to your report?

Letter of Transmittal

The letter of transmittal (or memo of transmittal) conveys the basic idea of the report to an audience. This would be directly addressed to the person who has authorised the individual to write the report. It is personal and follows personal pronouns such as you, I, and we, and use of conversational language. In a book, this section is what we normally refer to as the *Preface*.

As the letter of transmittal is personal, it should not be affixed in copies of all reports. It can be used only in selected copies of reports.

The letter of transmittal begins with the main idea, summarises its purpose, presents the scope of the report, spells out the method used to complete the study, and specifies the limitations.

Many other factors can also be included in the letter of transmittal. Side issues, suggestions, follow up studies, and any other details that might make the report more meaningful to the reader can be suggested in the letter of transmittal. Occasionally, if the report is very brief, the synopsis too can be included in this letter of transmittal. This would effectively contain the major findings, conclusions and recommendations.

Note: The letter of transmittal is personal in style.

Table of Contents

This section would effectively contain all the major or relevant sections and sub-sections within the text. It also includes the sections preceding the page. Depending on the complexity of the report, the Table of Contents may only include a few brief first level headings. Occasionally, the brevity in the Table of Contents may go against the writer if the reader is keen to know the detailed contents of the report before reading it. It is important that the headings and the sub-headings be listed in exactly the same format and style as they appear in the original text.

Warning! You will lose your reader if your headings and sub-headings do not match your original text.

Contents	
Acknowledgements	*ii*
Letter of Authorisation	*iii*
Letter of Transmittal	*iv*
List of Illustrations/Exhibits	*vi*
Executive Summary	*vii*
1. Background	1
2. Objective	2
3. Alternatives	2
4. Evaluation	6
5. Conclusions and Recommendations	15
6. References	17
7. Bibliography	18
Annexure 1 Production Cost Table	19
Annexure 2 Sales Cost Table	20
Annexure 3 Break Even Analysis	21

Exhibit 5.2   Table of contents.

List of Illustrations

Many reports contain a number of illustrations or exhibits that add to the aesthetic appeal of the report. In fact, visual aids also make the report easy to comprehend. To grasp a point and to understand the analysis accurately, a visual presentation is always a better method of depiction and description. In case the report writer so decides to use five or over five illustrations, it is always prudent to have a separate list indicating the exhibits used.

As far as possible, the illustration should be on the same page as the description that precedes it. If that is not possible, then it should be close to the description. Preferably a heading should be given to an illustration that captures the essence of the analysis.

Note: Guide your reader to the illustrations by providing a list on a separate page.

Executive Summary/Synopsis

A summary is a gist or a condensation of the report. The matter presented in the report is in brief, stated at the beginning of the report. This familiarises the reader with the contents of the report and facilitates in taking a decision: to peruse the entire text or shelve it.

A summary can be written in either paragraph format or in a point format. When we follow the paragraph style, it should be ascertained that no sentence or paragraph, as it exists in the main body of the report should be used to communicate. The main idea behind this stipulation is that each and every concept, as used in the main body of the report, has a certain context in which it is formulated. When we lift it from its context, and decide to use it in a restructured context, the meaning maybe lost. In a summary the emphasis should be on stating the idea in its accurate form without any copying or lifting from either the original or borrowed material.

Paragraph format

There is yet another form of writing a summary. Here we use the point format. This type of executive summary will normally be written for a top official who probably has little time to go through it. A mere glance at the summary will provide information on the report content. In such instances we normally script the points as they exist in the main body of the report. The basic purpose in observing this type of formulation is that as few changes as possible should be brought about in the summarisation process. The reader would definitely be closer to the text of the report if the points presented in point format are in their original form.

Point format

Occasionally, summary is confused with synopsis. Both terms can be used interchangeably. However, we normally label the gist of any piece of literary work or research paper as synopsis. It has academic connotations. A summary, on the other hand, can be used on almost all occasions when we resort to condensing the original and presenting it. The key findings of the report are paraphrased and stated in the same sequential manner as they appear in the original. In fact, sufficient emphasis should be laid on providing information so as to lure the reader into reading the original. This would hold good more specifically for the executive summary where the executive, merely on reading it, should be able to take a decision. It may also contain headings if the need to show the divisions and sub-divisions is great at the time of presenting facts in a condensed form. Normally a summary is expected to be one-third the size of the original report.

Summary and synopsis

Note: A summary may be written either in point or paragraph form. A summary can be used in any context while a synopsis has academic connotations.

Within the framework of drama stylistics an attempt has been made in the present work to study real-life and theatre-talk from the point of view of goals, structure and

| *Main aim/ objective* |

principles governing them. A model that analyses the organisation of naturally occurring talk has been proposed and applied to simulated talk in three absurd plays. The differences between the two kinds of conversations have been identified and explained.

Data for the study of ordinary conversation constitutes ten pieces of interaction, each

| *Methodology* ↓ *application of model for ordinary talk to simulated conversation* |

of forty minutes duration, taped in natural circumstances. The findings relate to the goal, the structure, and some principles governing interaction, such as the Cooperative and Politeness Principle. These pieces of conversation have been categorised as empty and non-empty. Empty interaction is that verbal exchange which is conducted with the purpose of strengthening social relationships. The goal is "remote" in the sense that it does not involve the fulfillment of an immediate purpose. Non-empty

| *Empty conversation* |

conversation is that exchange in which the interaction is conducted with the purpose of transmitting a message, eliciting information on some issue, exchange of opinions and the like; in short, there is always an immediate purpose.

The characteristic features of empty conversation are as follows:

- It is relationship oriented.
- There is no main-topic around which the interaction is built upon.

Non-empty conversation is characterised by the following features:

| *Non-empty conversation* |

- Its goal is transaction-oriented.
- There is a main-topic around which the topic revolves.
- The closing is marked by a repetition of the main-topic that serves as a reminder to the called, emphasising the purpose of the visit.

Both these types of interactions closely observe the Cooperative Principle and the

| *Principles observed/ violated* |

Politeness Principle, and a few violations of these principles found in the data generate implicatures which are not hard for the hearer to work out.

The selected absurd plays have been studied from the point of view of the above. The deviations from the norm, which the plays exhibit,

have been accounted for in terms of theme, vision of life, manipulation of characters and language. A number of differences have been identified which are as follows:

1. The goal of the conversants is neither relationship-oriented nor transaction-oriented.
2. The strategies employed by the characters for the purpose of negotiating the

| *Difference between ordinary and simulated talk* |

interaction in the plays are different from those in real-life interaction. There is literally a verbal tug-of-war in the plays. Here one interactant applies some strategies, trying to hold and engage the other interactant in the interaction, whereas the other interactant applies retreat strategies, trying to opt out of the same.

Exhibit 5.3   *(Contd.)*

3. The treatment of the main topic in the plays is different from that in ordinary interaction. To the very end it is not made explicit.
4. The Leave-Taking and Contact-termination in the closing sequence are both unusual. The Leave-Taking comes abruptly and the Contact-Termination gives no indication whether the interaction closed on a healthy note or not.
5. Action-related-exchange which has a minor role in ordinary conversation, plays a significant role in the thematic development of the plays analysed.
6. The two Principles, the CP and the PP, which are closely observed in ordinary conversation are constantly violated in the plays. Interestingly enough, despite these violations, the conversation does not come to an abrupt halt.
7. The implicatures generated as a result of the violation of these principles are hard for the hearer to work out and, further, despite the hearer asking for clarifications, the speaker does not provide the same at the time of occurrence.
8. In the plays nothing is superfluous or redundant. Although certain statements convey this impression at the time of occurrence, they cease to appear to be so when the play is seen in its entirety.

These differences reveal an artistic manipulation of the interaction for a literary purpose. The playwright, by these deviations, tries to portray the meaninglessness of human existence in an equally meaningless cosmos in which man is both alienated and isolated. The protagonist is viewed as lacking a purpose in life, where actions, more than words, determine behaviour.

Conclusion

Exhibit 5.3   Summary/Synopsis.

Warning! Do not reuse sentences from the main text in the summary or synopsis.

ABSTRACT

TOPIC OBJECTIVES
Learn to structure the abstract as the essence of the report
Gain an insight into strategically writing an abstract

"Easy reading is damn hard writing."
—Nathaniel Hawthorne

Occasionally, the report writer may be asked to write a one page abstract prior to handing in the report. Many of the characteristic features of writing an abstract are similar to that of a summary. However, there is a minor difference. While the summary is a mere condensation of the original report, the abstract is presentation of the essence of the report. The abstract usually contains three paragraphs. The first paragraph talks about the main aim of the report or discusses in brief the objective in writing the report. Paragraph two discusses in brief the methodology adopted to achieve the objective. The third or the last paragraph merely spells out the conclusions but does not elucidate on the same.

The main aim of the present work is to study real-life and theatre talk from the point of view of structure, goals and principles governing them. A model that captures the

*Main aim/
objective*

organisation of naturally occurring talk has been proposed and applied to simulated talk in three absurd plays. The differences between the two types of conversations have been identified and explained.

Data for the study of ordinary conversation constitutes ten pieces of interaction, each of forty-five minutes duration, taped in natural circumstances. Two types of conversations were identified and categorised as empty and non-empty. These pieces

Methodology

of conversations were studied in relation to their adherence to a different set of goals, structure and some Principles governing them. Two different models were proposed, which were then applied to three plays in the absurd theatre, namely, The Zoo Story, The Chairs,

Conclusion

and the Endgame. It was found that the deviations from the norm that the plays exhibit can be accounted for, in terms of theme, vision of life, manipulation of characters and language. The differences have been identified in the following areas:

1. Adherence to goals.
2. Strategies employed by the characters.
3. Treatment of the Main Topic, Leave-Taking and Action-related-exchange.
4. Observance of the Cooperative Principle and the Politeness Principles, and the generation of implicatures. These differences reveal an artistic manipulation of the interaction for a literary purpose.

Exhibit 5.4   Abstract.

A key strategy for writing an abstract, after completing the report, is to read it thoroughly and look for the key points pertaining to the aim or

*Look for key
points*

purpose of writing a report. Subsequent to this, jot down the methodology you adopted to achieve the aim and, finally, the key points of the conclusion. Close the report and then go about attempting to write the abstract without using references from the report.

If you make an attempt to copy sentences straight from the report, you are bound to provide either too much or too little information. There should

*State nothing
original*

be a logical coherence in the sequential arrangement of the sentences. The reader should not be left with the feeling that there is more to it than is evidenced through the naked eye. The chronology observed in the report is strictly adhered to in the writing of the abstract. It should also be kept in mind that just as in a summary, no new information is provided, similarly, in an abstract there is absolutely nothing original which is stated. It is merely a condensation of the material presented in a report, albeit in a structured manner, following as far as possible, the three-paragraph rule.

Abstracts can be informational or descriptive. The basic difference between the types of abstracts is in their length. An informational abstract is slightly long in the sense that it caters to a large report with massive chunks of information to be imported to the audience. It is normally 10% the size of

Informational abstract—10% size of original report

Descriptive abstract—150–250 words

the original report or slightly lesser and is written in a manner which enables the reader to take a decision if the report is worth reading or not. However, a descriptive abstract is briefer and of approximately 150 to 250 words. While it introduces the subject to the reader, it also cajoles the reader to browse through the report and study the results.

If one were to compare and contrast a summary and an abstract one can observe a few differences. In a summary the linear progression of idea is presented with substantial details. However, in an abstract, points are merely stated and concepts presented. Their progression and development is not dealt with.

Warning! No new information must be provided in the summary or abstract!

MAIN PARTS OF THE REPORT

TOPIC OBJECTIVES
Outline the component sections of the introduction
Comprehend the function and scope of the introduction

"Either write something worth reading or do something worth writing."   —Benjamin Franklin

Introduction

This is the preparatory section of the report that prepares the reader for analytical reading. If the report is very brief, there is no need to make sub-sections in the introduction. A few lines can be presented on the context with the background material or information. It has the following sections:

1. Background/History
2. Objective/Purpose/Problem statement
3. Scope
4. Limitations

Background/History

This section provides the backdrop for the report and spells out the basic purpose for which the report was written. The required history of the situation that will help in analysing or understanding the case more effectively is spelt out. It, in a sense, introduces us to the canvas on which the case is then sketched.

The Andaman & Nicobar Administration established a canning factory in Andaman Island in 1969 for tuna fish with an investment of ₹ 645,000. The factory had 45 workers. It canned Skipjack tuna in cans of 200 g net in refined vegetable oil/brine. Malabar Fisheries Project (henceforth, MFP) was the only competitor for the Andaman Factory. Unlike Andaman Factory, MFP had a wide range of products. MFP canned the yellow fin tuna in 112 g and 200 g cans. The 112 g cans were made of aluminium and were received free from Norway. MFP was planning to introduce 400 g tins to cater to the institutional market. It had a dealer network of 57, spread all over the mainland. Andaman Factory, on the other hand, did not have a very good dealer network. It had tried to contact institutional purchasers like Defence and hotels through letters and occasional meetings, but without any significant success. The yearly installed production capacity of Andaman Factory is 180,000 cans and the factory operates only for six months in a year from November to April during the fishing season. The Administration has set up two boat building yards and provides boats to the local fishermen through a subsidised loan scheme.

Exhibit 5.5   Background information.

Objective/Purpose/Problem Statement

Immediately after giving the background history, the purpose of writing the report or a one-line problem statement is made which helps in giving the entire report a proper direction and thrust.

The objective/purpose can be written in the following manner: The main objective of the Andaman canning factory is to find out the best way of marketing the tuna fish cans and operating the factory at its peak capacity. This would reduce operating losses and help local fishermen as their employment opportunities would not be affected.

Problem statement: A problem statement can be made in three ways:

1. *Question form:* What is the best way of marketing canned tuna fish and operating the factory at its peak capacity?
2. *To infinitive:* To find out the best way of marketing the tuna fish cans and operating the factory at its peak capacity.
3. *Declarative form:* Andaman Factory is currently facing a decline in sales of its canned tuna fish. Andaman Factory wants to find out the cause for the same and solicit recommendations/suggestions for the best marketing strategy.

Exhibit 5.6   Problem statements.

Scope

It spells out the area to be covered and not covered by the report. It familiarises the reader with the complexity and the size of the report.

The report outlines a number of steps that could reduce Andaman Factory's expenses and help in operating the factory at its peak capacity. However, it is difficult to project the precise financial impact of these measures at this stage.

Exhibit 5.7   Outlining scope.

Limitations

A report cannot be all-inclusive. There are bound to be shortcomings or limitations in a typical report. It is always prudent to spell out the limitations right in the beginning. This helps the reader as the reading process is smoother and facts and figures fall in place.

At the time of writing an inductive report, a statement to the following nature could be made:

> The report is limited in scope as would be any text written in the inductive style. Further, details pertaining to financial implications have not been precisely spelt out as they would entail in-depth analysis, and this would fall within the specialised domain of a project consultant.

Exhibit 5.8   Limitations.

Note: Draw up the limits of your study clearly so that the reader is not left considering/anticipating other factors.

Methodology

The methodology observed for conducting the research or writing the report should be clearly outlined. The report could be an analysis of certain samples collected for a study of the marketing potential for product X. In this case the exact strategy needs to be spelled out as to the manner in which the data was collected.

> A questionnaire with 50 open-ended questions was distributed to hundred men selected at random from the middle class segment to test their sensitivity to smoking. This data was analysed and compared to analysis conducted in the same area earlier by reputed sociologists.

Exhibit 5.9   Methodology.

Design

Depending on the nature of the report, there will be a discussion on the problem for which the report was written. In Chapter IV, we have discussed two types of reports, the informational and the analytical, which will help to determine the progression of the material in the text section. The discussion would then centre on the presentation of collated material or an analysis of the problem.

TERMINAL SECTION

"Please be good enough to put your conclusions and recommendations on one sheet of paper in the beginning of your report, so I can even consider reading it."
                                                                —Winston Churchill

Conclusion

TOPIC OBJECTIVES

Learn to come to conclusions and give shape to the findings. Know how to argue your case in the report to make your recommendation credible

The significance of this section cannot be undermined. It is the most important part of the report. It both excites the reader to read and signals analytical robustness in the writer. This section is derivative in nature and, whatever analysis has been carried out in the previous sections, is brought together and given a definite shape. At the time of writing the terminal section, care should be taken to avoid errors of logic. The results of the analysis should be stated in exactly the same manner as they appear in the body of the report. As conclusion is the final stage of putting together the results derived in the report, there should not be variations nor should any new idea or concept be introduced.

In a report the terminal section could also contain recommendations or suggestions, plan of action or future directions.

Recommendations/Suggestions

There is not much of a difference between recommendations and suggestions save the nature in which they are stated. The distinction between the two seems to be getting blurred. However, only a senior executive can make a recommendation while a suggestion moves from the lower ranks to the higher one. An example is given below.

On analysing the various problems faced by the Andaman canning factory, and considering the various alternatives stated in this report, it is recommended/suggested that the management of the Andaman canning factory observe the following steps:

1. Increase the production up to 80% of the plant capacity, as the plant will still be operating below its installed capacity, no capacity expansion would be required for the time being.
2. Operate at such a point that the break-even point is achieved within one year.
3. Introduce flexible pricing policy.
4. Open liaison office at Cochin and establish dealers network in the mainland.
5. Purchase 25-tonne reefer container to operate the plant for the whole year.

Exhibit 5.10   Recommendations/Suggestions.

Plan of Action/Future Directions

Occasionally the report may act as a stepping stone for tackling future issues. In such a report, after the conclusions, we also point out or make a reference to the time frame by which the activity should be completed. In other words, we specify the Plan of Action, e.g. in a report on the Five-Year Plan, a similar strategy can be observed. Further, a report could have implications for the future. In such instances, we spell out the future directions.

It is difficult to predict the economic future shape of Europe, but some educated guesses can be made based on the developments up to the end of the century.

1. Negotiations with the countries of Central and Eastern Europe have been dragging on from 1998 and would probably spill into the beginning of the next century.
2. The European Union of 25 members is expected to be a reality by the end of the next decade. A political, commercial, monetary, and strategic Europe may take shape.

The vision of Europe at the beginning of the 21st century is obviously speculative. It assumes that the member states will be prepared to allow the Union to act as the driving force for the entire continent and the prospective members will commit themselves unreservedly to the political objective set in the treaty. For the European Union, the only way to achieve these ambitions is to continue, without a backward glance, along the route mapped out for the community from the beginning.

Exhibit 5.11   Future directions.

Summary

A summary is used in the terminal section if the report is an informational one. As there is nothing new stated in the report and the entire study is a collation of material, the concluding section merely summarises the detailed findings.

SUPPLEMENTAL PARTS

TOPIC OBJECTIVES

Apply the rules of formatting to organise references and consulted research

Learn to supply extra but necessary information in Annexures

"Sometimes it seems like there's more footnotes than text. This isn't something we're proud of, and over time we'd like to see our footnotes steadily shrink."

—Barry Diller

References

This section is optional. It refers to the published texts that the report writer has cited in the text. Either the writer decides to indicate the references as a footnote on the same page or have a special page at the end of the report. If a statement has been literally lifted from another text due credit should be given. The borrowed line is placed in double quotes, at the end of which there is either a number in superscript or an asterisk mark or a number in parentheses. Either of the strategies can be followed. If an asterisk mark is used on a particular page, further references are indicated on the same page by an increase in the number of the asterisk marks. In a strategy of this kind, details on the cited reference are given as a footnote. In instances where there is some kind of numbering pattern which is followed either as a superscript or in parentheses the choice rests with the author. Details can be

Citations can have superscript, asterisk mark, or a number in parentheses

provided in a footnote or at the end of the report on a separate page as 'Endnotes".

Occasionally, a quote that is being cited from another text exceeds 100 words. In such instances the quote cannot be incorporated in the paragraph containing the point which necessitates further explanation. It is started on a separate line and indented on both sides. We even reduce the space between the lines. If we were using a 1½ line space, we narrow it down to 1 line space.

Further, if we decide to use a quote in which we borrowed the first line of a page from a book and then decided to use the last line on probably the same page to get the message across, we could use either of the two strategies mentioned below. One, give two references for the same page, which is extremely tedious, or show continuity between the two ideas by using only three dots between the two sentences or four in case there is a period preceding the second statement.

Manner in which references are stated is as follows:

1. Grice, H.P., Logic and conversation, *in* Peter Cole and Jerry L. Morgan (Eds.), *Syntax and Semantics*, Vol. 3, New York: Academic Press, 1975, p. 45.

    The full name of the author (surname first) followed by a comma. One style is to put the name of the article in double quotes and the name of the text or book either in italics or underlined. In the example cited above, it is the name of a chapter and is hence not used in quotes. A colon, name of the publishers and the year, follows the name of the place. Some authors put this information in parentheses. As it is a reference, the page number from which the reference has been taken is also cited. If the reference is to two or more pages, it would be preferable to give the inclusive page numbers, e.g. pp. 21–22. The spacing between the lines in the same reference is always single. However between two references it is 1.5 or double.

2. G.N. Leech, *Principles of Pragmatics*, London and N.Y.: Longman, 1983, p. 82.

3. Grice, *op.cit.*, p. 50.

    Op.cit. (*opere citato*) means "in the work cited" and is used with author's last name. It refers to an earlier cited reference that is followed by at least one reference about another source. It is best avoided.

4. Eugene Ionesco, *Notes and Counter-Notes*, trans. Donald Watson, New York: Grove Press, 1964, p. 138.

5. *Leech, loc. cit.* (*loco citato*), the place cited, refers to the same work and page, and is used with the authors last name. It is best avoided.

6. Ken Davis, *Better Business Writing,* Toronto: Charles E. Merrill Publishing Co., 1983, p. 14.

The reference style stated above is a Modern Language Association (MLA) style. There are other styles of referencing as American Psychological Association (APA), Chicago or Harvard. MLA is used primarily for Humanities. APA, Chicago and Harvard styles of referencing can be used for management and other disciplines. The only point that is worthy of consideration is that when the writer decides to reference in a particular style, it should be followed consistently. A mix and match style cannot be followed.

Bibliography

The formatting for a Bibliography varies slightly from that of reference though the differences are minor. It is always arranged in alphabetical order. Care should be exercised in citing the details concerning place and the year of publication. The formatting is as follows:

Austin, J.L., *How To Do Things With Words.* Cambridge (Mass.): Harvard Univ. Press, 1962.

Brater, Enoch. "The 'Absurd' Actor in the Theatre of Samuel Beckett." *Educational Theatre Journal*, **27**, 2, 197–207, 1975.

———. "Still Beckett: The essential and the incidental." *Journal of Modern Literature*, **6,** 3–16, Fall, 1977.

Lamont, Rosette C. (Ed.), *Ionesco: A collection of critical essays.* Englewood Cliffs (NJ): Prentice Hall, 1973.

Searle, J. Indirect Speech Acts. in *Syntax and Semantics*, Vol. 3. Peter Cole and Jerry Morgan (Eds.), New York: Academic Press, 1975, pp. 105–121.

If there is a repeat of the name of the author, but a different text or article, one style is to use a dash instead of the name of the author; the other is to repeat the name.

For Bibliography once again there four styles of writing: MLA, APA, Chicago and Harvard. The writer has to select which of the styles is appropriate for the text which is being compiled.

Annexures

Many a time, the report writer may feel that there are certain details in the report which are best left aside at the time of tempering the report. However, they are essential details with which the reader should be familiar. In such instances, annexures with necessary information are provided at the end of the report with a mention of the same at the point where its reference is being recorded.

SAMPLE COPY OF A REPORT

NILGIRIS—LAWN AND PARK PROJECT

Prepared for
Dr. Asha Kaul

Prepared by
Shirish Chandra Srivastava

Management Development Institute
Gurgaon
September 18, 1999

Contents

EXECUTIVE SUMMARY

Nilgiris shopping centre is currently facing the problem of dropping sales. Market research shows that these dropping sales can be attributed to Nilgiris, neglecting its ambience and facilities. Nilgiris' upcoming competitor—Himalayas shopping complex—is rated above Nilgiris on the ambience scale by the customers.

This greater perceived customer value of the Himalayas can be attributed to its better lawn and park facilities. The present work analyses Nilgiris park and lawn project in detail. From this analysis it is evident that Nilgiris would gain in short- as well as long-term by going ahead with this project.

This report recommends that Nilgiris shopping centre should immediately go in for developing its lawn and park facilities. It has been finally recommended that Nilgiris should go in for completing formalities for this project, as per the details, at the earliest.

Nilgiris Lawn and Park Project

1. INTRODUCTION

Nilgiris shopping centre was set up in the year 1981. It was developed to satisfy the needs of the growing number of customers in the Colaba area of Mumbai. Nilgiris shopping centre was developed as a three-storied arcade with different sections that stock almost everything a customer requires. The ground floor deals with food products, vegetables, groceries, stationery and other items of daily use. The first floor stocks clothing and footwear. For clothes there are different sections dealing with ready-mades, and there is also provision for tailoring. The top floor stocks premium gift items, jewellery shop and other niche items.

The Nilgiris shopping centre did good business for seventeen years after which another shopping arcade called "Himalayas" came up in close vicinity. This new shopping complex set up almost ten years ago made a dent in the sales of the Nilgiris shopping centre. From the market survey it was concluded that the major factor which resulted in boosting the sales of Himalayas was their excellent lawn and park facilities, which it offered to the customers free of cost. The primary cause for this was the great perceived demand for parks and lawns by people of Mumbai who viewed it as a luxury. Himalayas cashed on this idea around three years back and gained substantial profits.

Nilgiris has a plot of 8000 sq. feet just in front of the shopping centre. Nilgiris once used this plot as a park for children. With time Nilgiris concentrated only on their shopping centre and completely forgot about the fringe benefits they were offering to the customers.

This huge plot of land in this part of Mumbai is a very valuable asset and it is not being exploited to its full potential.

1.1 Purpose

The basic purpose of this report is to study the reasons for declining sales of Nilgiris shopping centre and to consider the alternatives for arresting this trend. It has been seen from the market research that improvement in lawn and park facility is bound to bring about escalation in its sales figures vis-à-vis its competitor Himalayas. For

Exhibit 5.12   (*Contd.*)

bringing about such a change, the following aspects have to be planned and analysed before entering into any contract.

The size of the area which is proposed to be developed as a lawn cum park.

- The present physical condition of this area
- The soil condition
- The planned improvements to be brought about
- The methodology for bringing about such a change
- The perceived benefits to Nilgiris by bringing about such a change
- The break-even analysis for this project

1.2 Limitations

This report studies in detail the reasons for dropping sales of Nilgiris' in comparison to Himalayas. The factors considered and studied in this report are only in comparison to the Himalayas shopping complex. It does not take into account other factors in the environment like changing tastes and preferences of the customers, and the influence of other shopping centres in the area.

2. METHODOLOGY

The trends and sales patterns of Nilgiris shopping centre for the past ten years have been studied in detail. It has been observed that the decline in sales has been more rapid in the last two years. Figure 1 shows the yearly sales figures for the Nilgiris shopping centre.

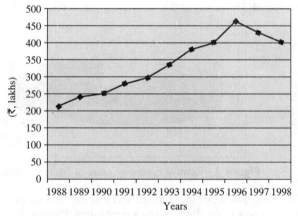

Figure 1   Sales of Nilgiris shopping complex.

Though Nilgiris was maintaining its tradition of offering lower prices, better quality of service and greater care for customers, still it was losing its sales very rapidly to Himalayas. This forced Nilgiris to rethink and refocus its strategies and analyse the causes for decline in sales. Nilgiris has realised that if this trend continues for another two years, the company will end up making huge losses.

To assess the reasons for the switching over of customers from the Nilgiris to the Himalayas, a market survey was conducted. From this survey it was found out that Nilgiris was rated higher than Himalayas on service, quality of products, and

Exhibit 5.12   (Contd.)

price competitiveness. The only parameter on which Nilgiris had a lower rating was its ambience and facilities provided to customers by its competitor Himalayas. The comparative results are shown in Figure 2.

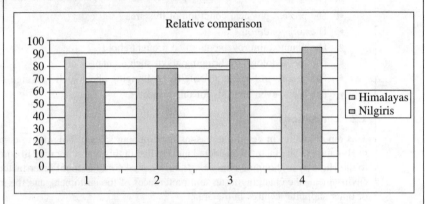

Figure 2   Relative comparative results.

Working on this cue, a further study was conducted to assess the parameters that the consumers valued the most in the category of facilities and ambience. The study conducted compared various benefits provided to the customers in the shopping centre and their relative value for them. Various factors like decor, provisions of lawns and parks, refreshment stalls, drinking water, air-conditioning, music etc. were considered. The results of this study are given in Figure 3.

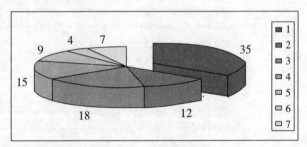

Figure 3   Relative customer value of facilities and ambience (%).

It was found that the consumers valued the presence of a large well-maintained lawn and park in the Himalayas to a great extent. Perhaps this was the only difference in the facilities provided by the two shopping centres. In the survey, most of the customers said that they came to the shopping centre in the evenings with their families and for them the ambience was very important. The presence of a nicely maintained lawn gave them an opportunity to leave their children there while they shopped. Many of the customers said that they themselves liked to relax in the lawns before or after they had shopped.

2.1   Nilgiris Lawn and Park Project

The lawns in the Nilgiris shopping centre have been lying in disuse for the past seven years. The detailed analysis of various factors has been done and is as follows:

Exhibit 5.12   *(Contd.)*

Present physical condition. For the past seven years no attention is being paid to this area. At present this plot of land, approximately 8000 sq. feet, has a lot of wild and unmowed grass. Apart from this a lot of wild vegetation has grown in this area. The wild bushes, creepers and shrubs give it a very shabby look. At present it is a haven for all varieties of insects and reptiles.

This "lawn area" has a boundary wall with railings. This boundary wall as well as railings are in a very bad condition. The boundary wall has plaster, which is peeling off. The wall and railings have not been painted for a number of years, which further adds to its shabby look.

Present soil condition. A few samples of soil were collected and were tested in laboratory. The laboratory report shows that the soil is rich in sodium, potassium and phosphorus. The soil is also rich in nitrates. The only constituent it lacks is organic waste. This organic waste can be supplemented by addition of artificial fertilisers and manure. The soil analysis shows that the soil is suited for the growth of carpet grass and seasonal flowers.

Planned improvements. The requirements of customers in relation to the lawn and park were studied in detail and it was concluded that the following improvements could be brought about. These planned improvements are proposed to be undertaken by a contractor at the earliest. After these improvements have been brought about, regular maintenance of these facilities is also proposed. The proposed planned improvements are as follows:

Land development. This plot of land has to be cleared first of all the wild shrubs and bushes. The land has to be levelled and graded before it is ready for soil treatment.

Soil treatment. The soil analysis shows that the land is deficient in organic wastes. The soil treatment has to be done to make up for the deficient nutrients. Provision for regular watering in the lawn should also be made. Apart from this the soil has to be treated with insecticides and anti-termite spray.

Carpet grass plantation. Analysis of soil sample shows that the condition of soil is extremely favourable for the growth of carpet grass. Growth of carpet grass is a slow process and takes a lot of time. It is a prerequisite for any lawn and park to provide the right kind of ambience. Hence to begin with, carpet grass must be planted in the whole area after soil treatment.

Lawn and park development. After the whole area of 8000 sq. feet is developed and planted with carpet grass, future development of lawn and park can be planned. This area should be subdivided into two equal parts. Each part will have a separate entry. One part shall be called " Nilgiris Park" and the other "Nilgiris Lawns".

Nilgiris park will be developed in the area just facing the shopping centre. This area shall be tastefully decorated with garden lights and small lamps. A small fountain shall be provided in the middle of the park. The sides of the park shall be lined with flowerbeds, which will have seasonal flowers. Maintaining seasonal flowers will not be very difficult. This area will also be provided with some children's recreational equipment like swings, slides and see-saws. Facility of Nilgiris park will be available to all customers of Nilgiris shopping complex free of cost. This park can be used by them for relaxing or for leaving their children there while they are shopping in the Nilgiris. In the Nilgiris park two small 50 sq. feet stalls should be provided. One of them should stock eatables like burgers, sandwiches and hotdogs, and the other should stock fruit juices, cold drinks and ice creams.

These stalls can be given on rent to outside operators. These operators shall be responsible for maintaining all the facilities in their stall. This will not only add to the revenue of the Nilgiris but also create goodwill for them.

Exhibit 5.12   (*Contd.*)

Provision of safe drinking water should also be planned in the Nilgiris Park. For this, two water coolers shall be provided at suitable locations. The contractor, maintaining the park shall maintain these water coolers.

Nilgiris lawns development and, finally, the park and lawn development will entail a lot of expenditure. Apart from this there shall be a recurring expenditure of maintenance charges paid to the contractor. Though it is assumed that the provision of these facilities will give a fillip to the sales of Nilgiris shopping centre, but initially a lot of expenditure is required to be incurred on this project. Revenue generation in the short and long run has been planned from these lawns.

Nilgiris lawns shall be developed and maintained with a view to letting out this area for garden parties, marriage functions and other such occasions. This part of Mumbai has a shortage of space. Thus there is a perceived demand for such lawns as party venues. This 4000 sq. feet area of Nilgiris lawns can be used to earn revenue for Nilgiris shopping centre. The lawns can be used as a mini golf course. To allow "putting practice" the golf course could have a membership fee which can be used to provide for the development and the recurring maintenance charges for the Nilgiris lawns and park.

Customers hire Nilgiris lawns in the night. In the morning and daytime these green and lush lawns can provide entertainment for children and thereby earn additional revenue for the Nilgiris.

2.2 Methodology for Change

The development of Nilgiris Park and Nilgiris lawns will be carried out by a contractor, based on a plan designed by an architect. The maintenance of these facilities shall also be given on contract on payment of monthly charges. Offers from willing contractors shall be invited, based on open tender, and the contract shall be awarded to the most suitable offer.

2.3 Perceived Benefits by this Change

We have already seen in the initial sections that this provision in lawn and park facilities by the Nilgiris shall help in boosting its sales. It is expected that Nilgiris, which is currently facing the problem of declining sales, shall once again acquire a comfortable position in the market. Its major threat from its competitor Himalayas will also be overcome.

Special discounts in lawn hiring charges can be given to regular customers of Nilgiris. This will further increase the loyalty of Nilgiris customers. The customers will view it as a great positive development towards customer care. The goodwill generated by such a step is difficult to quantify.

3. BREAK-EVEN ANALYSIS

A break-even analysis for the "Nilgiris park and lawn" project has been done. The purpose of this analysis is to find out whether this project is economically viable or not. Further, it also aims at finding out how much time it will take for the project to repay its own cost.

In this analysis we have not considered the resulting increase in sales of Nilgiris by provision of these facilities. The analysis has been carried out in such a way that the project should pay for itself in the shortest possible time and the resulting increase in sales should be net additional profits for Nilgiris.

Exhibit 5.12   *(Contd.)*

A detailed study of estimates for the Nilgiris lawn and park project was carried out. The break-even analysis has been carried out at present rates in consultation with M/s Allahabad Architect Company.

3.1   Total Costs

Fixed Costs

1.	Land development, levelling and grading cost (including plantation of carpet grass)	₹ 3,25,000
2.	Provision of two refreshment stalls and water coolers	70,000
3.	Initial preparation of flower beds	10,000
4.	Installation of children's recreation equipment	1,00,000
5.	Painting of walls and preparation of signboards	20,000
Total Fixed Costs		**₹ 5,25,000**

Quotations for regular maintenance of these facilities so created were invited from the leading contractors of Mumbai.

Mehta & Co., a reputed contractor, has quoted a rate of ₹ 45,000 per month for maintenance of these facilities after their installment. So the estimated Variable Cost per month is ₹ 45,000.

$$\text{Total Cost} = \text{Total Fixed Cost} + \text{Total Variable Cost}$$

or

$$\text{Total Cost} = ₹ 5,25,000 + nx \, (₹ 45,000)$$

where n is the number of months in which Nilgiris lawn and park project will break even.

3.2   Total Revenue

The current hire charges of lawns for parties (market rate) is ₹ 20,000 per day. On a conservative estimate it is assumed that the lawns shall remain booked for at least 10 days in a month. So the revenue from the rental charges of lawns per month shall be

$$₹ 20,000 \times 10 = ₹ 2,00,000$$

Revenue from refreshment stall

$$= ₹ 20,000 \text{ per month (Conservative estimate)}$$

Revenue from mini golf course

$$= ₹ 10,000 \text{ per month (Conservative estimate)}$$

Total revenue per month $= ₹ 2,00,000 + ₹ 20,000 + ₹ 10,000$

$$= ₹ 2,30,000$$

Total Revenue $= ₹ 2,30,000 \times n$, where n is the number of months
For break-even point,

Total Cost = Total Revenue

or $\qquad 5,25,000 + n \times 45,000 = 2,30,000 \times n$

or $\qquad 1,85,000 \times n = 5,25,000$

or $\qquad n = 2.84$

or $\qquad n = 3$ months

Hence the Nilgiris lawn and park project will break-even in three months.

Exhibit 5.12   *(Contd.)*

---

4. CONCLUSION AND RECOMMENDATIONS

Nilgiris shopping centre is continuously losing its sales to its newly established competitor—Himalayas shopping complex. An analysis of Nilgiris' declining sales shows that better ambience and facilities provided by Himalayas shopping complex have been instrumental in attracting Nilgiris' customers to them.

Nilgiris has to assiduously work on improving its 'perceived value' and image in the minds of its customers. The report spells out in detail the various aspects that Nilgiris must consider while designing the lawn and park project. The break-even analysis of this project shows that Nilgiris would recover its cost within three months of starting this project. Apart from this it will certainly help in boosting Nilgiris' sales.

It is recommended that Nilgiris shopping centre should observe the following steps:

1. Develop the required land.
2. Treat soil by addition of sufficient nutrients.
3. Plant carpet grass.
4. Divide 8000 sq. ft. land into two sections, Nilgiris Park and Nilgiris lawn.
5. Cultivate Nilgiris Park for providing fun and frolic for children.
6. Develop Nilgiris lawn for garden parties.
7. Develop Nilgiris lawn as a mini golf course.

This project should be completed at the earliest as any further delay will result in losing out more customers—implying a further drop in sales.

Exhibit 5.12   A sample copy of a report.

SUMMARY

Choose a brief, but stimulating title that provides the right quantum of information to the reader.

Use the Acknowledgements section to express a word of gratitude for support during the time of writing the report.

Affix a letter of authorisation to the report, if required. The letter of transmittal (or memo of transmittal) conveys the basic idea of the report and is directly addressed to the person who has authorised the individual to write the report.

The table of contents contains all the major or relevant sections and sub-sections within the text. Use visuals to enable your reader to grasp a point and understand the analysis accurately. Itemise them separately in a list.

Condense the report to a concise summary so as to facilitate the decision-making process. A summary can be written in either paragraph format or in a point format.

The summary condenses the original report but the abstract presents its essence.

The abstract states the main aim or the objective in writing the report, outlines the methodology, and spells out the conclusions.

The introduction is the preparatory section of the report. It comprises the background/history, purpose/problem statement, scope, and limitations of the report.

The main text briefly discusses the methodology and the design of the report.

The terminal section of the report gives shape to the findings.

The recommendations provide steps to implement the findings.

The report closes with a correctly formatted bibliography, a list of references and annexures.

CHECKLIST

Do's	Don'ts
Provide just the right amount of information in the report title	Use wordy titles
Give credit to those who contributed to the report	Repeating expressions when thanking multiple people
Phrase the letter of authorisation as a direct request	Omit to specify the problem, scope and deadline, if any, in the letter of authorisation
Use a personal tone in the letter of transmittal	Be curt and abrasive in the letter of transmittal
Be brief and concise in your summary	Exceed one third the size of the report in the summary
Use key points to write your abstract	State new ideas in the abstract
Provide the essence of the report in the abstract	Be detailed in the abstract
State the main objective of the report in the introduction	Spell out the scope as well as the limitations of the report at the very beginning
Take care to avoid errors of logic while providing the results of the analysis	Introduce variations in the conclusion
Visually separate a long quote by indenting and reducing the space between sentences	Weave in the quotes in the main body of the report
Provide annexures if the details are essential for the reader to comprehend the analysis	Be brief and avoid details either in the main body of the report or in the supplemental parts

RAPID REVIEW

A. Fill in the Blanks

1. The three parts of a report are _____, _____ and _____.

2. Informational abstract is _____ in size of the original report.

3. Descriptive abstract should be of _____ to _____ words.

4. The opening paragraph of a summary/abstract should state the _____.

5. An abstract should have on an average _____ paragraphs.

6. The date, month and year on the cover page are written at the _____ of the page.

7. A summary is a _____ of the original report and an abstract is the presentation of the _____ of the report.

8. A problem statement can be made in _____ ways.

9. Conclusion is _____ in nature.

10. Citations should be followed by an _____ , _____ or a number in parentheses.

B. True or False

1. The report makes greater impact if the title is in question form.

2. Title of a report should not exceed fifteen words.

3. Letter of transmittal is addressed to the person who has authorised the individual to write the report.

4. The writer can be innovative in the table of contents and write creative sub-headings.

5. The words, summary and synopsis, can be used interchangeably.

6. Visual presentations distract rather than capture attention.

7. An abstract presents the essence of a report.

8. An abstract and a summary are one and the same.

9. An abstract is a creative introduction to a report.

10. Consistency in approach is looked for in Bibliography.

C. Match the Following

A	B
1. Main parts of a report	(a) You reference
2. Letter of transmittal	(b) One third size of original report
3. Length of summary	(c) Essence of report
4. Abstract	(d) Introduction, text and conclusion
5. Headings	(e) Roman numerals
6. Problem statement	(f) Method and design
7. Text of a report	(g) Informational or descriptive
8. Annexures	(h) To infinitive
9. Prefatory parts	(i) Affixed to the report
10. Main part of a report written in	(j) Arabic numeral

Answers

A. 1. prefatory; main; supplemental   2. 10%   3. 150; 200
   4. Main idea   5. Three   6. bottom
   7. condensation; essence   8. three   9. derivative
   10. asterisk mark; superscript

B. 1. False   2. True   3. True   4. False   5. True
   6. False   7. True   8. False   9. False   10. True

C. 1. (d) 2. (a) 3. (b) 4. (c) 5. (g) 6. (h) 7. (f) 8. (i) 9. (e) 10. (j)

QUESTIONS FOR DISCUSSION

1. What is the significance of an impactful title to the report? How would it help in drawing the reader to the text? What are the factors that need to be considered when writing the title of the report?
2. What information is included in the middle or discussion section of a report?
3. What is an executive summary and how is it written?
4. What is an abstract? What information should it contain?
5. What is the difference between an executive summary and an abstract?
6. Discuss the relevance of scope and limitations in a report.
7. Enunciate the importance of the methodology and design section? Why should it be detailed? What is the message communicated to the reader through these two sections?
8. Why should a report carry a section on plan of action and future directions? What is the value add?.
9. What information is included in the terminal section of a report?
10. What are annexures and what details should be included in them?

EXERCISES

1. Prepare a problem statement in the question form, with a to infinitive and in the declarative form.
2. Pick up a brief report on the growing trends in the FMCG sector and write a summary on the same.
3. Select any article from a business journal and write a 200-word abstract.
4. You have just conducted research on the causes for failure of a power plant located at Corba. In the terminal section of your report give five recommendations and suggestions and draft a plan of action for the same.
5. Write a page of acknowledgements for a minimum of eight people who have helped you in writing the two reports.

6. As the team leader of your sales force you have been assigned the task of preparing a report on the daily fluctuations in sales. How would you structure the report? Indicate the sub-topics you may use.

7. Assume that you are the President of the Mess Committee in your college and have received several complaints from students concerning quality of food and timings for various meals. The nature of complaints is as follows:
   - Unhygenic conditions
   - Overcrowding
   - Tasteless food
   - Excessive oil used
   - Too spicy
   - No variation

   Write a report for the Director of your Institute on the basis of the data procured and suggest means through which conditions can be improved.

8. Prepare an outline of a report using the descriptive and informational sub-headings for hypothetical data concerning existing policies for promotion.

9. You are a management trainee in an MNC dealing with marketing of software. There has been a slight change in the market as a result of which you need to change your strategies. Write a brief report to your Project leader and your MD concerning the changes that need to be brought about. Identify differences, if any, in the style of writing the report.

10. Consult a minimum of five books for a report on Kaizen and prepare a Bibliography.

6

Circulars, Notices, Memos, Agenda and Minutes

CONTENTS

- Introduction
- Circulars and Notices
- Memos
- Agenda
- Minutes

LEARNINGS

After reading this chapter you should be able to:

➤ Discern when and with whom to use the circular and the memo

➤ Determine when and how to use a notice

➤ Plan for a proper meeting by making use of an agenda

➤ Compose a format for an effective memo

➤ Provide accurate, detailed and relevant minutes for a meeting

KEYWORDS

Circular, Direct Ordering (memo), Full Block Memo, Indirect Ordering (memo), Inter Department Communication, Intra Department Communication, Point Format, Minutes, Record, Semi Block Memo, Topical Minutes

INTRODUCTION

Written communication within an organisation should be drafted with utmost care. A written message can and does act as a precedence to further messages of a similar nature. Besides, it also goes on record. Intra- or inter-departmental written communication can be in the form of circulars or notices that are either circulated to all employees or displayed on a board for all to read. Inter-office memos are another form of important written communication for accomplishing multiple tasks. While there might be printed forms for filling in the memos, familiarity with the structuring of the message is always helpful.

Communication within organisations can also be in the form of meetings that need to be properly planned. For this, it becomes imperative for the agenda to be properly drawn up and the minutes of the meeting to be prepared early for maximum benefit to all concerned.

All these forms of transmitting messages require meticulous drafting and proper revision of the message and a careful understanding of the following:

1. Purpose of writing
2. Manner of writing
3. Pattern of tone and style that is adopted

CIRCULARS AND NOTICES

TOPIC OBJECTIVES

Learn to use circulars and notices within an organisation
Recognise the key components of both forms of writing

"By sending out more circulars, more circulars to file!"
—Bel Kaufman

Circulars and notices form part of intra-departmental communication. Informational messages are transmitted to the members of an organisation through circulars or put up as notices for everyone to read.

Specify day, date, time, place, and purpose of business

The various components of a circular or notice are as follows: day, date, time and place of the meeting and the purpose of the business to be transacted. Occasionally, the notice is displayed on a board and the same information is also circulated to all concerned within the organisation. The tone of both the circular and the notice is always objective, polite and courteous. A directive tone is avoided.

Note: Use circulars or display notices to share information within an organisation.

Malibu Industries
Bijwasan, New Delhi
NOTICE

Members of the Marketing Division are requested to gather for an important meeting on Saturday, 4 December 2014 to discuss the latest marketing strategy for our new product.

M.C. Sharma

Exhibit 6.1   Notice.

Malibu Industries
Bijwasan, New Delhi

Dated: 30 October 2014

Circular No. 423/56

The wives of five Kargil martyrs would be visiting the organisation on November 2, 2014 to familiarise us with their problems and grievances. They would also be suggesting ways to help other bereaved families of the Kargil soldiers.

Employees are requested to be present and to extend their cooperation for this noble cause.

Sd/-
Mahesh Gidwani
Manager
(Personnel)

Exhibit 6.2   Circular.

MEMOS

TOPIC OBJECTIVES

Distinguish between a memo and a letter

Learn to compose the memo using a converstaional style with appropriate structuring and formatting

"By the time you get a job, you know how to behave in a meeting or how to write a simple memo."
—Howard Rheingold

Memo, which is an abbreviaton of memorandum, forms part of inter- and intra-departmental correspondence. Derived from the Latin word "*memorare*", changed to "*memorandus*" (notable), means to provide information. A memo is a written statement that provides information by a person or a committee to other people. Literally translated in the organisational set-up, it is a brief official note circulated to one or more than one person, depending on the nature of the information to be circulated.

Memos provide information, make requests, invite suggestions and put on record

Though the basic purpose of a memo is to inform, make requests, put on record, report and invite suggestions, it is quite different from a letter. The variance is in the nature of the tone as well as the style. A letter is more formal in nature but a memo ensures that the tone is more conversational. This trend is away from the stiff, formal style of writing that characterised written communication several years ago. The tone adopted is contingent upon the topic under discussion

Conversational tone

and the relationship shared between the sender and the receiver. In fact, a good technique of ensuring that the memo communicates the desired effect is to read it aloud and see whether it can be categorised as a piece of conversation that is transcribed. However, if a memo is being sent to the President of the company, a slightly more formal style will be preferred than that for peers or colleagues. Hence, evaluate the position of the receiver, and critically analyse the topic prior to determining the tone of the memo.

Evaluate position of reader

The second pronoun "you" is used so as to add to the nature of informality. Further, names of people instead of their titles or prefixes are used, if the memo is addressed to one single person. Opening and close of a memo are also different from a letter. It does not have a salutation or a complimentary close as is present in a letter. However, the objective is clear and, if need be, is also underlined to draw attention.

Use of pronoun "You"

A memo is similar to a letter in the postulation of the subject and the points discussed. The language is polite and courteous and there is no breach of good will.

Many companies have their own printed format in which the message is written and sent across to other members. This format is more like that of a letter. It can be either in the full block or semi-block style.

Warning! Determine the position of the reader of your memo before deciding on the tone to be adopted.

NAME OF COMPANY
INTEROFFICE MEMORANDUM

Date: ....
Ref: ....
To: ....
From: ....
Subject: ....

....

....

....

NAME

SIGNATURE

cc.

Exhibit 6.3   Memo—full block format.

The three most important components of a memo are

   1. Heading
   2. Reference, date and subject
   3. Message

```
┌─────────────────────────────────────────────────────────────────────────┐
│                         NAME OF COMPANY                                   │
│                       Interoffice Memorandum                             │
│   To: .................................        Ref: ....................................... │
│   From: ...............................        Date: ...................................... │
│       (Designation)                                                       │
│                         Subject: .....................................    │
│   ....................................................................... │
│   ....................................................................... │
│   ....................................................................... │
│                                                                           │
│                                              Name                         │
│                                                                           │
│                                              Signature                    │
│   cc.                                                                     │
└─────────────────────────────────────────────────────────────────────────┘
```

Exhibit 6.4   Memo—semi-block format.

Heading

Reference to sender and receiver

This will include reference to the sender and the receiver. Normally, the official designation is used to address the sender. There are also instances when the prefix Mr., Ms., Dr., and so on may be used. This, however, is rare and, even if the addressee is addressed by a courteous prefix, the same rule cannot be applied to the sender. The formatting of the memo should be consistent. If a name is being used for the recipient, then a similar pattern should also be observed for the sender.

Reference, Date and Subject

Provide reference No. and full date

The reference number for a memo should always be given. It helps in filing and recording of documents, making cross-referencing easier. Full dates are important from the point of view of future reference. Further, specifying the same also prevents miscommunication.

Make the subject matter brief

The subject of a memo is extremely important. It should be brief and be able to communicate the basic intent of the message. This prepares the reader for what is to follow. It should be stated in a concise manner. Avoid use of full sentences. Instead, follow a "sentential shorthand" to send forth the message, e.g. purchase of 48 computers.

The Message

Direct ordering— Purpose followed by details

The message is direct and brief, and is phrased in short and simple sentences. It follows a direct style of writing, that is, the purpose and the necessary details to support the opening sentences. Subsequently, there is a request for action or specification of a deadline for the completion of the task. However, when a request has to be made or bad news is transmitted, the style of presentation of information is reversed. Details are presented prior to purpose. The reader is gradually and logically led to the conclusion. In case a direct plan of organisation is followed, the reader would not read the entire memo. In the reverse ordering, it is easier to maintain the goodwill of the reader by proceeding logically and systematically and at the same time transmitting the information.

Indirect ordering— Details followed by purpose

JAM: Have you structured the memo as per the purpose of message?

Malibu Industries
Interoffice Memo

Date: November 12, 2014
Ref: 563/45
To: H.R. Department
From: Purchase Department
Subject: Purchase of 48 Computers

Thank you for your suggestion to purchase 48 computers for the Marketing and Accounts Departments. Your suggestion has been evaluated and the cost implications also worked out.
The proposal sent across is definitely of great value as it will facilitate the functioning of the above.

We are in the process of finalising the budget for the current financial year. It will probably take another couple of weeks. As soon as it is cleared, we will be in a position to purchase the computers.

L.N. Gupta

cc. Mr. M.H. Mohanty, President

Exhibit 6.5   Memo with direct ordering: full block format.

Malibu Industries
Interoffice Memo

To: H.R. Department   Ref:563/45
From: Purchase Department   Date: November 12, 2014
Subject: Purchase of 48 Computers

Thank you for your suggestion to purchase 48 computers for the Marketing and Accounts Departments. Your suggestion has been evaluated and the cost implications also worked out.
The proposal is definitely of great value as it will facilitate the working of two departments.
You must be aware of the fact that there has been a severe financial crunch in the company. We are still analysing the causes for this problem. Probably it will take us a couple of weeks before we can take a final call.
In this situation it is very difficult for us to purchase computers at this juncture. However, we shall keep the proposal in mind for necessary action at an appropriate time.

L.N. Gupta

cc: Mr. M.H. Mohanty, President

Exhibit 6.6   Memo with indirect ordering: semi-block format.

Present statistical information in tabular form

Occasionally, statistical information needs to be presented in the memo. The writer should present the information in a tabular form so that it is easier for the reader to grasp.

Malibu Industries
Interoffice Memorandum

To: Manager, Accounts Department   Ref: 496/32
From: Deputy Manager   Date: November 1, 2014

Subject: Monthly Expenditure on Stationery

We decided to conduct a bi-annual review on monthly expenditure incurred on miscellaneous items. Information regarding other items such as travelling and halting allowance, courier charges, electricity and telephone bills, etc. have been reviewed.

In the current fiscal year, the following is the monthly expenditure on stationery in our company.

This is the first in the series of calculations.

Month	Expenditure
April	₹ 5000.00
May	₹ 10,000.00
June	₹ 6000.00
July	₹ 5000.00
August	₹ 10,000.00
September	₹ 6,000.00
Total	₹ 42,000.00
Average	₹ 7000.00

As you can see, the average monthly expenditure on stationery is ₹ 7000.00 (Seven thousand only) which is 5% more than what it was during the corresponding period of the previous year. You will agree that this exceeds the stipulated increase of 3%.

We trust that all departments will ensure that overall increase in expenditure during this year would not exceed 3% such expenses as were incurred in the previous year.

M.N. JOSHI

Exhibit 6.7 Memo with statistical details.

AGENDA

TOPIC
OBJECTIVES
Prepare an agenda that communicates desired objective
Identify the components of the agenda

"The secret of your success is determined by your daily agenda."   —John C. Maxwell

An agenda for a meeting should be prepared well in advance. It should include a list of things to be discussed. The purpose of having the agenda circulated sufficiently in advance is that it enables the participants to mentally prepare themselves for the meeting. Preparing the agenda and sending it ahead of time is always advantageous. Unnecessary

Circulate the agenda in advance

time is not wasted in browsing over the issues during the course of the meeting. The agenda in such cases is affixed to the circular and sent to all the members.

An agenda should contain the following components:

1. Name of the organisation and location
2. Day, date, year, time and place of meeting to be convened
3. Minutes of the previous meeting
4. Various issues to be discussed
5. Signature of the concerned authority or Secretary

In case the agenda is one in a series for meetings held on any specific issue, the number of the meeting could also be mentioned.

Note: Circulate your agenda well in advance to help the participants prepare themselves for the meeting.

Malibu Company
Gurgaon

A meeting of the HR Department is scheduled to be held on Thursday, April 8, 2014 at 2:30 p.m. in the Zen Hall. The agenda for the meeting is:

1. Confirmation of the minutes of the last meeting
2. Review of the recruitment process
3. Finalisation of the training calendar
4. Revision of pay scale

All members of the HR Department are requested to be present for the meeting.

J.K. Mushran
Secretary

Enclosure: Minutes of meeting held on March 4, 1998

Exhibit 6.8 Agenda.

MINUTES

TOPIC OBJECTIVES

Learn the purpose of keeping minutes
Grasp strategies to draft an objective and relevant record

Minutes—Formal record of the proceedings of a meeting

"A meeting is an event where minutes are taken and hours wasted."
                                        —James T. Kirk

Minutes are a formal recording of the proceedings of a meeting. They are written to ensure that all relevant issues being discussed are put on record and can be cross-referred to by the members of the organisation at a later date. The minutes provide a detailed record of the discussion. They are always written in reported speech form. Direct quotations are avoided.

Basically, minutes emphasise the main points of the discussion, the conclusions arrived at, and the recommendations made. They are written by the Secretary of the company or by the council or a person especially designated for the task. The minutes of a previous meeting are either circulated prior to or read aloud for everyone at the time of the meeting.

Recording of details—Point format, topical headings or with main points underlined

The Chairman is the first person to sign the minutes. In case there is any controversy regarding the recording of issues or even details, there is further discussion. Only when everyone is satisfied, do they sign the minutes which acts as a seal indicating acceptance.

The task of jotting down the minutes is tedious. Copious notes are taken down which can later be read and re-read for correct scripting of information. Care has to be taken to ensure that all relevant points are written in the right context. In the meeting there can be unnecessary interruptions or digressions from the main topic. These constitute irrelevant matter and need not be taken into consideration. Sentences need to be rephrased, restructured and given a logical ordering. The sifting, sieving and positioning of the issues discussed in the meeting are all part of the job of the person writing the minutes. It is what we refer to as presenting the ideas in a condensed form or a "shorthand".

Recording of details can be done either in the point form, with topical headings or, for greater emphasis, underlining the beginning of the point. Highlighted points can be underlined or put in italics to give the statement importance. The names of people are cited at the time of reporting a statement, e.g. Mr. Sharma emphasised the importance of..., Mr. Gupta concluded by stating... . Occasionally, these sentences may also become judgemental or biased. There are some companies, though, that prefer ambiguity to specificity in mention of names. The minutes are written in the third person. For example, "It was stated…" "The problem was discussed by the committee members…" etc. As they are a record for posterity, it is essential that the essence of the meeting be captured. Hence, there is first a formulation of the draft of the minutes which is either circulated to the members or read aloud in the subsequent meeting for approval. As stated earlier, if the current meeting is a continuation of a series of similar discussions, the minutes are numbered so as to act as a guide for further reference.

The details that should be present in minutes are as follows:

1. Name of the organisation.
2. Specification of the place, date, month, year and time.
3. Name of members, listed in order of seniority. The designation of the officers may also be specified. In flat organisations the names are written in an alphabetical order.
4. Name of presiding officer should be listed above the names of the members for greater emphasis.
5. Names of members who were invited for the meeting and could not make it are also listed in a separate column.
6. Specification of agenda.
7. Details of dissent, if any.
8. Record of details.

9. Signature of the secretary (which is in the right-hand column) and the Presiding officer (which is in the left-hand column).

10. Vote of Thanks.

Note: Distinguish between digressions and interruptions to present a condensed version of the key ideas discussed in the minutes.

Malibu Industries
Bijwasan
New Delhi
Minutes

A meeting of the members of the HR Department of Malibu Industries, New Delhi was held at the Zen Hall at 2:30 p.m. on 8 April 2014.
Presiding: Dr. L.M. Motwani, President
Present: Mr. H. Kaul
       Mr. Suresh Kichlu
       Mr. M. Subramaniam
       Ms. Nandita Roy
       Ms. Achla Mahalwar, Secretary
Absent: Mr. S. Narayanaswamy
      Ms. Suniti Maini

No. of minutes	Subject of minutes	Details of minutes

Exhibit 6.9 Minutes of a meeting (point format).

Malibu Industries
Bijwasan
New Delhi
Minutes

A meeting of the members of the HR Department of Malibu Industries, New Delhi was held at the Zen Hall at 2:30 p.m. on 8 April 2014.
Presiding: Dr. L.M. Motwani, President

Present: Mr. H. Kaul
       Mr. Suresh Kichlu
       Mr. N. Subramaniam
       Ms. Nandita Roy
       Ms. Achla Mahalwar, Secretary

Absent: Mr. S. Narayanaswamy
      Ms. Suniti Maini

1. Confirmation of the Minutes of the Previous Meeting
The minutes of the meeting held on 25 March 2014 were approved and duly signed by the President.

2. Review of Recruitment Process
Ms. Nandita Roy suggested that the recruitment process be made more stringent. Five levels of interviews were proposed by Mr. Suresh Kichlu. The proposal was seconded by Mr. H. Kaul.

Exhibit 6.10 (Contd.)

3. Finalisation of the Training Calendar
The secretary reported that approximately twenty training programmes/workshops were held in the previous year. If the number was increased by ten, they would be able to cover the entire workforce. Dr. L.M. Motwani agreed to this suggestion. Mr. M. Subramaniam expressed his reservations about training the entire workforce but was soon convinced on the feasibility of the proposal, keeping in view the current international trends. Finally, all the members agreed to increase the number of training programmes.

4. Revision of Pay Scales
Mr. S. Subramaniam proposed that the pay scales be reviewed in the light of the prevalent pay scales of other organisations. Mr. Suresh Kichlu seconded the proposal. Dr. L.M. Motwani agreed to study the revised pay scale pattern of other organisations before taking a final decision.

5. Next Meeting
It was decided to hold the next meeting on 3 May 2014.

6. Vote of Thanks
The meeting ended with a vote of thanks to the President.

Dr. L.M. Motwani   Ms. Achla Mahalwar
President   Secretary

Exhibit 6.10   Minutes of a meeting (topical headings).

Malibu Industries
Bijwasan
New Delhi

Minutes

A meeting of the members of the HR Department of Malibu Industries, New Delhi was held at the Zen Hall at 2:30 p.m. on 8 April 2014.
Presiding: Dr. L.M. Motwani, President

Present: Mr. H. Kaul
          Mr. Suresh Kichlu
          Mr. N. Subramaniam
          Ms. Nandita Roy
          Ms. Achla Mahalwar, Secretary

Absent: Mr. S. Narayanaswamy
          Ms. Suniti Maini

The minutes of the meeting held on 25 March 2014 were approved and duly signed by the President.

Ms. Nandita Roy suggested that the recruitment process be made more stringent. *Five levels of interviews were proposed by Mr. Suresh Kichlu.* The proposal was *seconded by Mr. H. Kaul.*

The Secretary reported that approximately twenty training programmes/workshops were held during the previous year. If the number was increased by ten, they would be able to cover the entire workforce. Dr. L.M. Motwani agreed to this suggestion. Mr. M. Subramaniam expressed his reservations about training the entire workforce but was soon convinced on the feasibility of the proposal, keeping in view the current international trends. Finally, all the members agreed to the increased number of training programmes.

Exhibit 6.11   *(Contd.)*

Mr. S. Subramaniam proposed that the pay scales be reviewed in the light of the prevalent pay scales of other organisations. *Mr. Suresh Kichlu seconded* the proposal. Dr. L.M. Motwani agreed to study the revised pay scale pattern of other organisations before taking a final decision.

It was decided to hold the *next meeting on* 3 May 2014.

The meeting ended with *a vote of thanks to the President.*

Dr. L.M. Motwani   Ms Achla Mahalwar
President   Secretary

Exhibit 6.11   Minutes of a meeting.

SUMMARY

Written communication within an organisation has to be thoughtfully drafted as it also goes on record.

To share informational messages within an organisation, circulars are transmitted or notices are displayed for everyone to read.

A memo is a written statement, a brief official note circulated to one or more than one individual by a person or a committee, depending on the nature of the information to be circulated.

Agenda includes a list of things to be discussed. It is circulated sufficiently in advance to enable the participants to prepare themselves so that the meeting may proceed smoothly. The agenda in such cases is affixed to the circular and sent to all the members.

Minutes are a formal recording of the proceedings of a meeting. They are written to ensure that all relevant issues being discussed are put on record and can be cross-referred to by the members of the organisation at a later date.

CHECKLIST

Do's	Don'ts
Send a circular if you want to ensure the information reaches everyone	Use a tone of command in the circular or notice
Be sure of the difference between a circular and a memo	Use the same style of writing a circular and a memo
Use a circular or a notice for intra-departmental communication	Adopt the style of writing a circular or a notice for interdepartmental communication
Check if your memo can work as oral communication	Omit to take the position of the receiver of the memo into consideration before adopting a conversational tone
Use "you" to retain informality in the memo	Use a salutation or complimentary close as in a letter

Do's	Don'ts
Follow the style of writing that is governed by organisational norms	Be creative in structuring the memo
Circulate the agenda ahead of the meeting	Omit to mention the number of the meeting on the agenda in case there have been several
List down all the points in the agenda	Be selective in scripting the agenda
Represent the discussion of a meeting in the right context in the minutes	Be haphazard with recording the minutes. Use the point form with topical headings
Be concise yet comprehensive in recording minutes	Be in a rush while recording or writing minutes

RAPID REVIEW

A. Pick Your Choice

1. The tone of the circular and notice is in the form of
    (a) command   (b) request   (c) order

2. The word "memo" is derived from the Latin word
    (a) memor   (b) memorandum   (c) memorare

3. The difference between a memo and a letter is in the
    (a) tone and style   (b) message   (c) addressee

4. In a bad news memo/letter
    (a) details should be avoided
    (b) purpose should follow details
    (c) details should follow purpose

5. Minutes are written by the
    (a) President
    (b) Vice-President
    (c) Secretary of the Company

6. Minutes should be signed by
    (a) Presiding officer and Secretary
    (b) President and Vice-President
    (c) Vice-President and Secretary

7. At the time of reporting a statement
    (a) the name of the person should be cited
    (b) counter arguments should be specified
    (c) reactions of the Presiding officer should be recorded

8. Circulating the agenda in advance helps the participants to
    (a) streamline their activities

(b) saves time

(c) makes the participants well focussed

9. (a) Names of people   (b) Titles   (c) Prefixes

are used in a memo.

10. The message in a memo follows:

(a) direct organisational plan

(b) indirect organisational plan

(c) none of the earlier stated

B. True or False

1. A memo is very different from a letter.

2. The reference number for a memo helps in filing and recording.

3. In bad news messages the purpose should be stated right at the start of the memo/letter.

4. Minutes are a formal record of the time of a meeting.

5. Minutes should not be judgemental or biased.

6. Agenda for a meeting should be circulated in advance.

7. The words memo and circular are synonyms.

8. The tone of a memo is stiff and passive.

9. The format of a memo resembles that of a letter.

10. The agenda for a meeting should specify all the topics to be discussed in order of importance or manner of presentation.

C. Match the Following

A	B
1. Message in a memo	(a) Topical headings
2. Statistical information	(b) To put on record
3. Minutes of a meeting	(c) Direct and brief
4. Purpose of a memo	(d) Tabular form
5. Tone of a memo	(e) Intra-departmental communication
6. Circulars and notices	(f) Conversational
7. Tone of the circular	(g) Displayed on board
8. Agenda	(h) Read aloud or circulated
9. Draft of minutes	(i) Issues to be discussed
10. Notice	(j) Polite and courteous

Answers

A. 1. (b) 2. (c) 3. (a) 4. (b) 5. (c) 6. (a) 7. (a) 8. (c) 9. (a) 10. (a)

B. 1. True   2. True   3. False   4. False   5. True
    6. True   7. False   8. False   9. True   10. True

C. 1. (c) 2. (d) 3. (a) 4. (b) 5. (f) 7. (j) 8. (i) 9. (h) 10. (g)

QUESTIONS FOR DISCUSSION

1. What is the difference between circulars and notices?
2. A memo is in the nature of a letter and is yet not a letter—Discuss.
3. What are the advantages of a memo over a letter?
4. What is the relevance of circulating the agenda well in advance of the meeting?
5. Minutes are a formal record of the proceedings of a meeting. What factors are emphasised in minutes and what is the order in which they are structured?
6. Spell out differences between a full-block and semi-block format of a memo. What are the advantages of one over the other?
7. In how many forms can minutes be written? Which do you prefer and why?
8. Circulars and notices are getting outmoded with the growing trend of using e-mails. Discuss.
9. How is an agenda for a meeting different from its' minutes?
10. What are the components of a memo?

EXERCISES

1. Write a notice for students of your college informing them of a student committee meeting.
2. Prepare a circular for the student advisory committee informing them of the decisions taken by the Student body.
3. You are the Secretary of the Student Council. A meeting has been fixed for 16 December 2014. Prepare an agenda of three issues to be discussed in the meeting.
4. As a student representative in the faculty meeting you were also expected to prepare minutes of the meeting. The issues discussed were as follows:
   - Grades
   - Attendance

- Discipline
- Vacations

Write the minutes (a) *with topical heading,* (b) *in point format,* (c) *underlining the start of the point.*

5. Assume that you are heading the Accounts Division of your Company. Prepare a memo for the Chairman of the Company with statistical details concerning the expenditure incurred in the last six months and expected expenditure for the next six months.

6. Collect minutes from three different organisations. Analyse all three and study the methodology observed in them. Which of the formulations do you think is the most effective and why?

7. Suppose you are the head of the marketing division and are to conduct a meeting in a week's time. Call your secretary and issue instructions concerning the specifications in the agenda.

8. You have recently hired a Secretary and are in the process of training her to work according to your requirements. Instruct her on how to take down minutes of a meeting.

9. Write a bad news message to an employee in the memo format and a letter format. Compare and contrast the two.

10. Post your exit interview, you have been requested to provide feedback to the HR in the written format. You would like to share the same with the rest of the members in the organisation and the President. Which form of written communication will you adopt and why? Prepare the text for your communication and share with the rest of the students/participants for their comments.

CHAPTER

7

Writing Letters

CONTENTS

- Introduction
- Business Letter Format
- Styles of Letter Arrangement
- Types of Letters
- Telegrams
- Telex Messages
- Facsimiles (Fax)
- Electronic Mail
- Maintaining a Diary

LEARNINGS

After reading this chapter you should be able to:

➤ Use the appropriate business letter format to best reflect company/writer

➤ Learn of different styles of letter arrangement

➤ Use the relevant style of composition for the purpose at hand

➤ Adapt the message to the medium

➤ Follow the AIDA principle

KEYWORDS

Attention Line, Opening, Complimentary Close, Enclosure, Carbon Copy, Postscript, Full Block, Semi Block, Open Style, Request Letter, Inquiry Letter, Letter of Transmittal/Receipt, Sales Letter, Good/Bad News Letter, Telegrams, Telex, Fax, Email, Diary

INTRODUCTION

Business correspondence forms an integral part of everyday dealings with clients and customers. The formatting of the letter, the style of arrangement of the various components as well as the manner of composition, lend either a positive or a negative image about the writer and the company being represented. Letter writing can prove to be one of the most challenging, interesting and creative ways of transmitting messages. With the emergence of new techniques, some styles of letter writing have become outmoded. These changes in writing need to be understood and brought about so as to keep abreast with the new methodology of business correspondence.

BUSINESS LETTER FORMAT

TOPIC OBJECTIVES

Understand the component parts of a business letter
Identify the format, function and purpose of each component
Illustrate with examples the correct use of each

"In an age like ours, which is not given to letter-writing, we forget what an important part it used to play in people's lives."   —Anatole Broyard

Most companies and organisations follow their own style of writing and formatting a letter. Whichever style is followed, all letters can be broadly broken up into four components:

1. Heading
2. Opening
3. Body
4. Closing

Heading

The heading is a very important component of a letter as it contains vital information on the company/sender, reference number and the date. Many companies ensure that the same be provided in such a manner that the

Letterhead— Logo and name of the company

image of the institution is further enhanced. The *logo*, the formatting of the name of the company on the letterhead—all add up to create an impression in the mind of the reader. The importance of this initial information can be gauged from the fact that professional artists are hired specifically for the creation of the logo and the formatting of the company name and address, which is subsequently printed on all letterheads. Once the logo is created it becomes representative of the company and is rarely, if ever, changed.

In non-official letters, not written on the official pads, the personal or company address should be provided. Either of the two ways of writing the address can be followed:

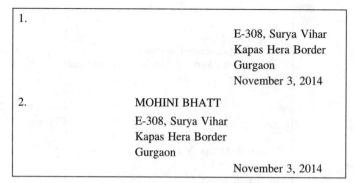

Exhibit 7.1   Non-official letters.

In the second example, the name and address are centred and the date continues to be in the right-hand margin.

This initial information, which is part of the company profile, has to be separated from the main letter by the reference number and the date. Mostly all official letters have both "your reference" and "our reference" numbers on the letter. This helps both the sender and the reader as they are able to refer back to the earlier correspondence, and file it in an appropriate manner.

The date line is normally typed three lines beneath the letterhead. There are two ways in which the date can be written:

- 3 November 2014
- November 3, 2014

While putting down dates, it is not correct either to use the number of the month or to add st, nd, rd, or th after the day of the month. For example, neither should one write first, second, third, tenth, etc. in the date line, nor should one write, for instance, 3.11.2014.

Note: Use reference numbers to help track the correspondence and file it in a proper manner.

Opening

The opening comprises the inside address of the recipient, the attention line and the salutation. All three are extremely important from the point of view of the reader.

Inside address

The inside address of the recipient is always written on the left-hand margin of the letter. The name of the recipient together with the designation is also spelt out. The job title is written on the same line after a comma or it is written on the next line in the inside address. These details are accompanied by the full address of the reader. For example:

Name of the writer, job title and address

The Amelius Company
E-308, Surya Vihar, Kapas Hera Border
Gurgaon 122002

November 3, 2014
Ref no:12/FF2/34

Mr. Suresh Mehta, M.D.
Premium Industries
416, Sector 14
Gurgaon—122016

Exhibit 7.2   Opening of the letter.

JAM: Correct any addition of st, nd, rd, or th after the day of the month!

Attention line

> *Letter addressed to a company*

An attention line is used in the letter when it is addressed to a department in the company instead of a specific person. It helps in expediting the process. This line is always typed below the address and above the salutation. It begins in the left-hand margin. Its format is as follows:

> **ATTENTION: FINANCE DEPARTMENT**
>
> or
>
> *Attention: Finance Department*

The "attention" line can be written in capitals, or in italics or underlined, if done on computer or it can in bold.

Salutation

There are several ways in which the salutation is written. If an attention line has been used and the name of the addressee is either not known or not put in the letter, the salutation should be in the form of:

Madam:

Sir:

As far as possible, efforts should be made to find out the name of the receiver so that the salutation carries the correct name. Of course it goes without saying that the name should be correctly spelt. In business and formal letters, there is always a colon that is used after the salutation while in informal letters a comma can be used.

The Body

While the opening sets the pace for the letter, the body or the middle sustains the interest. The body of a letter has two parts: the Subject Line and the Message.

The subject line

The writer may so wish to prepare the reader for the main content of the letter by adding a subject line immediately after the salutation. It is written in a manner almost similar to the attention line. Either it is written in capitals or underlined. It starts on the left-hand margin and the word "Subject" is always followed by a colon, e.g.

> *Main content in brief*

The Amelius Company
E-308, Surya Vihar, Kapas Hera Border
Gurgaon 122002

                                        November 3, 2014
                                        Ref no: 12/FF2/34

Mr. Suresh Mehta, M.D.
Premium Industries
416, Sector 14
Gurgaon—122016

Sir:

Subject: *Training Review*

Exhibit 7.3   Body of the letter.

One can also avoid the italics and put the subject in bold as given below:

Subject: Training Review

It may be noticed that unlike the word "Attention", the word "Subject" is not underlined or typed in italics.

The message

While the opening developed interest in the reader and cajoled him/her to read on, the message section transmitted the details. For effectiveness in main message transmittal, normally a two paragraph scheme is followed. In the first, the writer tries to build on the attention that has been captured by the subject line and in the second tries to furnish the reader with details so that interest can be sustained.

> *Main message elaborated in two paragraphs*

> The Amelius Company
> E-308, Surya Vihar, Kapas Hera Border
> Gurgaon 122002
>
> November 3, 2014
> Ref no: 12/FF2/34
>
> Mr. Suresh Mehta, M.D.
> Premium Industries
> 416, Sector 14
> Gurgaon—122016
>
> Sir:
>
> Subject: *Training Review*
>
> Trainings are an integral part of any organisation. While there are many vendors who do provide the training, there are a few who actually get into reviewing the process.
>
> We at Amelius believe that a training review provides both the trainer and trainee a handle on what happened, success measures and ways in which the training can be augmented. Apart from 360 degree feedback on the training and trainer, we have developed various tools for assessment.
>
> We are keen to interact with you and discuss the feasibility of working with your organisation.

Exhibit 7.4   The message.

Closing

In written communication, at the time of writing letters, there is leave-taking, as in oral communication. The difference lies in the manner in which this technique is followed.

The complimentary close

> **Close matches the salutation**

The close varies in tone and style. It is contingent upon the salutation. With a change in the latter, the complimentary close also undergoes a change. Some examples of the same are:

Salutation	Close
Dear Rohini:	Cordially,
Dear Ms. Hukku:	Sincerely,
Madam:	Yours truly,
Sir:	Yours truly,
Dear Sir:	Yours faithfully,
Dear Sir:	Respectfully yours,

After the complimentary close, it is worth noting that there is a comma that is used.

The company and the writer's signature

Many companies follow a system of putting the company signature beneath the complimentary close in capitals. This is of course optional and indicates that the company is legally sending the letter and all responsibility lies with the company. An example for the same is provided below:

Normally, the writer after the complimentary close puts his/her signature in hand writing which is followed by the identification, that is, the job title and the name of the department of work. The writer's identification below the signature can be typed on the letter in the following ways:

> Anand Kaul, Vice President
> Marketing Department
> or
> Anand Kaul, Vice President
> or
> Anand Kaul
> Vice President
> or
> Anand Kaul
> Vice President
> Marketing Department

Warning! The close must always compliment the salutation.

Reference initials

Writer's/Typist's initials

The reference initials are used only if the writer's name is not included in the letter. When the writer's name is omitted from the letter, the initials are written first and are followed by the typist's initials. If there are three initials, the first indicates the person who signed the letter, the second initials belong to a person who wrote the letter, and the third indicates who typed it. The reference initials can be put in either of these forms:

> RKMahalwar/am
> RKM/AM
> RKM/am
> RKM/ft/am

Enclosure notation

Notation for additional papers or documents affixed

When something is affixed to the letter in the same envelope, an enclosure notation is used. This helps the receiver to ascertain that all the references made to in the letter have been attached. The manner of writing this notation is as follows:

> Enclosure
> Encl.
> Enclosures:

Carbon copy and blind carbon copy notation

There may be a number of copies of the original letter meant for different people. Details should be indicated in the letter through which the recipient also gets to know the people who will be reading the mail. This notation is normally made below the enclosures notation. The manner in which it is written is as follows:

Notation for copies sent to other people

> cc
> CC
> cc:
> CC:

The blind carbon copy notation or bcc is written when the sender does not want the receiver to know that the same mail is being sent to someone else. This notation does not appear on the original. It is typed on the upper left-hand corner of the letter. However, both cc and bcc notations should appear on the writer's copy of the letter.

Postscript

This is the last part of the letter, which is an afterthought. Many a time the writer forgets to include an important detail and wishes to include it at the end. This technique is adopted when there is a need to jot a point as a postscript. Occasionally, certain writers deliberately omit a detail to which they want the reader to pay attention and include the point at the end of the letter in the form of a postscript. The letters PS represent the word postscript and are written as PS:

Notation for additional information

The Amelius Company
E-308, Surya Vihar, Kapas Hera Border
Gurgaon 122002

November 3, 2014
Ref no: 12/FF2/34

Mr. Suresh Mehta, M.D.
Premium Industries
416, Sector 14
Gurgaon—122016

Exhibit 7.5   (*Contd.*)

Sir:

Subject: *Training Review*

Trainings are an integral part of any organisation. While there are many vendors who do provide the training, there are few who actually get into reviewing the process.

We at Amelius believe that a training review provides both the trainer and trainee a handle on what happened, success measures and ways in which the training can be augmented. Apart from 360 degree feedback on the training and trainer, we have developed various tools for assessment.

We are keen to interact with you and discuss the feasibility of working with your organisation.
Sincerely yours,
THE AMELIUS COMPANY

Enclosures: 1
CC: Mr. Mahavir Sood
P.S: Please return the enclosed document by post by January 2015.

Exhibit 7.5   Postscript.

"A woman seldom writes her Mind, but in her Postscript."
—Richard Steele, Spectator

STYLES OF LETTER ARRANGEMENT

TOPIC OBJECTIVES
Illustrate different layouts for the business letter
Analyse the need for various layouts

"To find out your real opinion of someone, judge the impression you have when you first see a letter from them."
—Arthur Schopenhauer

The style of arrangement of a letter varies from person to person with some adopting the full-block formatting style and some going in for a semi-block. The style also demonstrates the tone of the letter. The more formal the tone, the greater is the need to adopt a full-block format. The amount of white space around the words typed reveals the level of formality or informality, e.g., in a full-block style where all the paragraphs begin on the left-hand margin, there is little that is left to imagination. On the other hand, in the indented paragraph or open style where some notations are put on the left-hand side, some on the right-hand side with indentation of paragraphs, the white space left becomes symptomatic of the informal tone. Let us take a look at the different styles of writing a letter.

Full Block Style

All notations and messages start on the left-hand margin

In this form of writing a letter, all notations and paragraphs begin on the left-hand margin. This is comparatively easy to type as no paragraphs are made and it also saves on the typing time. It looks neat and has a business like tone to it.

```
                              IMMI
November 4, 2014

Mr. Rohit Basu, General Manager
Industrial Consultancy Services
Daryaganj
New Delhi

Dear Mr. Basu:
Subject: Enlistment in the Directory of Industrial Consultants

Please refer to your letter No. 1425 dated October 20, 2014 on the captioned subject.

In this connection, we wish to inform you that IMMI, on behalf of the all-India financial
institutions maintains a Directory of Financial Consultants with the main objective
of providing guidance to financial institutions, banks, government departments,
entrepreneurs, etc. for selecting suitable candidates for their consultancy need.

The enlistment of consultants in the Directory is generally done on the basis of their
experience, duly supported by documentary evidence in the form of reports, studies,
notes, drawings, etc. prepared by them for their clients in the fields in which they seek
enlistment.

Keeping the above in view, you may please return the enclosed application form, duly
filled in, alongwith the necessary enclosures to enable us to consider your request for
enlistment.

We assure that the report, etc. submitted by you will be kept in strict confidence by us.

Thank You.

Yours Sincerely,


Protima Mahajan
General Manager

Nmp
Encl: 1

cc: Mr. Mahavir Sood
```

Exhibit 7.6   Full block style.

Semi-block Style

> *Partly traditional and partly non-traditional*

This style of writing a letter is also very common as it encompasses the traditional style of writing and brings together with it the ease in formulating the message that is present in a full-block style. In a semi-block style of writing a letter, lists, addresses or quotations are incorporated by indenting the same.

IMMI

November 4, 2014

Mr. Rohit Basu, General Manager
Industrial Consultancy Services
Daryaganj
New Delhi

Dear Mr. Basu:
Subject: Enlistment in the Directory of Industrial Consultants

Please refer to your letter No. 1425 dated October 20, 2014 on the captioned subject.

In this connection, we wish to inform you that IMMI, on behalf of the all-India financial institutions maintains a Directory of Financial Consultants with the main objective of providing guidance to financial institutions, banks, government departments, entrepreneurs, etc. for selecting suitable candidates for their consultancy needs.

The enlistment of consultants in the Directory is generally done on the basis of their experience duly supported by documentary evidence in the form of reports, studies, notes, drawings, etc. prepared by them for their clients in the fields in which they seek enlistment.

Keeping the above in view, you may please return the enclosed application form, duly filled in, along with the necessary enclosures to enable us to consider your request for enlistment.

We assure that all the details submitted by you will be kept in strict confidence by us.

Thank You.

Yours Sincerely,

Protima Mahajan
General Manager

Nmp
Encl: 1

cc. Mr. Mahavir Sood

Exhibit 7.7   Semi-block style.

Open Style

No fixed paragraph formulation scheme

This is the most traditional as well as informal style of writing letters. It does not adhere to the fixed paragraph formulation scheme. In fact, all the paragraphs are indented with some notations on the left and some on the right. However, gradually this style of writing is getting outmoded.

Note: The choice of layout reflects the degree of formality that has been adopted.

IMMI

November 4, 2014

Mr. Rohit Basu, General Manager
Industrial Consultancy Services
Daryaganj
New Delhi

Dear Mr. Basu:

Subject: Enlistment in the Directory of Industrial Consultants

Please refer to your letter No. 1425 dated October 20, 2014 on the captioned subject.

In this connection we wish to inform you that IMMI, on behalf of the all-India Financial institutions maintains a Directory of financial Consultants with the main objective of providing guidance to financial institutions, banks, government departments, entrepreneurs, etc. for selecting suitable candidates for their ventures.

The enlistment of Consultants in the Directory is generally done on the basis of their experience duly supported by documentary evidence in the form of reports, studies, notes, drawings, etc. prepared by them for their clients in the fields in which they seek enlistment.

Keeping the above in view, you may please return the enclosed application form, duly filled in, along with the necessary enclosures to enable us to consider your request for enlistment.

We assure that the report, etc. submitted by you will be kept in strict confidence by us.

Thank You.

Yours Sincerely,

Protima Mahajan
General Manager

Nmp
Encl: 1

cc. Mr. Mahavir Sood

Exhibit 7.8 Open style.

TYPES OF LETTERS

TOPIC
OBJECTIVES
Discuss strategies of achieving the purpose of the letter
Differentiate different kinds of business letters on the basis of intent
Indicate letters that are distinguished by the mode of transmission

"It seems a long time since the morning mail could be called correspondence."
—Jacques Barzun

There are different types of letters, each with a different task to be accomplished. What is, however, common among all of them is the desire to expedite matters through written communication. For this, it is essential that the letter be planned in a manner to generate interest and lead the reader into taking appropriate action. Let us consider the acronym AIDA for achieving the above-stated goal.

A—Capture Attention
I—Arouse Interest
D—Create Desire
A—Inspire reader into taking Action

This is also what we refer to as the four-paragraph construct. In the opening or the first paragraph, the writer employs techniques to capture the attention of the reader. This can be done if the letter is reader-oriented. As soon as the reader senses the element of benefit, there will be motivation to take some action. For this, it is essential that the letter should focus on the reader, on a 'you' attitude.

> **Capture the attention**

The second and the third or the middle paragraphs focus on developing interest in the subject matter and creating desire to perform the requisite task or take subsequent action. If the attention of the reader has been captured in the first paragraph, the next couple of paragraphs build on the same. In other words, the basic theme with which the letter began should be developed. There would be conviction about the feasibility of the proposal only if there is evidence to support that the statements made are true and beneficial to the reader.

> **Develop interest and create desire**

The last paragraph persuades the reader to take some action. Throughout the letter, the writer has been trying to convince the reader. This paragraph is now a culmination of the initial efforts. Clear statements need to be made as to what should the reader do if there is a desire to comply with the request of the writer.

> **Propel the reader into taking action**

With a change in purpose, the manner of writing a letter also undergoes a change. The organisational pattern varies from letter to letter. Let us take a look at the different types of letters.

Direct Requests

> **Be persuasive**

Direct requests need to be persuasive in nature. Before writing a request, the sender should gather some information on the reader and his/her needs. This would help in drafting the letter and making it reader-friendly. The letter has to be very carefully drafted by the sender as a request is being made. All sentences and ideas should be linked coherently. The reader should not get the impression that the letter is a long and convoluted one. For this, the statements should have clarity and brevity so that the receiver does not spend much time in trying to decipher the actual content. If it is not clearly formulated, the reader may lose interest in the letter and the request may be left unattended.

> **Link ideas and sentences**

> **Be clear and brief**

Question yourself, "Why should the receiver comply with the request unless there is an envisioned benefit?" If you secure an answer to this query, it will help in composing the letter with a you-orientation.

For a request letter to make a direct impact, the main idea should be stated first with all the necessary details. The idea requesting action needs to be worded very carefully so that there is no scope of ambiguity. Once

| *State the main idea first* |

the opening has been formulated, the next stage is of writing the middle. Draw the attention of the reader to the letter in hand. The sender should indicate, while giving details of the request, the manner in which the reader would gain by complying to the request. If the

| *Indicate advantages to the reader* |

letter is successfully drafted keeping the above stated points in mind, almost half the problem is solved. The request on more than one occasion will be complied with.

Often there is more than one request embedded in the one, formal request. It should be broken down into smaller points so that there

| *Use a pattern of listing for sub-points* |

is clarity in the message. It can also be expressed using a pattern of listing or sub-headings with a statement or two providing details.

The arrangement should be logical and coherent with the most important point stated first. This can then be followed by points that are less important which should necessarily relate to the main request.

The closing of the letter should contain a specific request for action and be coupled with an expression of appreciation for the time spent in considering

| *Specific request for action* |

the request or at least going through the same. As far as possible, a letter should be addressed to a specific person rather than to a company or institution. This at least ascertains that the letter has reached the concerned person and follow-up action becomes easier. The receiver, in such instances, is bound to take more responsibility when a message is addressed directly rather than when the letter is addressed to the company.

It goes without saying that there should be a lot of tact involved in formulating any letter and more specifically a request letter. Avoid

| *Be tactful and polite* |

expressions of the following nature that violate the politeness principle: "Thanking you in advance...", "Waiting for a positive response..." Statements like the following would be more appropriate: "I would be grateful if...", "I would appreciate..." All these expressions come towards the end of the letter when the sender is specifically making a request for some action.

Note: For a request letter to make a direct impact, the main idea should be stated first with all the necessary details.

Inquiry Letters

These letters are written when the sender wishes to make an inquiry either about an issue or a policy. There should be clarity about the purpose of writing the letter. Suppose he/she wishes to ask for details about the policy for equipment refinance, there should be clarity in the statement. There

should, at no cost, be an intermingling of issues or policies. The

Clarity in making a request

subject should be clearly stated, and the purpose for making that request be explicitly stated. This makes it easy for the reader to understand the motive behind the inquiry. It even expedites the process of compliance or rejection. Suppose the purpose for the inquiry is not clearly addressed. Then the reader would probably assign his/her own motive and the speed of the response would be contingent upon the implicit intent.

The Close in the letter of inquiry should adhere to the principles of

politeness as brashness on the part of the sender could probably result

Adhere to principles of politeness

in non-compliance of the request. As this letter is a request, even though written in the form of an inquiry, it should observe the politeness principle.

The letter of inquiry will probably have a number of questions to which answers are sought. All queries should be specific and related to one another. If there is more than one question, it should be numbered or written under a sub-heading. Questions should be framed in such a manner that they can elicit an answer that is more than a "yes" or "no". The reply to these inquiry letters then would help the reader in chalking out further strategies. If the response is a monosyllable, all avenues to further correspondence are closed.

Warning! Do not intermingle issues while making an inquiry in the letter.

Letters of Reference

There are many Institutes and companies that require a reference letter for the candidate applying for admission or a job. The candidate, prior to citing

a name, should secure consent from the proposed referee. Once the

State the position you are applying

permission is granted, then only should the name be cited in the documents requiring reference details and letters. If, you wish to secure a reference letter from a referee with who you had been in touch a few years back, refer to the relationship that you enjoyed; if possible, specify the dates or the year and any special event that will help the referee to place you in right focus.

The opening paragraph of the letter requesting a reference clearly states the position for which the application is being made. The letter should be

"you-oriented". If expressions such as the following can be added:

"You"-orientation

"Your recommendations would greatly enhance...", "Your reference would definitely count..." you have a greater chance of securing for yourself a positive recommendation letter.

Some details like resumé, and the job that you wish to apply for, should be enclosed. The resumé will definitely help in forming a positive opinion about the candidate as the reader may not be able to recollect much about the candidate. In case the current resumé is not ready, the writer should

provide the reader with some current information about the self in the letter so that an effective recommendation can be made. Details of the Institute or company in which admission is sought will help the referee decide the tenor of the message.

| *Enclose resumé and details of job* |

As this is again a request, a courteous and polite close should accompany the main message. A stamped, self-addressed envelope should also be attached to the letter so that it becomes easy for the reader to dispatch the reference letter.

| *Courteous and polite close* |

Jam: Have you enclosed your resume and other details for your referee while making a request for a recommendation?

Legal Transactions

Letters concerning legal transactions are formal and there is a stipulated format for the same. The letter is written in the passive voice with possibly an appendix that spells out the legal formalities in detail. What is important in these letters is that they should be honest and fair. All facts and details should be presented truthfully. Let us take a look at a sample letter:

| *Letter written in passive tone* |

Dear Sir

Subject: *Sanction of Financial Assistance—Formalities to be completed*

Please refer to our letter of Intent No. .... dated .... conveying sanction of ***term Loan/Line of Credit/Foreign currency term loan** not exceeding ₹ .... lakh (Rupees .... lakh only) ***US$/DM .... equivalent to ₹ .... lakh** to your ***Company/Firm/Concern/Society/ Trust** relating to documentation and creation of security for availing the said ***Loan/ Line of Credit/Foreign currency term loan** are set out in the Appendix. You are requested to comply with the same at the earliest.

Should you require any clarification/information on any of the requirements, please ***contact our office** at Tel. Nos. .... or write to us immediately.

Yours faithfully,

XYZ

*Delete if not applicable
**Applicable only to foreign currency loans

Exhibit 7.9 Legal transactions.

Letters of Transmittal

Accompanying letters to cheques or documents

Letters of transmittal are those letters that accompany any cheque or business documents. They are important as they provide a record for future reference. A good transmittal letter should be able to accomplish the following tasks:

1. Identify what is being sent
2. Specify any action to be taken
3. Identify the purpose for which the papers or the cheque is being dispatched.

Dear Dr. Maini

Enclosed is Cheque No. 678921 for ₹ 8,000/- (₹ Eight thousand only) as consultation charges for four hours workshop conducted on 20 October 2013.
Kindly acknowledge the receipt.

Sincerely,

XYZ

Exhibit 7.10   Letter of transmittal

Sales Letters

Streamline the objective and identify the people

Drafting and composing a sales letter is very tough. There are a lot of facts that need to be taken into consideration at the time of writing a sales letter. The basic purpose of writing should be clear. Streamlining the objective is followed by an identification of the people to whom the message is to be transmitted. The last and the final stage is the composition of the letter in a systematic, logical and easy to comprehend pattern.

The purpose of writing a sales letter is that direct, face-to-face interaction with all customers is not always possible. It is written with the purpose of:

1. Attracting new customers
2. Retaining interest of old customers
3. Creating a good impact
4. Facilitating retention about the product and the company

Be innovative and creative

With a change in the purpose, the manner of writing the letter also undergoes a change. If the purpose is to get an immediate response, the letter could make use of "attention grabbers", e.g., "A free gift with purchase of items over ₹ 500". "A free coke for children below the age of 15."

The more innovative and creative the letter is, greater are the chances of it being read by the customer.

Dear Ms. Patnaik

Congratulations! You are the lucky winner of the day. There is a free gift hamper worth ₹ 5,000 waiting to be collected from our Avalon office on Mehrauli-Aya Road.
We would be highly obliged if you could possibly have coffee with us on 2 November 2014. It would be extremely nice if at the same time you could attend a brief presentation of 50 minutes at our resort.

Sincerely,

XYZ

Exhibit 7.11 Sales letter.

In this particular example, the purpose of the writer is to introduce the resort to the sender by way of presentation. The bait of a free gift hamper has been used.

The writer can use many techniques to capture the attention of the reader. Primary among them could be the use of fancy and non-traditional stationery and one-liners written both on the envelope and the letter. Next is the composition of the message that is dependent on the unusual juxtaposition of ideas and concepts. The more creative the writer is in this technique, the greater will be the receptivity of the message, e.g., "Zero to josh", "Catch you there", "Who says you can't land a catch!" Certain other techniques like making use of startling sentences or statements or using questions to capture the attention of the reader can be employed, e.g., "Satisfaction guaranteed *or* your money back", "Twist and Shout", "Why go to movie when they can come home to you?" "How important is your child's health to you?"

Composition of message
1. Unusual combination of words
2. Startling sentences
3. Questions

The choice of the strategy is contingent upon the following:

- Product
- Company
- Market segment

The sales letter typically follows the AIDA plan of organisation. Once the attention of the reader has been captured, interest needs to be sustained. At this stage the positive qualities of the product must be emphasised. As market survey has already been done and the market segment identified, the drafting or composition of the middle section would not be so tough, e.g. the middle section of a sales letter for a new electrical appliance that prepares snacks in 20 seconds can be drafted in the following manner:

You come back home after a long and tiring day. You are feeling hungry but do not have the energy or stamina to make food. Just flip the switch of the Marino snack maker with 20 gm uncooked rice. Before you can get a plate in your hand, the tasty, crunchy snack is ready to eat. You can relax and listen to music, with the delicious snack by your side.

Exhibit 7.12 Promotional material.

The desire to take action has been created in the customer and finally in the closing there is an additional line stating how, where, and when to get in touch with the sales department of the Marino company. Besides, probably there would be the early bird incentive thrown in—a 25% discount on purchase of every product. Offer open till 8 December 2014.

Note: Make use of attention grabbers if you need to solicit an immediate response.

Good News Letters

It is comparatively easy to write good news letters or replies. A direct approach can be adopted, which comprises three stages:

1. State the main idea or the best news. The reader has probably been waiting for it so that it can act as an effective device to capture the attention.

2. Provide the explanations or the details. In such letters not much effort would be needed to sustain the interest of the reader.

3. Close on a positive, friendly note, together with a clear statement of action desired, appreciation, and a willingness to help further.

| *Maintain a "You"-emphasis* |

In these letters once again there should be a "you"-emphasis instead of an "I"-emphasis. Contrast the two statements, both of which are part of good news letters.

> 1. Congratulations! I was really happy to hear that you had secured 90%...
> 2. Congratulations on your exemplary performance...

Exhibit 7.13   Good news letter.

The first statement deals with the pleasure accorded to the writer, but the second one commends the reader on the great performance. Which would you prefer? Wherein should you focus?

Good news replies should always begin with compliance with the reader's request rather than an expression of gratitude or pleasure. In the middle section it should be clearly stated that either you are in the process of complying with the request or have already complied with it. Subsequently, provide explanations to build conviction and garner receptivity.

Bad News/Refusal Letters

| *Do not begin on a negative note* |

When there is some bad news to be transmitted, the job ahead of the writer is pretty tough. Chances are high that the reader will not read the reasons for the bad news if the letter begins on a negative note. The letter will be more acceptable if the following points are kept in mind at the time of writing the letter:

1. The goal of writing the letter should be clearly emphasised
2. The language used should be positive
3. There should not be direct statement of the word "no"
4. There should not be a hint of apology

This letter can be written either in an indirect or direct form. In the indirect form the opening paragraph is always in the form of an acknowledgement of probably the efforts that have been put in and appreciation of the same. Apart from acknowledgement and appreciation, there can be other ways to open a bad news letter. The letter can also begin with something positive or favourable to the reader, or on a note of praise. It can also begin on a note of understanding the goals and needs of the reader. For example: "Thank you for your interest in Proline Industries."

Opening— Acknowledge- ment, appreciation, note of praise, understanding goals of reader

The middle section is normally an elucidation of reasons and explanations as to why the proposal or the project, though definitely good, cannot be considered. At the time when the reasons are being presented, it is crucial to reveal how the decision is reasonable and fair. The writer can even go to the extent of indicating to the reader how this decision may have positive future repercussions. In this section negative language should be avoided and the tone should be positive. Avoid direct statements with a you-reference. Contrast the two statements:

Middle— Elucidation on reasons

> 1. You shouldn't have sent the sales letter.
> 2. The dispatch of the sales letter ...

Exhibit 7.14 Refusal letters.

The first statement is accusative, while the second is neutral. In the latter example, the reader is going to be more receptive to reasoning and explanation. The reasons that are provided should be detailed and tactfully presented.

In the closing section the bad news should not be repeated, nor should the statements be backed up with apologies. Be as sincere as possible. If no further communication is desired, do not close on a false note of promise of getting in touch at a later stage.

Do not repeat or apologise

The primary reason for following this structure is that as soon as bad news is conveyed, the mind of the receiver stops accepting any other information input and closes to any further explanations or reasoning. Thus, if maintaining the goodwill of the reader is important, it is necessary that the explanations precede the bad news.

Maintain goodwill

In a direct approach, the writer comes directly to the point. The opening itself has a brief statement on the bad news that is followed by a brief reason or explanation and a stiff and formal close. The only advantage of this form of writing is that the message is brief and the reader arrives at the message almost immediately. It can only be followed in instances when the message does not create a direct personal impact and the writer wishes to drive home the point clearly, directly and in no time.

The close should be courteous and polite.

At the time of writing a bad news letter, certain points should to be kept in mind. The goodwill of the reader has to be maintained and there should be a feeling that the writer has, in all fairness, has been responsive but now is firm on the stand taken and will not be swayed.

Note: While a direct approach is best with good news letters, an indirect approach may be more feasible for bad news/refusal letters.

Letters of Acceptance/Acknowledgement

Acknowledge all correspondence

There should always be acknowledgement of business papers, letters, documents, etc. after receipt of the same. The three-fold advantage of sending these acknowledgement letters is that they

1. Provide a record,
2. Show courtesy, and
3. Avoid misunderstanding.

State all details

As they are mostly routine letters, they follow the routine procedure of writing. The sender first acknowledges the receipt of the letter, provides the necessary details and backs it up with a complimentary close that indicates a desire to maintain the goodwill of the reader.

Dear Mr. Mukherjee:

Thank you for the cheque No. 894632, dated 9 November 2014 for ₹ 10,000 (₹ Ten Thousand only) as professional charges.

Your promptness in making payments is appreciated, and we hope that we will be able to serve you again.

Sincerely,

XYZ

Exhibit 7.15   Letter of acceptance/acknowledgement.

All facts should be clearly stated in letters of acknowledgement. In the above example, all details pertaining to the cheque, the date of issuing the cheque, the amount and the purpose are presented. This information is necessary as letters of acknowledgement are records for further transaction of business.

TELEGRAMS

TOPIC OBJECTIVES

Understand the techniques for writing a Telegram

Learn to differentiate the writing of a telegram from a letter

A telegram is a quick and easy way of transmitting a message. However, it is different in many ways from a letter. It is a very brief message that neither adheres to the rules of grammar nor observes punctuation. There is a printed form on which the message, together with the details of the sender and the receiver, are filled in.

Brief and condensed message

Chandigarh Post Office		
NAME AND ADDRESS OF THE ADDRESSEE	NAME ADDRESS	Rajan Gupta Sector C, Pocket III, House No. 3053 Vasant Kunj, New Delhi
	TELEGRAPH OFFICE TELEPHONE No.	Vasant Kunj 6896527

MESSAGE:

1. FIVE PROFESSORS ARRIVING DELHI FROM CHANDIGARH TUESDAY FIFTH DECEMBER IC219 0600 STOP LEAVING NEW DELHI FRIDAY EIGHTH DECEMBER 1C319 1800 FOR ENGLAND
2. ARRANGE ACCOMMODATION FOR NIGHTS OF FIFTH SIXTH AND SEVENTH
3. ARRANGE ITINERARY TO LOCAL AND NEARBY PLACES STOP PARTY ARE MOSTLY ELDERLY
4. CONFIRM STOP SEND DETAILS BY TELEGRAM

SENDER'S NAME   SHRABANI BASU

NOT TO BE TELEGRAPHED   SECTOR 14
SENDER'S ADDRESS   MAIN SQUARE, CHANDIGARH

Exhibit 7.16 Telegram.

The message, the sender's name and the address are all in capitals or block letters. Instead of a period the word "STOP" is written to indicate break between sentences. Time is mentioned by way of a twenty-four hour time scheme and dates are always written in words. For example, in the above telegram, the time specified is 0600 and 1800 and the dates mentioned as "fifth" and "eighth". As a telegram is a costly affair and each word is counted separately, brevity should be maintained. This does not mean that clarity and accuracy can be sacrificed at the cost of brevity. Words with prefixes such as un-, im- and in- can be used to economise on use of words. For example:

Undermentioned	Unacceptable
Impermanent	Imperfect
Inapplicable	Inappropriate

Jam: Have you filled in the telegram in block letters?

TELEX MESSAGES

TOPIC OBJECTIVES
Comprehend the technique for writing a telex message
Modify message to match telex style of writing

By definition a telex message is an electronic message that is typed on a word processor, and is directly sent through telegraph lines to the recipient. It is in fact fast replacing the letter as it reaches its destination almost immediately or as soon as the message is keyed in. Sending telex messages is

Electronic message typed on a word processor

an expensive affair and is worked out in terms of the time the operator takes to transmit the message. Hence, for telex messages, brevity, clarity and accuracy are absolutely essential. Further, the grammatical and punctuation necessities in a letter are usually not adhered to in a telex. As in a telegram, the entire message is written in capitals or in block letters. A period is used instead of the word "STOP". Some of the techniques of writing a letter are observed. For example, the attention line and the complimentary close are used. While in a letter the attention line is written when it is to be addressed to the company, in a telex the name of the receiver is used. Depending on the relationship observed between the sender and the receiver, the complimentary close is written, which is followed by the name of the sender.

Be brief, clear and concise

A telex message operates on code numbers unlike a telegram. Many details are provided prior to the actual beginning of the message, but almost all of them are in the form of numbers or alphabetical representations, e.g., there is a code for the place from where the telex message begins and to the place where it is being sent. Time once again is written in the form of numbers, using the twenty-four hour time scheme. As more and more people have started using a fax or e-mail, this mode of sending message is gradually becoming outmoded.

Note: Write the name of the receiver in the attention line of a telex.

FACSIMILES (FAX)

TOPIC OBJECTIVES
Understand the advantages of sending a fax
Apply understanding of fax for message transfer

A fax is again an electronic device for transmission of message. Most organisations have a fax machine through which they can transmit the message almost instantly. A fax can also be sent by the computer provided there is a modem attached to it. The advantage of a fax is that visuals and graphics can also be transferred. An attempt should be made to make the fax as brief as possible so that maximum number of pages are faxed. The advantage of a fax over a letter is that it can be transmitted immediately. While a letter by ordinary post, takes on an average three to four days to reach its destination, the fax reaches as soon as it completes its circuit through the fax machine. There is also the provision of an activity confirmation line in the fax machine that confirms the accurate transmittal of the message.

Electronic message

A typical fax would look like a letter with the name of the recipient and the fax number on top of the letter in the following manner:

Immediate transmittal of message

Kind Attn:	Mr. Mohit Ambisht
Fax No.:	(011) — 6133156

ELECTRONIC MAIL

TOPIC OBJECTIVES

Identify key aspects of email writing

Use learning of writing emails to professional message transmittal

Electronic or e-mail is one of the fastest means of transmitting the message. There has to be an internet connection on the computer for the sender to send the message. The advantage of an e-mail is that simultaneously it can be sent to a number of people, and the message can be retrieved at will. There is almost no paper work or filing of letters. There is also a system of Auto archive through which selected messages can be sent to a different folder and the unnecessary messages deleted.

Electronic mail— One of the fastest means of transmittal

No paper work or filing of letters

Another advantage of an e-mail is that at the time of sending a reply there is no need to send in the reference number. The original message to which a reply is being given is also displayed. This helps the receiver to view the response in the correct perspective.

Almost all material, whether it is in the form of visuals or graphics, can be transmitted through an e-mail, which makes it one of the most accessible and the easiest forms of communication. In fact, today it is one of the most accepted form of communications.

Avoid capitals and block style

Jot down comments on the letter

Brief messages

Just as there is a format for the letter so also is there a format for the e-mail. The salutation and reference in an e-mail, after the first and second round of exchange is normally dropped. The same is the case in an informal exchange. Care should be taken to ensure that the message is not written in capitals or block style as is done in a telegram or telex message. According to the e-mail formatting, if all words are in capitals, e-mail users feel that the sender is shouting at them. As an e-mail is almost second to oral communication, messages are very brief and can also be one liners, e.g., "No, I did not receive it."

Some organisations have *Local Area Network* (*LAN*) connection. This lessens paper work, facilitates transmittal of message to a number of people simultaneously, and reduces the necessity of secretaries and assistants. Accessing or sending e-mail is a relatively simple process provided the sender has an internet connection. The various steps are as follows:

1. Login to the computer
2. Get connected to the internet
3. Feed in the user name and password
4. Click on the site through which e-mail facilities can be obtained
5. Feed in your login name and password
6. Type the name of the receiver and e-mail address

7. Type the subject line

8. Feed in the brief message

9. Re-read and review

10. Click the mouse button on send.

If you, as a sender, want to store the material, you also have the provision in the computer to do the same. It is something like the filing of the original letters. If the message is saved, you can refer back to the folder whenever you need to refer to it or when you are unable to get a response.

Material stored on the hard disk

On the part of the receiver if the internet connection is switched on and is working on the computer, a small beep would inform that a message has been received. To retrieve messages a receiver has to again logon, reach the site and then open mail after feeding in the login name and password.

Warning! Do not use capital letters for an e-mail as it may visually offend the reader.

Handling Mail

Large organisations have a separate department for incoming and outgoing mail, which is referred to as the *Receipt and Dispatch section*. All incoming mails are sorted out in this section, entered into a register, and then transferred to the concerned person. If it is a letter that is marked to a particular department, the head normally opens it and marks it to the concerned person.

A letter received by a particular department is either filed or circulated to other people within the department or outside for their comments. In a company or organisation there are different files or folders dealing with different issues. All letters or correspondences are marked and then entered into the folder according to the date of receipt. Prior to filing the letter, the concerned officer notes down suggestions or comments so that subsequent action can be taken either immediately or postponed for future use. All files are marked in alphabetical order and placed in a systematic order. This is done so as to ensure quick and easy retrieval of information at a later date.

Different files or folders for different issues

Whenever a letter or proposal is circulated to other people, a note is added to the original letter. In this note the receiver condenses the letter or proposal in the form of points and then circulates it. References are made to other points made on that particular issue and the file numbers with the reference numbers cited in the left-hand margin so as to make it easier for the reader to access the material in case there is a need. When the entire file is circulated for reference, small flags are affixed to the pages which bear a connection between the current mail and the previous correspondences. The notes which are sent across for perusal normally come back with an additional note, either accepting the proposal or showing dissent. Further action is then taken upon the recommendations or suggestions.

Affix a note when message is circulated to other people

Now with the usage of electronic mail on the increase, different files on the computer are created and most information is stored in what is referred to as the data bank from where it can be retrieved easily. Once again this system uses up almost no space, except on the computer, greatly reduces paper work and obliterates all problems pertaining to maintaining, locating and retrieving of files. Further, when cases are resolved and closed, the file can be deleted from the computer by a mere click of the mouse button.

MAINTAINING A DIARY

TOPIC OBJECTIVES

Manage a diary with details

Learn to frame the content suitably for future reference

"What is a diary as a rule? A document useful to the person who keeps it. Dull to the contemporary who reads it and invaluable to the student, centuries afterwards, who treasures it."   —Sir Walter Scott

Beginning the process of writing a diary and then maintaining it, in the initial phase, seems to be a rather a tedious task. However, as one climbs up the ladder of success, one realises the importance of this small task which can have far reaching effects. Writing a diary is an informal task and is more in the nature of letter writing. The receiver is the diary itself as the salutation and the message is addressed to the diary.

An informal process of writing

It follows no strict pattern and the writer can jot down the happenings of the day either in point format or in paragraph form. It has two distinct advantages:

1. It helps the writer to unburden
2. It acts as a record of the happenings of the day

With stress and tension mounting and inability to communicate, writing a diary helps the writer to unleash emotions by penning them down.

Pages should have dates

As a diary also acts as a record of the activities of the day, the date should of necessity be put on the page. This helps the writer in maintaining a record of the daily procedures and happenings.

As writing and maintaining a diary are personal and confidential, the writer can give vent to personal emotions while expressing feelings. The page is written in the first person and is based more on the comments, feelings and observations rather than statement of actual facts. Some

Statement on feelings and observations

organisations require that personal/formal diaries be maintained in the form of a log book. Such a diary is different from the informal, personal narrative shown in Exhibit 7.17.

Note: Even though informal in nature, writing a diary helps keep track of professional and personal events.

November 8, 2014

Dear Diary,

The day was hectic as we had two meetings today and the papers for the conference also had to be dispatched by noon. I was quite happy with the pace of work and I think was able to perform to the best of my capabilities.

The two meetings that we had were in connection with:

1. Sanction of loan to project proposed by Shilpa Industries. It was held in the forenoon and everyone was energetic and full of suggestions and comments. This went on rather smoothly and there was no dissent. I felt it went off too smoothly. In fact, I wanted to make a few suggestions but felt no one would be receptive to them. So I maintained a diplomatic stance and kept quiet.

2. The second meeting was held in the post-lunch session and was in connection with planning the farewell programme for Mr. Ahuja, Vice president, Marketing division. As he is not a very popular person, there was a lot of dissent concerning the amount of money that was to be collected for his farewell gift. Mr. Mahajan was extremely vocal. I personally do not blame Mr. Mahajan for his outburst. There have been moments when Mr. Ahuja has also been nasty to me. In fact, this morning he called me just to tell me that whatever I had achieved so far was a result of his guidance and once he was gone I would really be in a soup. I am terribly happy he is leaving our organisation. I don't want to sound mean, but I hope he gets what he actually deserves.

Mahesh Mulchandani

Exhibit 7.17 Diary writing.

SUMMARY

Business correspondence is an integral part of client-customer interaction. The manner of composition, the formatting of the letter, the style of arrangement of the various components—the heading, opening, body and close—reflect the image of the writer and the company, and affect the purpose of the communication.

The choice of style for the letter arrangement depends on the purpose and tone of the writer. There are three such styles that she can choose from—the full block style, the semi-block style and the open style. While in the full block style all components of the letter begin from the left side margin, the open style has no fixed paragraph formulation. The semi block style is a mix of both these styles.

It is essential that the letter be planned in a manner to generate interest and lead the reader into taking appropriate action. With AIDA—Capture *Attention,* Arouse *Interest,* Create *Desire,* Inspire reader into taking *Action*—this goal can be effectively achieved. There are different types of letters, each with a different task to be accomplished.

Direct requests need to be persuasive in nature. The message should be structured to make a direct impact. The closing of the letter should contain a specific request for action and should be coupled with an expression of appreciation.

An inquiry letter should be clearly stated, and the purpose should also be explicit. This helps the reader to understand the motive and expedites matters. Questions should be framed in a manner to elicit an answer that is more than a "yes" or "no". The close in the letter of inquiry should adhere to the principles of politeness.

A request for a letter of recommendation is accompanied by a tone of confidence and professionalism. Orienting the letter towards the receiver will help convey the importance of the recommendation for the purpose. The close must be polite and courteous.

Letters concerning legal transactions are formal and follow a stipulated format. Letters of transmittal are those letters that accompany any cheque or business documents and provide a record for future reference.

A sales letter is written when direct interaction with all customers is not always possible. If the purpose is to get an immediate response, the letter could make use of "attention grabbers". The letter will be effective if written innovatively and creatively.

A good news letter is easier to write. A direct approach can be adopted. It usually begins with a statement of good news, continues into an explanation of related details and closes on a positive, friendly note.

The structure of the bad news/refusal letter is important as the receiver may not absorb any other information once the bad news is stated. It is useful to open with acknowledgement, praise or a neutral statement. This can be followed by the news itself along with explanation and other details. Care should be taken that there be no direct refusal, and the text is positive without a sense of apology. This helps maintain goodwill despite the refusal.

After receiving business papers, letters, documents, acknowledging receipt is important. The three-fold advantage is that they provide a record, show courtesy and avoid misunderstanding.

Letters may be distinguished by the mode through which they are transmitted. This also affects the way they are composed. Telegrams, Telex, Fax, Emails are cases in point. In the email for instance, the salutation and reference can be done away with as the original message is transmitted on the screen, It should not be written in capitals or block style as is in a telegram or telex message.

CHECKLIST

Do's	Don'ts
Use the heading to provide vital information about the company	Forget to provide this information if the official letterhead pad is not being used
Indicate the name of the recipient	Right align the recipient's name and address details
Use a colon after "Subject"	Underline "Subject"
Follow the same formatting style in close and salutation	Mismatch the close and the salutation
Left align all notations and paragraphs in the Full Block style	Use the Full Block style for an informal letter
In a request letter compose a message in a systematic and coherent manner	Give the impression of a convoluted long winded request
Attach letters of transmittal to business documents	Omit to state in the letter what is being sent
Use the AIDA plan of organisation for the sales letter	Lose the interest of the reader through bad formulation of the sales message
State the best news first in a good news letter	Be long winded in a good news letter
Condense messages for the email	Painstakingly keep to the salutation and close format in an email

RAPID REVIEW

A. Pick Your Choice

1. A business letter can be formatted under
    (a) three heads   (b) four heads   (c) none of these
2. The letter should be based on a
    (a) I attitude   (b) You attitude   (c) We attitude
3. Direct request should be
    (a) stated bluntly   (b) persuasive   (c) neither of the two
4. The arrangement of requests in a letter should be logical and coherent with the
    (a) most important point   (b) details   (c) purpose stated first
5. Letters of transmittal are those letters
    (a) through which information is transmitted
    (b) through which message is transmitted
    (c) that accompany any cheque or business documents

6. The choice of the strategy for writing a Sales letter is contingent upon
   (a) the product   (b) the company   (c) the market segment
   (d) all of these advantages
7. Electronic mail is
   (a) quick
   (b) saves time
   (c) can be retrieved easily
   (d) has all these advantages
8. Diary writing helps the writer to
   (a) unburden   (b) unleash creative instincts
   (c) prepare for the next day
9. A diary is written in a
   (a) formal
   (b) informal
   (c) partly formal and partly informal style
10. A letter of acknowledgement
    (a) provides a record
    (b) shows courtesy
    (c) avoids misunderstanding
    (d) serves all these purposes.

B. True or False

1. The close in a letter is contingent upon the salutation
2. The notation bcc never appears on the original but appears on the carbon copies.
3. In a full-block style all notations and paragraphs begin on the left-hand margin.
4. Reader-friendly letters rarely, if ever, achieve targets.
5. More than one request should not be stated in a letter.
6. The inside address of the recipient is always written on the left-hand margin of the letter.
7. Altering the purpose of writing a letter does not bring about a change in the manner of writing.
8. A bad news letter should begin with something positive or favourable.
9. Subject, reference and date need not be used in an e-mail.
10. Whenever a letter or proposal is circulated to other people a note is added to the original letter.

C.   Match the Following

A	B
1. cc	(a) Blind carbon copy
2. bcc	(b) Carbon copy
3. PS	(c) Personal and confidential
4. Encl	(d) Enclosure
5. Open style	(e) Simple and brief
6. Close in a letter	(f) Traditional and informal
7. E-mail	(g) State purpose
8. Fax	(h) Postscript
9. Diary writing	(i) Polite and courteous
10. Opening paragraph	(j) Facsimile

Answers

A. 1. (b)   2. (b)   3. (b)   4. (a)   5. (c)   6. (d)   7. (d)   8. (a)   9. (b)   10. (d)

B. 1. True   2. True   3. True   4. False   5. True
        6. True   7. False   8. True   9. True   10. True

C. 1. (b)   2. (a)   3. (h)   4. (d)   5. (f)   6. (i)   7. (e)   8. (j)   9. (c)   10. (g)

QUESTIONS FOR DISCUSSION

1. What are the advantages and disadvantages of (a) telegrams, (b) telex messages, (c) facsimiles, and (d) e-mail?
2. Which part of the letter, according to you, is the most important from the point of view of capturing reader's attention?
3. What is the difference between a block, semi-block and open style of letter? Discuss the advantages and disadvantages of all the three types.
4. A sales letter best captures the AIDA Principle—Comment.
5. Identify the similarities between letters of request and inquiry letters.
6. What is the advantage of a facsimile over a telegram?
7. What are the various steps of sending an e-mail?
8. How has it become easier for us to maintain records and add or remove excessive e-mail to our folders? Compare and contrast this with traditional and conventional methods of handling mail.
9. What are the advantages of a letter of transmittal? Why is it used as a covering letter for cheques or important business documents?
10. Discuss the various stages in drafting a letter of request and compare the same to a sales letter.

EXERCISES

1. You are working in the marketing division of a cosmetic company. Identify the market segment and draft a sales letter propagating the extra plus in your latest talcum powder.

2. A letter of refusal needs to be drafted for a client requesting for a loan for a project. As a project manager how would you soften the impact of the negative news?

3. You have been working for the last five years and now intend going to Boston University for further studies. Two recommendation letters need to be sent to the University from your last academic institution. Draft two letters for your Professors requesting them to give recommendation letters. One of them has probably forgotten you as your interaction with her lasted for only one semester.

4. A letter of transmittal has been sent to you together with a cheque of ₹ 30,000 as consultation charges. Draft a letter of acknowledgement.

5. Send an e-mail to your boss informing him/her of your travel plan.

6. Select a partner and discuss briefly on any topic asking questions and giving short answers. Try and translate the discussion into e-mail correspondence.

7. The day has been hectic for you. The following have been the happenings in the day:
   - low grades
   - heated argument with Professor
   - misunderstanding with a friend

   Write a page of your diary keeping the above in mind.

8. Browse through your e-mail over the last one week and then ponder over the following questions:
   - How much space in the computer does it take?
   - How much time does it take to retrieve the relevant mail?
   - To what extent does it reduce paper work?

   Now discuss the relevance of e-mail over ordinary mail.

9. Your boss is about to arrive in New Delhi for five days and intends to visit the plant in Jaipur you are heading. You want to play it safe so you send a fax and an e-mail to your Jaipur office. Prepare a draft of both, the fax and the e-mail.

10. You have invited a consultant for a one-day workshop on communication. On the invoice prepare a letter in semi block style to be attached to the cheque for consultation charges.

Applying for a Job

CONTENTS	LEARNINGS
• Introduction • Solicited and Unsolicited Letters • Curriculum Vitae (CV) • Resumé • Filling up Employment Applications	After reading this chapter you should be able to: ➢ Craft an appropriately written and designed letter ➢ Strategise to convince in an unsolicited application ➢ Apply the norms of objectivity to a CV ➢ Learn to innovate with the format of a resumé ➢ Use the standard form to advantage and highlight desirable traits

KEYWORDS

Achievements, Action Words, Clarity, Goal Orientation, Innovation, Learning, Resumé Categories, Solicited Letters, Standardised Forms, Unsolicited Letters, Summary

INTRODUCTION

Designing and formatting a Curriculum Vitae (CV) or a Resumé is a painstaking task. To a great extent it determines the suitability of a candidate. It is a passport to a good and attractive job. Whenever an organisation advertises for certain posts, it normally, receives a large number of CVs or Resumés. To make a proper selection a weeding criterion is applied by which only a few resumés are accepted for a final round of screening. The determining factor for signalling first level acceptance is the appropriately written and designed accompanying letter. To capture the interest of the employer, something strikingly different should be presented in the letter. This covering letter is then affixed to the CV/resumé which becomes the medium for encapsulating and presenting the major qualifications as well as capturing the attention of the reader.

SOLICITED AND UNSOLICITED LETTERS

TOPIC OBJECTIVES

Understand the aspects of writing application letters
Distinguish between solicited and unsolicited applications
Learn to frame the application suitably

"If you call failures experiments, you can put them in your resume and claim them as achievements."
—Mason Cooley

Letters of application either in response to an advertisement or in the form of a self-initiated proposal are referred to as solicited and unsolicited letters respectively. These are the most important job-search letters. If well-drafted, they can easily elicit a positive response. However, if badly written, they would, without doubt, remain ignored.

The features that need to be kept in mind at the time of writing application letters are as follows:

- **Make your letter individualistic.**   Each individual possesses certain traits that are specific to the self and make him/her specially suited for a particular job. Highlight these qualities and

  Highlight specific traits

  present them in a fashion that makes you specially suited for that post. A conventionally written letter will only produce a disinterested response. Contrast this with a letter that is innovative and spells a dynamic personality. The balance would definitely tilt in favour of the latter.

- **Catch the reader's attention.**   At the time of writing a letter, ask yourself a simple question, "Why should the reader go through the

  Innovate and apply strategies in the opening paragraph

  letter and shortlist me as one of the suitable candidates?" There may be hundreds of other applicants with almost the same qualifications. There has to be something in the writing that will attract the

reader to the application in hand. In a solicited letter, the attention line can be reference to the advertisement. In an unsolicited one writing techniques should be different and can vary from initiating the letter with a reference to the product they manufacture to probably expression of a desire to make concrete and worthwhile contribution to the growth of the company. These should, as far as possible, be spelt out in clear and unambiguous terms. In the first instance, it will indicate the knowledge of the writer concerning the product while in the second, reveal a sincere and humble desire to contribute to the company as well as act as a pointer to the capabilities of the candidate.

- **Highlight your educational/professional qualifications.** Once the attention of the reader has been caught, it is necessary that interest be

sustained. The middle paragraphs help the writer to present captivating content. For a HR professional looking for a suitable candidate, educational or professional qualifications of the candidate and the organisational fit are the most critical. Present these

Sustain interest by spelling out your strongest qualification

details with accuracy and in a manner that appeal to the reader. The strongest point in favour of the candidate is on-the-job experience. From the perspective of the company, a candidate with experience is always preferable. This point should be highlighted in detail and correlated to the needs of the company. Spell out details of projects, if any, that add to the job requirements.

Specifying one's strong professional qualification is sufficient as an overtly long letter can literally put off the reader. As far as possible, be brief and succinct. The candidate can further refer the reader to the resumé or CV if there are other strong points that would make the candidature more appealing or acceptable.

Refer to the CV/resumé

Note: Highlight those qualities that show you as suitable for a particular job.

At the time of writing the letter, the candidate should remember that the time to make an impact is less than a minute. Within that time frame the application form and the resumé remain either on the table or are discarded. For this it is necessary that the letter be drafted in an impressive manner, following the general accepted rule of three sections:

1. Opening
2. Middle
   - (a) Spells strongest qualification
   - (b) Summarises other relevant qualifications
   - (c) Conjoins qualification with needs of the company
   - (d) Presents any other brief accomplishment and
   - (e) Refers back to the resumé/CV
3. Closing

Between the two types of letters there is not much of a difference except in the opening paragraph. In a solicited letter as applications are invited, the source needs to be specified from where the candidate obtained the information. Together with this the opening paragraph should also specify the reason for writing the letter and the job applied for.

Warning! The time frame for the desired impact that the letter must make is only one minute!

This is with reference to your advertisement No. 123 in the Sunday Edition of the *Economic Times*, dated 7 November 2014. I would like to apply for the post of *Information Technology Trainee*. My engineering background would allow me to serve your organisation well.

Mr. Pradeep Verma from Midas Touch, in our marketing session, stressed the point that at this time of the year you needed fresh marketing graduates to conduct your survey.

In the opening of this letter, together with the reference number, there is also present a "you" attitude that definitely appeals to the reader.

Contrast this with the opening of an unsolicited letter where the need for inducting a new candidate has to be created. In this case the organisation has not announced a job opening. Yet, the candidate has decided to send forth personal documents for there is an impression that the qualifications and experience are suited for the applied position.

There are a number of techniques that can be applied in such instances. The most popular is one of using references. Taking names of people who are either friends or have a say in the functioning of the organisation is a popular strategy.

Another technique could be to refer to some innovative and much publicised activity or achievement or policies of the company.

Today's issue of the *Times of India* carried a page on the HR and Training policies adopted by your company. These strategies are truly innovative and representative of a growing organisation like yours.

Applying for areas where ingenuity and creativity is desired, the opening too can be creative and different. Imagine yourself to be in a position where you have to screen hundreds of applications. It would be a welcome change if a letter introduced a candidate in a noveau manner. You would be tempted to pause and further browse through the details.

There is little difference between a solicited and an unsolicited letter when it comes to the middle or the closing section of the letter. In the middle

section, specify the educational qualifications or work experience that will help you to perform the job to the best of your ability. Do not merely state that you possess all the required qualifications to perform the job to its
satisfaction. This alone will not suffice. Spell out your strong points so as to make a greater impact. In case you do not possess the requisite qualities but would still like to apply for the job, specify other strengths so that the reader is able to position you in the correct perspective.

> *Middle section deals with the educational qualification or work*

Whatever is written in the letter should always be in the form of knowledge acquired or skills developed instead of completion of various courses. By merely stating that "I have two degrees and four diploma certificates", "I" do not stand to gain much. Suppose the manner of presentation is changed and on-the-job experience is discussed, there are higher chances of success than otherwise.

JAM: Check if you have stressed knowledge and skills over and above degrees and qualifications in the covering letter.

Certain qualities are looked for in all candidates who should possess either some or all of the following traits, namely, diligence, capacity for
hard-work, honesty, responsibility, assertiveness, confidence, and leadership qualities. If these traits can be spelt out in the letter, they would definitely go in favour of the candidate. In the middle section there should also be a reference to the resumé. It can be in the form of referring the reader to the resumé at a certain point or towards the close with a polite request to look at the details. By this time the reader should be sufficiently motivated to browse through other details provided along with the letter.

> *Present the following traits: diligent, hard-working, honest, responsible, assertive and a good leader*

> *Closing section— Thank the reader and request for further action*

In the closing section the candidate should thank the reader for the time spent on reading the letter and request for further action either in the form of an interview date or follow-up action. In case it is the former, contact address and time should be specified.

Note: Refer to your resume or CV in the middle section of your letter.

CURRICULUM VITAE (CV)

TOPIC OBJECTIVES

Comprehend features of CV writing

Adopt brevity and clarity in scripting the points

"Life is the art of drawing without an eraser."
—John W. Gardner

The Latin words *curriculum vitae* (*CV*) literally mean "course of life". A CV is a summary of the candidate's qualifications and experience. It is objective in nature and provides no detailed insight

CV—Factual
record of
candidate's
qualifications
and experience
in the capabilities of the prospective applicant. A chronological statement of biographical details, the CV is now outmoded with most companies now going in for a resumé which is more descriptive and spells out contributions made by the candidate. The format of a typical CV is specified below:

Name:	Mahima Mitra
Date of Birth:	24 September 1975
Permanent Address:	37/4 Jai Singh Road, New Delhi - 110001 E-Mail: Mahima@hotmail.com Phone: (011) - 6896527

Educational Qualifications:

Degree	University/Institute	Subjects	Division	Year
BA	Lucknow University History	English, Psychology,	1	1999
XII Class (CBSE)	St Joseph's Convent High School, New Delhi Computer Science	English, Physics, Chemistry, Maths,	1	1996
Class X (CBSE)	St Joseph's Convent High School, New Delhi	French, English, Maths, Social Studies, Science	1	1994

Extra Curricular Activities:
1. Member of Rotary Club
2. Member of Quiz Club, Biological and Sciences Society, Delhi Magic Centre and Film Society
3. Captain of Tennis and Basketball teams
4. Took part in various junior state-level tennis tournaments

Projects Undertaken:
1. "Optimisation of Cutting Parameters" for Sundaram Clayton Limited
2. "Bio-materials and their Future Trends" for BITS, Pillani

Work Experience:
1. Programme Trainer for Cognizant Technology Solutions
2. Programme Analyst for Cognizant Technology Solutions

Exhibit 8.1 Curriculum vitae.

If the CV were to be analysed, it would reveal absolutely nothing about the personality of the candidate. What was the gain from the work experience and the projects undertaken? It is difficult to secure an answer from the biographical details cited in the CV. Though not much information can be culled out of a CV, there are still some companies that prefer a CV over a resumé.

In a CV, the educational qualifications are presented in the reverse order starting with the latest. People who have significant work experience and

| Present educational qualification in reverse order |

would like to switch jobs should, prior to their educational qualifications, specify their work experience. If the projects that they have undertaken are of significance and of direct relevance to the job applied for, they should be stated immediately after the work experience.

JAM: Have you listed your educational qualifications in reverse order in your CV?

RESUMÉ

TOPIC OBJECTIVES

Distinguish the CV from a Resume
Understand the function of various sections of the resume

A resumé is a one to two page summary of skills, accomplishments and education written to capture the attention of the reader, and its basic purpose is to secure an interview. Some of the characteristic features of a resumé are as follows: it can be tailor made for a company and the job that an individual wishes to apply for; it is original and geared towards a specific goal. As it is more descriptive than a CV and discusses the qualities of the candidate, viz. the

| Resumé— summary of skills, accomplishments and education |

positions held, the content has to be accurate and interesting, and related to the company objectives. The positive quality about a resumé is that it helps you to 'sell' your traits by providing pertinent and unique details that stand out, assists in relating skills and achievements necessary for the job.

There is no fixed style of writing a resumé. What is, however, looked for is a consistency in approach. At the time of writing a resumé, remember

| Be consistent in approach |

that the employer does not know a thing about you. The manner in which you present information about yourself will generate interest and heighten possibility of being summoned for an interview. Highlight information that you wish to emphasise, and omit unnecessary and unpleasant details. In short, make your resumé goal oriented and job specific.

Prior to beginning work on the resumé, a thorough self-assessment should be done, which will help you to relate your qualities, achievements and skills to the needs of the organisation. As you sift and sieve through these, keep in mind the expectations of the reader. This will help you to gear yourself in the right direction.

Note: There is no fixed style of writing a resume; the emphasis is on making it goal oriented.

The various sections within a resumé include:

Name and Address

Name, Institute address, Permanent address, E-mail address and Telephone number. The full, legal name should be written. It is normally centred on the page. If the applicant so wishes to present both the addresses, then the current address can be written in the left-hand column with the e-mail address and the permanent address in the right-hand column. If only the permanent address is to be mentioned, then it is written in the centre of the page immediately beneath the name. Do not provide information concerning your age, marital status, sex or children. The employer may not be interested in these details and you may put him/her in an awkward situation by volunteering to provide additional or unnecessary information.

Note: Omit mentioning your personal details; the employer may not be interested!

Career Objective or Career Goal

The career objective or goal should be related directly to the job for which you are applying. Make the statement highly focussed and related to the goal of the organisation. Avoid use of pronouns such as "I" and "my" in your objective. Details to be included in your career objective are: the tenure of the position you are seeking, the job title, and the field in which you wish to work.

> A summer job as a research assistant with an academic institute, which requires skills in conducting field study, researching and preparing project reports.

Educational or Professional Qualification(s)

If you have certain professional qualifications that will aid you in securing this job, stress them before you move on to other educational qualifications. The name of the institute, degree and graduation date, and the marks or percentage or degree should be highlighted. The manner of formatting must be consistent. Suppose your score for your B.A. is very high and you would like to stress that, then you should ensure that you observe a similar and consistent pattern throughout for all other degrees as well. Avoiding a mention of average scores for some degrees while including them for some sends a negative signal to the employer.

JAM: Is your format consistent?

Related Course Work, Special Projects, Academic Awards

This section is optional. In case you have done some related coursework or special project or have won an academic award, you could list it down and indicate what you gained as a result of it. Contrast the two statements:

1. Completed a summer project on Marketing Strategy of Liberty.
2. Project Assistant for promoting Marketing Strategy of Liberty, a project undertaken as part of Summer job. Assisted clients with selection of shoes, developed and promoted special marketing events. Sales increased by 7 per cent in the six-month period.

The first statement is dry and does not actually tell much about the contributions made by the candidate. On the other hand, the second statement specifically stresses through *action words* the work undertaken by the candidate and the results.

Work Experience

If the work experience is significantly more than the educational or professional qualifications, it should be put prior to the latter; else it should be positioned after a reference to academic qualifications. This section should include:

1. Date and year
2. Name of the organisation
3. Job title
4. Responsibilities held
5. Any significant contributions made to the growth of the company

Some candidates may not have any work experience. In such cases they can be innovative and use headings such as Language Proficiencies, Computer Competency, Special Skills, Professional Memberships, and various Accomplishments. The candidate can think of any number of categories and use the one that is most suitable and able to create an impact.

Note: Innovate to create resume categories that make an impact.

Skills, Abilities

Not all resumés carry a section on skills. If you feel that some of the acquired skills can be suitably stated under various headings, proceed confidently. To write this section a five-tier process needs to be worked on.

1. List jobs and activities or special posts that you have held
2. Jot down skills that you have acquired in the process of completion of the task
3. Group them into three to five categories
4. Think of suitable headings for all and list all the skills under these headings
5. Arrange headings in order of importance as they relate to your career goals

Activities and Awards

All the activities in which you have participated and the awards that have been won need not be stated. Select only those that have a direct bearing on your career goals. List them in order of importance. Do not indulge yourself in this section. Make it brief and meaningful.

References

Unless the employer asks for the references, do not mention them.

Nayantara Mohanty

268, Sector 16-A   W 19 B, Greater Kailash
Chandigarh 160015   New Delhi 110048
E-mail N.Mohanty@hotmail.com   Ph: (011) 6412772

Career Objective. To become a research scholar in the area of corporate communication with a multinational company, which requires skills in media planning.

Education

Magdalene College, University of Cambridge, England   **1992–1993**
Degree: Master of Philosophy
Subjects: Sociology and Politics of Development
Faculty: Social and Political Sciences
Commonwealth Scholar
Courses divided into three: essays in international politics, development economics and dissertation of 15,000 words. Topic of research: Kashmir

Mount Holyoke College, South Hadley, Massachusetts, USA   **1986–1990**
Degree: Bachelor of Arts
Subjects: Economics and International Relations
Mount Holyoke College International Student Scholar
Courses reflect a diverse curriculum: Industrial Economics, Nationalism and Communism, American Foreign Policy

Wellesley College, Wellesley, Massachusetts, USA   **1988–1989**
Selected for junior exchange programme. Attended classes at **Massachusetts Institute of Technology (MIT),** including some at the **Sloan School of Management**.

Bishop Cotton Boys' School, Bangalore, India   **1984–1986**
Examination: Indian School Certificate (ISC)
Subjects: Economics, Accountancy, Commerce, Maths, English and Hindi

Sophia High School, Bangalore, India   **1973–1984**
Examination: Indian Certificate School Leaving Examination (ICSE)
Subjects: Arts, Sciences, Social Sciences and Languages

Work Experience

The Ford Foundation, New Delhi   **Jan'97–Jan'99**
Programme Assistant for the Forestry and Water Resources Management Programmes.
Responsibilities included:
Assisting in evaluating proposals, negotiating grants, preparing grant-related documents and monitoring and evaluating grants.

Exhibit 8.2 *(Contd.)*

Financial Times, London   **March 1996**
Freelance Journalist: Edited and rewrote copy for the regular pages and the Weekend Section.

British Broadcasting Corporation (BBC), Bush House, London Dec.'95–Mar.'96
R.P.A. (Radio Production Assistant)
Eight week attachment with the Bengali service, BBC World Service Radio. Mainly cutting and editing tape for the broadcast, (*Probaha*) banded packages and recording live interviews, under severe time pressure. *Probaha* is a current affairs programme, covering political events in Bangladesh and India.

Linguistic Proficiency

English, Hindi, French and (spoken) Bengali

Achievements

Recipient of the Charles Wallace (India) Trust award, 1996 and a scholarship from the Cambridge Commonwealth Trust, 1996 for research work on Kashmir.
Awarded the Mount Holyoke College Scholarship for international students ((1986–90).

Interests

Sports
Played for the first five (number 2) for the Magdalene College Squash team. Played for the Mount Holyoke College Squash team at number three.
Won badminton tournaments at college and school levels.

Travel
Solo back-packing through most of Europe: France, the Netherlands, Italy, and Portugal.

Exhibit 8.2   Resumé.

FILLING UP EMPLOYMENT APPLICATIONS

TOPIC OBJECTIVES
Understand the crux of the questions in employment forms
Learn techniques of self presentation

"I am afraid that the pleasantness of an employment does not always evince its propriety."—Jane Austen

Besides government departments, public sector undertakings, autonomous bodies under the government, some companies too have a standardised employment form that they may expect the candidate to fill mostly before the selection process. The accuracy with which the form is filled together with the manner in which the details have been provided help the organisation in assessing the true merit of the candidate.

These forms need to be filled carefully and re-read to ascertain that there is no factual error. It is prudent to get the form xeroxed and first fill the copy, check and re-check to ensure that all details required by the company have been provided and then to proceed with the completion of the original form. All instructions should be strictly followed at the time of filling up the form, e.g., in case it is stated that the name should be written in Block letters with last name first, the column should be completed exactly as per the requirements.

Together with the academic information, the application form also contains certain questions which help the employer to gauge about the candidate's personality and views. Let us take a look at some of the questions and manner in which they can be tackled.

1. Many people change their ideas about careers. What has influenced the course of your thinking so far?

    Suppose a candidate gave the following answer:

    > My father's appreciation of things around him as an engineer and my own aptitude for the same was the primary influence in shaping my career choice. Interaction with friends and relatives, especially an uncle who is the MD of a government undertaking, made me realise that I was not cut out for the private sector.

    A response such as this is very abstract. Try and be as concrete and specific as possible. In the example cited above, what are the "things" that have helped the applicant to give shape to his/her future? Further, as far as possible, name-dropping should be avoided. No one likes to hear of the well-placed "uncles" and relatives. The company is interested in the candidate as a person because of certain positive qualities and not because of connects to the illustrious "Uncle".

    The response could probably be drafted in the following manner:

    > General awareness, concern for human values, and ability to derive maximum out of given situation helped me in rethinking and making my career choice.

2. What are your short-term and long-term career objectives?

    In a question such as this the response has to be carefully drafted. Whatever you state should be in accordance with the needs of the company. It should not be divergent or unrelated to the company goals. For example, if a candidate was filling in a form for a Company providing consultancy services, the objectives could be stated as follows:

    > My short-term objective is to be part of an implementation team, in the Marketing Department of a company, where I would learn practical applications and concepts of management. My long-term career objective is to be responsible for strategic aspects of business and to direct or manage a team.

    It should be remembered that with a change in the company the manner of approach will also be different. All questions should be addressed to the expectations of the organisation from the candidate.

3. Describe a difficult and challenging project that you have undertaken. What did you do, why did you do it and what was the outcome?

This is a specific question. Efforts should be made by the candidate to present the project in a manner that it indicates growth, be it in terms of learning, innovating or contributing.

> I had undertaken a comprehensive study of the energy sector in India with special reference to hydro-electric power generation and supply. I chose this project as I have been interested in the power sector and the curriculum of my third year course in engineering provided me an ideal opportunity. The various sources of electric power were studied and analysed on parameters of technology, engineering and environmental implications. Have worked on a paper outlining this study and made recommendations for work.

Through a proper response to queries as above, the candidate can promote the self and market qualities that are appealing to the organisation.

Some additional questions can be as follows:

4. Describe a situation where it is necessary to involve others to achieve a task. What part did you play, and what was the outcome?

   In this question, leadership qualities are actually being looked for. Did you as a leader take on the responsibility of facilitating, *Display leadership qualities* involving and directing the entire group? If you can highlight these three qualities in your situational presentation you can definitely score high points.

> In my college days we were organising a marketing fair. All of us were excited about the project. Unfortunately, at the last minute some students decided to drop out as they realised that they had projects to complete on which they would be graded. I talked to them and we decided that we should approach the concerned faculty and request for a time extension. This would enable us to do justice to both the tasks. As representative of the group, I approached the faculty and after brief discussions was able to convince as well as get an extension of three days.

5. Describe a situation where you found yourself differing from others on how to achieve a goal. Why did you differ, what actions did you take and what was the result?

   This question tests assertive behaviour. Can the candidate stand alone and claim that the expressed point of view is right or is there a need to join the pack for fear of taking a stand? *Be assertive in tackling questions* Ability to say no, to differ from other members within the organisation, take responsibility for actions and not be scared of the results are all qualities of a strong assertive candidate. Description of a situation keeping these factors in mind will help the candidate go a long way.

> We were approaching sponsors for the inauguration of the Intellectual Club in which we had eminent personalities participating in a panel discussion. We were divided in our opinion. Some students felt that we should repeatedly contact organisations and the more we pestered them, the greater would be our chances of success. However, I disagreed with them. I felt that the programme was important for the business community. They should, after the initial approach, volunteer on their own. I further suggested that various industry organisations/associations be contacted. This would increase sponsorship and add value to the programme. The suggestion was accepted and we were successful in our approach as we got sponsorship from almost 50 companies.

Warning! The approach to the response needs to change if there is a change in the company applied to!

6. Looking at your life as a whole, indicate a key event or experience that you consider has been instrumental in shaping who you are. Describe how it has influenced you.

| Present motivational factors | Question 6 is really not interested in the "event" or the "experience". It is structured to find out the motivational factors. What are the factors that have shaped you and to what extent? |

> During my last year at College, I was faced with a challenging situation. The faculty advisor for the Annual Function met with a sudden crisis at home and found that she could not continue as coordinator. Since I had been working closely with her as student coordinator she asked me if I could handle the show on my own.
>
> There was a good deal left to do. The finances needed to be accounted for, there were the invitations to be dispatched and the logistics to be finalised. The burden of official responsibility cast a shadow of doubt over me.
>
> I had been working very hard for this and wanted the event to go well. I decided to take the bull by the horns. I worked around the clock for the next five days. Fortunately, the function was a runaway success and after this, many a laurel came my way. I have never looked back since then. I have taken upon tasks with the assured feeling that goals and objectives can be achieved despite all odds provided the will is strong.

7. Add anything about yourself that would be helpful by way of comment. Structure it to give leeway to yourself for incorporating anything by which you think you can capture the attention of the reader. This is the time for presentation of traits that have not been covered in the rest of the application form but which you feel are imperative for survival in any organisation. Some of these traits can be:

| Present positive personality traits | |

clarity of expression, ability to communicate effectively, determination to perform a certain task, strength of conviction, etc.

For all these questions, the candidate should present that part of the personality which will make him/her stand out among the rest of the candidates. Another point to be kept in mind is that you should not go too far back in personal history. If an incident or anecdote cited is one that took place five or six years ago, probability is high that the impact of it on the candidate would have weakened. As far as possible, narration of "influencing factors", "situations involving others" in which some kind of learning took place should be contemporary. Further, at the time of spelling out these incidents, do remember that the company is not interested in the event or episode but in the learning that took place.

JAM: Have you re-read your filled out form to ensure there is no factual error?

SUMMARY

Letters of application may be solicited or unsolicited.

Letters may be distinguished by their opening paragraphs. In a solicited letter, the source needs to be specified whereas in an unsolicited letter the need for inducting a new candidate is to be created.

The key to catching the reader's attention is by making the letter individualistic, and highlighting the desired qualifications and traits.

A CV is a summary of the candidate's qualifications and experience. It is objective in nature and provides no detailed insight into the capabilities of the prospective applicant.

A resumé is a one to two page summary of skills, accomplishments and education. It can be tailor made for a company and the job that an individual wishes to apply for; it is original and geared towards a specific goal.

The accuracy with which an employment form is filled together with the manner in which the details have been provided helps the organisation in assessing the true merit of the candidate.

Certain questions in the questionnaire help the employer gauge the candidate, personality traits, views and perspectives.

Concrete and specific responses aid the reader and make a good impression. Depending on the question, responses should be crafted which indicate an organisational fit.

Stress on leadership qualities and instances of assertive behaviour that are imperative for survival in any organisation, help the candidate secure a positive response.

CHECKLIST

Do's	Don'ts
Innovate with the conventional application for a position so as to stand out	Innovate at the cost of leaving the reader behind! Tailor your application to needs of the position
Be brief and succinct	Be overtly succinct and lose the interest of the reader
Spell out the source for a solicited letter	Omit to create the reason for an unsolicited application
Use the more descriptive resumé to your advantage	Be creative and forget the objective
Highlight information that you wish to emphasise	Be detailed and long-winded
Format the content of the resumé with consistency	Do data dumping
Situate the work experience before the educational experience if the former is sizeable	Shy away from innovating with categories to make up for a lack of work experience
Follow all instructions while filling standard application forms	Be inaccurate with professional details
Highlight individual achievements	Name drop to secure a position
Be concrete and specific	Use abstract phraseology

RAPID REVIEW

A. Pick Your Choice

1. Your
   - (a) skills, strengths
   - (b) educational qualifications
   - (c) work experience

   should match the job requirements

2. Letters of application in response to an advertisement are called
   - (a) solicited letters
   - (b) unsolicited letters
   - (c) covering letters

3. The attention of the reader can be sustained by highlighting
   - (a) educational qualifications
   - (b) work experience
   - (c) both of these

4. The difference between a solicited and unsolicited letter is primarily in the
   - (a) opening paragraph
   - (b) middle
   - (c) closing

5. Educational qualifications should be stated
   - (a) chronologically
   - (b) reverse chronological order
   - (c) in order of excellence

6. In a resumé the full legal name is
   (a) centred   (b) written in the left-hand margin
   (c) written in the right-hand margin
7. In a career objective avoid usage of pronouns such as
   (a) you   (b) we   (c) I and my
8. If the work experience is significantly important it should, while writing the resume be written
   (a) right at the top   (b) before the educational qualification
   (c) right at the bottom
9. Headings for skills should be arranged in
   (a) order of importance   (b) alphabetical order
   (c) chronological order
10. A letter can be made highly individualistic by
    (a) highlighting special traits
    (b) highlighting and presenting traits in an appropriate fashion
    (c) none of the above

B. True or False

1. Only those references should be listed who are willing to attest to your abilities.
2. While listing educational qualifications and work experience follow a chronological ordering.
3. A resumé highlights skills, strengths and abilities in relation to the job.
4. A career objective can change with a shift in application or job.
5. Spending time in drafting a covering letter is useless as it is thrown in the garbage bin.
6. One way of writing a good covering letter for a particular company is to talk to people in that organisation and draft it according to their needs and expectations.
7. An unsolicited letter is never considered.
8. Resumé should be neatly typed and error free.
9. The career path can be neatly chalked after you get a job.
10. A covering letter to a resumé is similar to a sales letter.

C. Fill in the Blanks

1. A resume is _____ and _____.
2. The manner of formatting a CV or a resume should be _____.

3. To write the section on skills and abilities a _____ process needs to be worked on.

4. All instructions should be strictly _____ at the time of filling up the application form.

5. Skills should be clubbed into _____ or _____ groups.

6. The section on related course work, special projects and academic awards is _____.

7. The determining factor for signalling first level acceptance of the resumé is the appropriately written and designed _____.

8. The attention line in a _____ letter is a reference to the advertisement.

9. A letter should, as far as possible, follow the general accepted rule of _____ sections.

10. In an unsolicited letter, the most popular technique used in the opening is to make use of _____.

Answers

A. 1. (a) 2. (a) 3. (c) 4. (a) 5. (b) 6. (a) 7. (c) 8. (b) 9. (a) 10. (b)

B. 1. True   2. False   3. True   4. True   5. False
    6. True   7. False   8. True   9. False   10. True

C. 1. Goal-oriented; job-specific   2. consistent   3. five-tier
    4. followed   5. three; five 6. optional   7. cover/accompanying letter
    8. solicited   9. three   10. references.

QUESTIONS FOR DISCUSSION

1. To what extent does work experience play a role in securing a job?

2. What is the relevance of the AIDA principle in drafting a letter?

3. Can an unsolicited letter secure a job interview?

4. How important is a listing of educational qualifications vis-a-vis work experience?

5. While a CV is a factual record of the candidate, qualifications and experiences, a resumé is a "sales letter". Discuss.

6. What is the difference between a CV and a resumé?

7. What is the importance of the Employment Application form? Why do many companies use these forms as a basis for short listing candidates?

8. Why should you avoid using "I" too frequently in a solicited application letter?

9. How can you make your letter of application sound impressive?

10. How should one best use the space for providing any other information on a standard application form?

EXERCISES

1. Prepare a resumé.
2. Write a fifteen-word career objective while applying for a job in a company in one of the following areas:
   (a) Marketing   (b) Finance
   (c) Operations   (d) HR
3. In an advertisement dated 14 July 2014, Malibu Industries has advertised for the post of Management trainees in the area of HR. Write a solicited letter applying for the job.
4. Amelius Company is a reputed company manufacturing medical equipments. Write an unsolicited letter to the Manager Personnel applying for the post of a Sales representative.
5. In not more than 150 words write down what you have learned most in the past three years.
6. Select a partner who has also prepared a resumé. Discuss each other's resumé threadbare and try to identify strengths and weaknesses.
7. Write a solicited and an unsolicited letter to IMMI (a financial institution) for the post of Accounts Officer. Compare and contrast the two letters and note down the similarities and dissimilarities.
8. Collect ten CVs and resumés and examine them. Which of the two make a greater impact and why? List ten reasons.
9. In approximately 300 words write about yourself—your areas of interest, career goals, key learning and work experience.
10. Discuss your areas of interest with your friend. Identify areas where you stand to gain or lose in terms of expression of the same for a job.

C H A P T E R

9

Writing to Communicate

CONTENTS	LEARNINGS
• Introduction • Reader Orientation • Coherence • Errors of Logic • Grammatical Flaws • Put on Your Thinking Hat	After reading this chapter you should be able to: ➤ Comprehend the rigour in the writing process ➤ Differentiate between correct and incorrect usage ➤ Use appropriate methodologies for writing ➤ Focus on logical reasoning ➤ Identify errors in your writing process

KEYWORDS

Reader Orientation, Flawed Logic, Genetic Fallacy, Circular Logic, Rushed Generalisation, Cause and Effect, Moral Equivalence, False Dilemma, Red Herring, Dead Wood, Strawman, Split Infinitive, Present Continuous, Conditional Sentences, Subject-Verb Agreement, Modifiers, Parallel Structure, Active Voice, Conjunctions, Parenthesis, Punctuation Marks, Transitional Words and Phrases

INTRODUCTION

Almost any and every person can write, provided there is familiarity with the language. But to make it live, vibrating and meaningful is tough and differentiates good writing from the bad one. The focus in this chapter is on writing to communicate effectively. The requirements, by far, are many with emphasis on the reader, the semantics, the logic, the syntax, the punctuation, misused words and expressions, and transitional words and phrases. If we further break up this list there are multiple subdivisions, all of which may be difficult to address in this chapter.

I have made an attempt to capture constructs in which we most commonly err. The list by no means is exhaustive. However, using this as a building block to further augment the business writing style is sure to make the process logical and rigorous.

> "Who wants to become a writer? And why? Because it's the answer to everything. ... It's the streaming reason for living. To note, to pin down, to build up, to create, to be astonished at nothing, to cherish the oddities, to let nothing go down the drain, to make something, to make a great flower out of life, even if it's a cactus."
>
> —Enid Bagnold

READER ORIENTATION

TOPIC OBJECTIVES

Comprehend reader orientation
Gear the writing process to match reader expectations

> "Writing is.... being able to take something whole and fiercely alive that exists inside you in some unknowable combination of thought, feeling, physicality, and spirit, and to then store it like a genie in tense, tiny black symbols on a calm white page. If the wrong reader comes across the words, they will remain just words. But for the right readers, your vision blooms off the page and is absorbed into their minds like smoke, where it will re-form, whole and alive, fully adapted to its new environment."
>
> —Mary Gaitskill

When we write a document, the text should be geared towards creating appeal for the reader. What are the reader expectations? What should I write so that it gels with the reader needs? How should I write so that I am on the same page as the reader? These are some of the questions to be answered before we begin the writing process. Too much or too little content, repetition of ideas or misplaced focus can tune the reader off. Plan before you pick up steam. Be confident of the content that you write—quantum of information should be right, do not use a tentative style of writing or incorrect use of expressions or gender insensitive language. If the reader finds the content appealing or as per expectations chances are high that it will be considered and action will be taken. However, if the document lacks reader appeal, it maybe trashed and all the effort that went into the composition may go a waste. Let us consider the following examples:

Inappropriate Quantum of Information

Incorrect Usage	Correct Usage
Henry Augener [President] and Eugene De Witt [Vice President] were at **loggerheads over** the question of how to manage the company. **De Witt** was of the view that the size of the management should be decided on the basis of company size whereas the **Augener** was of the opposite view.	The Company President and Vice President were **debating** the question of improving management of the company. **The Vice President** was of the view that the size of the management should be decided on the basis of company size whereas the **President** was of the opposite view.

Explanation: The report is submitted to the president, Augener. Citing the report readers' names and using a negative term 'loggerheads' shows insensitivity towards the reader. Use positive language.

CCD faces a particularly exciting summer season with a large growth opportunity. Macroeconomic conditions, policy decisions and growing environmental awareness of Canadians are positively impacting the car detailing service **industry. Currently,** he details about 142 cars annually. Due to a spike in demand for car detailing services in the summer, CCD's services have been booked in advance for a month, and Colin has had to refuse **customers. The** fact that CCD would feature in next week edition of 'The Outlook' will only bolster his reputation. Thus, CCD should focus on expanding its	CCD faces a particularly exciting summer season with a large growth opportunity. Macroeconomic conditions, policy decisions and growing environmental awareness of Canadians are positively impacting the car detailing service industry. **Currently,** he details about 142 cars annually. Due to a spike in demand for car detailing services in the summer, CCD's services have been booked in advance for a month, and Colin has had to refuse customers. **The fact** that CCD would feature in next week edition of 'The Outlook' will only bolster his reputation. Thus, CCD should
customer handling capacity. Not doing so may lead to loss of current and potential customers.	focus on expanding its customer handling capacity. Not doing so may lead to loss of current and potential customers.

Explanation: There are too many ideas in the original paragraph. It leads to reader disorientation. In a paragraph there should not be more than one or two ideas that are linked to one another. Break up the paragraph for clarity. It will enhance reader orientation.

JAM: Have you considered the reader expectations?

Tentative Statements—Touch of Uncertainty

Incorrect Usage	Correct Usage
Designers and engineers **are likely to be available.** Small number of replacements will be required for employees present in service businesses.	Designers and engineers **may be available.** Small number of replacements will be required for employees present in service businesses.

Explanation: The word 'likely' is tentative in nature. Replacing the word 'likely' with the modal verb 'may' will bring about a change in meaning. 'May' also conveys the sense of probability.

Managing RMTC **would be slightly difficult** as it would have varied businesses.	Managing RMTC **will be difficult** as it will have varied businesses.
Explanation: 'Would be' conveys a sense of probability. Adding 'slightly' to 'would be' makes the proposition highly tentative.	

Warning! Use of incorrect modal verbs will make the proposition tentative.

Inaccurate Juxtaposition of Words

Incorrect Usage	*Correct Usage*
Construct focus groups for each unit **comprising of** high performers.	Construct focus groups for each unit **comprising** high performers.
Explanation: "Comprising" in British English does not take "of".	
Given the **lack of prior** infrastructure development on the continent, potential for growth is tremendous.	Given the **lack of proper** infrastructure development on the continent, potential for growth is tremendous.
Explanation: There is no time reference and hence the word 'prior' does not convey meaning in this context. The emphasis in the point is on the adequacy of infrastructure development.	

Gender Neutral Language

Incorrect Usage	*Correct Usage*
Option: Advertise to **increase his customer** base rather than retain **his customers.**	Option: Advertise to **increase customer** base rather than **retain customers.**
Explanation: Avoid use of he/she, his/her. Use gender neutral language.	
Once the building is constructed, **he will work with his team** for interior decoration.	Once the building is constructed, **the team** will work on interior decoration. or **The work on interior decoration** will begin once the building is constructed.
Explanation: Either the sentence structure is reversed or the masculine/feminine pronoun is dropped to make the language gender neutral.	

COHERENCE

TOPIC OBJECTIVES

Focus on making the text coherent

Ensure that all parts are well knit

"The proverbial German phenomenon of the verb-at-the-end about which droll tales of absentminded professors who would begin a sentence, ramble on for an entire lecture, and then finish up by rattling off a string of verbs by which their audience, for whom the stack had long since lost its coherence, would be totally nonplussed, are told, is an excellent example of linguistic recursion." —Douglas Hofstadter

While writing a text or a document, it maybe possible that I have understood the reader expectations and have geared myself to addressing the concerns. However, the positioning of the ideas and the concepts may not be appropriate. If there is lack of clarity in my mind, it gets reflected in terms of long winded sentences, incorrect positioning of ideas, awkward constructs, use of dead wood or redundancies etc. The end result is always the same: lack of clarity in the mind of the reader/receiver. Let us analyse some examples that lack coherence.

Lack of Clarity

Incorrect Usage	Correct Usage
CCD **lacks** proper organizational structure, the work force is not enough and sometimes problem are caused by transition from friends to employers.	CCD **faces problems** of poor organizational structure, and small work force. **These problems** are compounded as many of the employees are friends and it is difficult to transition from one relationship to the other.
Explanation: In the example provided in the incorrect usage column, though there is brevity, it lacks clarity. Breaking up the sentence, placing emphasis at the right places and building connects can help the writer make the text coherent.	
Option 2: Give **successive discounts**	Option 2: Give **yearly discounts of 10%**
Explanation: Too vague. Options need to be substantiated for credible evaluation.	

Inappropriate Choice of Words

Incorrect Usage	Correct Usage
Statement of Options We have **three courses of action**	Statement of Options We have **three options**
Explanation: Courses are different from options. Clarity needs to be maintained	
Based on the evaluation of options, **the recommended strategy** is to retain machine tool, construction and their respective allied businesses under two divisions.	Based on the evaluation of options, **the recommendation** is to retain machine tool, construction and their respective allied businesses under two divisions.
Explanation: Strategy and option cannot be used as synonyms. Be careful in choice of words.	

Lack of Specificity and Concreteness

Incorrect Usage	Correct Usage
Enclosed is a copy of "Larson Inc.—Future of Operations in Nigeria" prepared as per your instructions.	**Enclosed is a copy of report titled** "Larson Inc.—Future of Operations in Nigeria" prepared as per your instructions.
Explanation: Use of specific and concrete words makes the report clear and specific.	

In order to make a decision on the feasibility of Larson's operations in Nigeria, **the profitability is the primary parameter that needs to be evaluated.**	In order to make a decision on the feasibility of Larson's operations in Nigeria, **long term profitability in terms of capital gains is the primary parameter that needs to be evaluated.**
Explanation: Terms like 'profitability' should be qualified by more specific terms.	

Note: Use specific and concrete language.

Inappropriate Emphasis

Incorrect Usage	Correct Usage
But given existing and living conditions, government restrictions on and union opposition to expatriate employment, **it is difficult to recruit and retain good candidates for the JV.**	**Recruiting and retaining good candidates for the JV** is difficult due to given existing and living conditions, government restrictions and union opposition to expatriate employment.
Explanation: The important element in a sentence should come first.	
His utmost priority was to devise and implement a course of action, **with only four months in hand,** that would ensure good customer base with higher profits needed to pursue higher education.	**With only four months in hand** his utmost priority was to devise and implement a course of action that would ensure good customer base with higher profits needed to pursue higher education.
Explanation: As the focus of the writer is on 'four months in hand', it should ideally be positioned at the head of the paragraph.	

Awkward Constructions

Incorrect Usage	Correct Usage
It contains a summary of the present situation, evaluation of options available **and a plan of action has been recommended.**	It contains a summary of the present situation, and evaluation of available options. **Based on the assessment a plan of action has been recommended.**
Explanation: Parts within a sentence should be linked to each other. Break up the sentence and delete redundant words to make the text coherent.	
Named in the top three detailing establishments by The Outlook he faced severe competition from others operating in the lower **mainland who** built a strong reputation especially among affluent customers by providing them all the conveniences as possible such as pick-up and drop at a price 3 to 4 times higher ($350-$450) than Colin's Car detailing ($80-$120).	He faced severe competition from others operating in the lower **mainland. The** competitors had built a strong reputation among customers, especially affluent ones by providing them all possible conveniences as pick-up and drop at a price 3 to 4 times higher ($350-$450) than Colin's Car detailing ($80-$120).
Explanation: The sentence is long and convoluted. There is no link between the point at which the paragraph begins and ends. Breaking up the sentence into three brings about coherence. Interestingly, the number of words used in the incorrect usage column is 56 and in the correct usage is 46.	

Misused Expressions

Incorrect Usage	Correct Usage
You **better** pay heed to your teacher's advice.	You **had better** pay heed to your teacher's advice.
Explanation: Words like *had better* and *would rather* are used to express advice or preference. An auxiliary verb is added.	
He had **a half** a banan(a)	He had **half** a banan(a) (or a half banana)
Explanation: The article 'a' is not used before half which is followed again by the article 'a'.	
Karan was standing **in between** the two benches.	Karan was standing **between** the two benches.
In back of the café is the residence gate.	**Back** of the café is the residence gate.
Explanation: Avoid using '*in between*' and '*in back*' of . 'In' is avoided in such cases.	
Rajat stepped **in** the train.	Rajat stepped **into** the train.
Explanation: '*In*' indicates "location within" and '*into*' refers to "motion" or "direction".	
This is a lesson **to each and every one** of us.	This is a lesson **for every one** of us.
Explanation: The usage of the phrase 'each and everyone' is inaccurate and should be avoided.	
The street was extremely crowded. **However, we finally succeeded to reach the office on time.**	The street was extremely crowded. **Finally, however, we succeeded to reach the office on time.**
Explanation: A sentence should not begin with 'however' when the meaning is nevertheless.	

Strawman Options

Incorrect Usage	Correct Usage
People who do not support the mid-day meal scheme of the ***government hate the*** poor children.	People who do not support the mid-day meal scheme of the ***government do not find it easy*** to attract students to the classroom.
Explanation: In the incorrect structuring, the argument is oversimplified and attributions are made without any reasoning or justification. Inevitably such statements are negated by the reader or listener.	
The company is facing major losses in its core business of manufacturing glass. It has two options before it: **to maintain status quo** or to diversify in manufacturing of cans.	**The company is facing major losses in its core business of manufacturing glass. It has the option of diversifying in manufacturing of cans.**
Explanation: As the company is facing losses, maintaining status quo will not help. It is a strawman option that has been set up merely to shoot down.	

Redundancy/Dead Wood

Incorrect Usage	Correct Usage
Subject: **Final report** on the future strategy of Neptune Gourmet Seafood.	Subject: **A report** on the future strategy of Neptune Gourmet Seafood.
Explanation: The word 'final' suggests that drafts of the same report have been submitted earlier.	
The new brand can be positioned as a low cost alternative with new **packaging and packing.**	The new brand can be positioned as a low cost alternative with **new packaging.**
Explanation: Repetition, can be avoided. Packaging and packing mean the same.	
Enclosed is the analysis report, **thoroughly investigated, along with** suggestions for future action.	Enclosed is a report **analysing the situation and providing** suggestions for future action.
Explanation: Use of 'thoroughly investigated' is redundant. The writer is expected to thoroughly investigate for analysis. As presented in the correct usage column, the sentence can also be revised for clarity.	

JAM: Have you re-read the text to avoid dead wood?

"You do not have to explain every single drop of water contained in a rain barrel. You have to explain one drop—H$_2$O. The reader will get it."
—George Singleton

ERRORS OF LOGIC

TOPIC OBJECTIVES
Follow a structured pattern of writing
Build on the stated premise

"All opinions are not equal. Some are a very great deal more robust, sophisticated and well supported in logic and argument than others."
—Douglas Adams

Have you ever heard the reprimand, "Be logical!" What is it that has been said or not said which has made the statement illogical or lacking in logic? To be able to provide an answer to the question we can state that in simplistic terms anything which is logical normally follows a systematic ordering, a progression from one idea to another in a structured pattern which leads to a conclusion derived from the stated facts. All statements are connected and missing out on any one makes the derivation incomplete or faulty. Logical errors, if any, can stem from many factors. Some examples have been provided below which address issues/ errors of logic.

Illogical Connection

Incorrect Usage	Correct Usage
The employees can be dressed in movie star costumes, which will attract children as well as create **an image** in whole market about the **company's dedication in the business.**	The employees can be dressed in movie star costumes, which will attract children as well as create **awareness** in the whole market about the **company products.**
Explanation: Logic needs to be established. Promotion does not necessarily lead to establishing "company's dedication in the business."	
Customer loyalty is important for AP as 90% of its revenue comes from repeat customers.	90% of AP's revenue comes from repeat customers. **Hence, it is important for the company to maintain customer loyalty.**
Explanation: The relationship between two clauses or sentences needs to be established. Use words as hence, to show the link and establish connects.	

JAM: Have you been able to establish the logical connect?

Flawed Logic

Incorrect Usage	Correct Usage
Effect on Neptune's reputation—**Neptune's reputation will increase due to expansion. Also** quality ready-to-eat food may increase its credibility in eyes of retail consumers also.	Effect on Neptune's reputation—**Successful expansion clearly indicates an increase in Neptune's reputation. Introduction** of quality ready-to-eat food will also increase its credibility in eyes of retail consumers.
Explanation: Company reputation does not increase/decrease because of expansion. Greater understanding of technical terms will make the writing coherent and logical.	
Discounts to restaurants and wholesalers Increase in demand: For those restaurants that consider NSG the supplier of choice for fresh seafood, a discount in prices will allow greater flexibility **with respect to menu and prices, and thus the amount they buy will definitely increase.**	Discounts to restaurants and wholesalers Increase in demand: For those restaurants that consider NSG the supplier of choice for fresh seafood, a discount in prices will allow greater flexibility **to the customers and thus the amount they buy may increase.**
Explanation: The menu and variations in a hotel are not determined by discounts. As there is no one to one correspondence between flexibility and purchase, "will definitely" can change to "may" to logically indicate probability.	

Note: Develop a connect.

Genetic Fallacy

Incorrect Usage	Correct Usage
Why should I listen to that guy? The guy comes **from Delhi, and we know that Delhites** are fraud.	Why should I listen to that guy? The guy **may be a fraud.**

Explanation: In a genetic fallacy the conclusion is based on the assumption that an idea, product or person is wrong because of the origin. Deleting the place of origin will accord objectivity to the sentence.

The current Director at one of the Medical Colleges was a football champion in his college days. With that kind of background, **his tenure at the college will be like a football game.**	The current Director at one of the Medical Colleges was a football champion in his college days. With that kind of background, **he may wish to encourage the sport in college.**

Explanation: The last sentence in the incorrect usage column builds an incorrect assumption based on an understanding of the past. The argument is fallacious and not based on sound logical reasoning. An accurate assumption is presented in the correct usage column.

Circular Logic/Begging the Question

Incorrect Usage	*Correct Usage*
Shyam Modi is a **good communicator because he speaks effectively.**	Shyam Modi is **an effective communicator.**

Explanation: The beginning and the ending of the argument are the same and it is restated without any proof.

All men are mortal **Mortality is death** **Therefore all men must die as they are mortal**	All men are mortal

Explanation: Circular logic or begging the question is a manner of stating what has already been stated or implied in the first clause. It makes the sentence construct and argument repetitive.

Red Herring

Incorrect Usage	*Correct Usage*
The level of adulteration is very high in unpackaged food. **But unpackaged food is cheaper and the vendors make a good living out of it.**	The level of adulteration is very high in unpackaged food as it is cheaper and helps vendors make a huge profit.

Explanation: In this example, the second statement attempts to reduce the intensity of attack of the previous sentence. A distracting tactic of detouring is adopted to avoid the key issues/arguments. In the correction the second sentence is replaced by an action-centric one.

There is no reason why drinking should be considered wrong when it provides so much pleasure to the drinkers.	Though drinking has been found to provide pleasure to many people, it has been found that when taken in excess it can cause damage to the liver.

Explanation: The logic in the incorrect usage column is fallacious, lacks depth and cannot be validated on sound reasoning. The sentence has been rewritten to make it credible and logical to the reader.

Rushed Generalisation

Incorrect Usage	Correct Usage
Even though it was only the first meeting with Rohit, **I can tell** that he is not going to be our good friend.	Even though it was only the first meeting with Rohit, **I guess** that he is not going to be our good friend.
Explanation: In the incorrect usage, the conclusion is based on inadequate or biased evidence that has been drawn without relevant evidence.	
I drank soda and now I am sick, *so* the soda must have made me sick.	I drank soda and now I am sick, **so I presume** that soda must have made me sick.
Explanation: Here, in the conclusion it is assumed that if 'X' occurred after 'Y' then 'Y' must have caused 'X.'	

Warning! A rushed conclusion can be fallacious.

Cause and Effect

Incorrect Usage	Correct Usage
Limited capacity at the Shouldice Hospital (SH) has resulted in other hospitals coming into competition with the SH in the market. They are claiming treatment with the same technique as used in the SH. **But the more recurrence cases from them shows their incapability which is bringing bad name to the technique and to the SH.**	Limited capacity at the Shouldice Hospital (SH) has resulted in other hospitals coming into competition with the SH in the market. They are claiming treatment with the same technique as used in the SH. **However, there are many cases of recurrence which indicates their incapability of handling the technique. It may bring a bad name to the SH.**
Explanation: The cause effect relationship should be carefully established. In the case of incorrect usage though the effect is directly attributed to the cause, the logical connect is missing. Either details or data should be presented to show a robust connect or a supposition. Check the correct usage column.	
The glass packaging industry is facing intense competition from PET cans. **As a result, the companies' profitability is steadily declining** because glass is its flagship product.	The glass packaging industry is facing intense competition from PET cans. **It will not be long before the companies' profitability will decline** because glass is its flagship product.
Explanation: The cause effect relationship is not well established in the incorrect usage column. The effect of the competition between the two industries has not led to a decline in the current business. Currently, it is not the cause but may possess the potential to impact the business.	

Moral Equivalence

Incorrect Usage	Correct Usage
Anyone who participates in a fashion show has loose morals.	**A recent survey of 100 fashion shows has found that 50% of the participants have loose morals. Based on the findings it can be predicted that many participants** in the fashion show have loose morals.

Taking drugs is suicidal: the person who takes drugs is voluntarily committing suicide.	**Recent medical journals have reported the impact of different drugs on mortality. Based on the conclusions, it can be predicted that** the person who takes drugs is voluntarily committing suicide.
Explanation: This is a logical fallacy as arguments in the two examples cited above are built on moral high ground. While these arguments carry emotional appeal, they cannot be validated through logical reasoning. Data and supporting arguments need to be provided to validate the claim.	

False Dilemma

Incorrect Usage	*Correct Usage*
Either you have broken the window or you have not. Which is it?	**The window has been broken.** Who has done it? How did it happen?
Either you can afford to go to the Pub or you cannot. Which is true?	Do you have the money to go to the Pub?
Explanation: Giving only two choices despite the possibility of other choices. Sentence can be rewritten so that it communicates the same message and yet provides more than just two options. This is also referred to as black and white thinking. In both the examples cited above the statements are structured in a manner that they do not accord the receiver a third option. This is a fallacious line of argument. For there to be conviction the statements should be open and accord the receiver an opportunity of giving a response that does not fall in the black and white category.	

Appealing, Therefore True

Incorrect Usage	*Correct Usage*
If you **were a true Indian** you would support Indian government in whatever foreign policies they choose against enemy countries.	**You should** only support those foreign policies of Indian government against enemy countries that are right.
Explanation: In the incorrect usage, the conclusion is based on emotional appeal (either positive or negative) rather than on the real issue at hand.	
As employees of a lead software company we should be the forerunners in forming policies. **We should not ape other companies which have a lower turnover.**	As employees of a lead software company **we should be the forerunners in forming policies**.
Explanation: There is no connection between the first sentence and the second in the incorrect usage. Lower turnover and policies need to be connected before the logic in the second sentence can be accepted.	

"It ain't whatcha write, it's the way atcha write it." —Jack Kerouac, WD

GRAMMATICAL FLAWS

TOPIC OBJECTIVES

Learn the types of grammatical errors

Re-read to remove all grammatical fallacies

"His sentences didn't seem to have any verbs, which was par for a politician. All nouns, no action."

—Jennifer Crusie

Identification of grammatical flaws is the toughest in any form of writing. This is more so with native speakers who often conceptualise in their native language and then translate the same into English. Many of the grammatical flaws stem from conversion of ideas from one language to another. Additionally, when we write, our focus is primarily on content development. This often leads to incorrect sentence formulations that rob the text of smooth flow. Some of the flaws relate to sentence constructions, modifiers, infinitives, conjunctions, active and passive voice, Transitional words and phrases, punctuation marks etc. Understanding of grammatical patterns of writing help in removing inadvertent errors that may surface in the writing process. Let us study the examples below.

Grammatical Correctness

Incorrect Usage	Correct Usage
As the new product introduced will not have **the ASPD gold seal of approval hence** its brand name is going to be affected.	As the new product introduced will not have **ASPD gold seal of approval** its brand name will be affected.
Explanation: Incorrect use of article before a proper noun. Use of the article 'a' and 'hence' in the same sentence is grammatically incorrect. Both are used to reason the effect of an action. Present progressive (is/am/are + ing with the verb) is used to express an action in progress. In the above case, the effect on brand name will take place in future and hence you need to use simple future tense.	
Even after demand touching all time high our inventories **had continued** to grow **and it increased up to 60 day's supply** twice the normal level.	Even after demand touching an all time high our inventories have continued to grow **leading to 60 days excess supply,** twice the normal level.
Explanation: Incorrect use of past perfect tense. In this case, use of present perfect tense is appropriate as we are talking about the current situation. Incorrect use of conjunction "and". It does not establish cause and effect relationship of the continued increase and excess supply. Syntax error: Sentence needs revision to establish the cause and effect relationship.	

JAM: Have you used the correct tense?

Complex Sentence

Incorrect Usage	Correct Usage
The crux of the problem is how to devise a plan to conglomerate the contra distinctive **businesses to enhance the efficacy of the entire Miller Empire and make it more concomitant with an objective of bringing back its eminence.**	The crux of the problem is how to devise a plan to conglomerate the contra distinctive **businesses. An understanding will enhance the efficacy of the entire Miller Empire and make it more concomitant.**
Explanation: Restructuring the business and management are two issues which can be stated in simpler terms. Breaking up the sentence into two makes it more readable. "... with an objective of bringing back its eminence" is redundant as it is embedded in the previous clause "enhance the efficacy of the entire Miller Empire".	
Operating out of Colin Ford's driveway, on a limited capital investment, the company requires customers to drop their vehicles and pick them back up, after detailing, and **hence, is unable to capitalise on the affluent customer base.**	**The company is unable to capitalise on the affluent customer base due to the following reasons.** It operates out of Colin Ford's driveway on a limited capital investment and requires customers to drop their vehicles and pick them back up, after detailing.
Explanation: The sentence has been broken up for brevity and clarity. The most important clause "unable to capitalise on the affluent customer base" has been put at the head of the paragraph to bring about clarity in the writing.	

Conditional Sentences

Incorrect Usage	Correct Usage
If **he will join** the team, we will definitely win the tournament.	If **he joins** the team, we will definitely win the tournament.
Explanation: This structure is used when there is a possibility and is very likely that the condition is fulfilled. Structure: If + simple present, will + present form of the verb	
If **he would join** the team, we would definitely win the tournament.	If **he joined** the team, we would definitely win the tournament.
Explanation: This structure is used when there is a possibility but it is unlikely that the condition will fulfill. Structure: If + past indefinite, would + present form of the verb	
If he **would have joined** the team, we would have won the tournament.	If he **had joined** the team, we would have won the tournament.
Explanation: This structure is used when it is impossible and very unlikely that the condition will be fulfilled. The situation is so as it refers to the past. Structure: If+ past perfect, would have + past participle form of the verb.	

If I **would know** his address, I will tell you.	If I **knew** his address, I would tell you.

Explanation: In the unreal and improbable situations of present and future, past tense is used in the if-clause (with present or future meaning) and would is used in the other part of the sentence.

Structure: If + past indefinite, would + present form of the verb

Subject-Verb Agreement

Incorrect Usage	*Correct Usage*
Eggs and milk **is** not sold in the supermarket.	Eggs and milk **are** not sold in the supermarket.
Explanation: The subjects joined by *and* require a plural form of verb	
Eggs and milk **are** a healthy breakfast	Eggs and milk **is** a healthy breakfast.
Explanation: The verb is singular when subject refers to the same things.	
The communication faculty **are** going out for dinner.	The communication faculty **is** going out for dinner.
Explanation: Collective noun takes a singular verb.	
The faculty **has** made different presentations in the conference.	The faculty **have** made different presentations in the conference.
Explanation: When the reference is to a number of activities (plural) performed by a collective noun, the verb is in the plural.	
There **are** no news about UFOs these days.	There **is** no news about UFOs these days.
Explanation: The nouns with plural forms but singular meaning take on a singular verb.	
The number of candidates enrolled for CAT exam **are** reducing.	The number of candidates enrolled for CAT exam **is** reducing.
A number of candidates enrolled for CAT exam **is** reducing.	A number of candidates enrolled for CAT exam **are** reducing.
Explanation: The word number is used as singular when preceded by 'and' and as plural when preceded by the article 'a'.	
My friend, along with his cousin, **are** expected to arrive shortly.	My friend, along with his cousin, **is** expected to arrive shortly.
Explanation: If the subject is separated from the verb with phrases such as 'along with', 'as well as', 'besides' etc., a singular verb is used.	
1000 rupees **are** a good amount to be paid for car detailing.	1000 rupees **is** a good amount to be paid for car detailing.
Explanation: Singular verb is used in instances when sums of money, distance and periods of time are used as a single unit.	

Use of Present Continuous

Incorrect Usage	Correct Usage
Sell units **having** low profits	Sell units **with** low profits
Explanation: Generally, static verbs (denoting status) and verbs of sensation (touch, smell) do not take 'ing'. In the above case, we can either say 'Sell units which have low profit' or still crisper 'Sell units with low profits.'	
Some of these businesses **are having** low growth potential, but they are also the ones contributing most cash.	Some of these businesses **have** low growth potential, but they are also the ones contributing most cash.
Explanation: Present progressive (is/am/are + ing with the verb) is used to express an action in progress. In the above case we find that there are certain businesses which have low growth. Businesses with low growth potential is a state and therefore we need to use the present simple (used to describe a habit, routine, universal truth, etc.).	

Split Infinitive

Incorrect Usage	Correct Usage
Ananya decided **to quickly remove** the CD player.	Ananya decided **quickly to remove** the CD player.
Mahatesh moved **to slowly empty** the can.	Mahatesh moved **slowly to empty** the can.
Explanation: Interposing an adverb between *to* and *the infinitive* it governs is acceptable, but the construct should be avoided unless the writer wishes to put extra stress on the adverb.	

Misplaced Modifiers

Incorrect Usage	Correct Usage
Excitedly waiting for the results to be declared, **Rohan's friends were called and talked to by Rohan** several times during the day.	Excitedly waiting for the results to be declared, **Rohan called his friends** several times during the day.
Explanation: The modifier modifies the noun. In this case, as it is improbable that Rohan's friends would share the same excitement as Rohan, the modifier is misplaced.	
Tired with the hard work at the Institute, **Ram's ecstasy was evidenced by Ram** when his Prof. informed him that course work was over.	Tired with the hard work at the Institute, **Ram was ecstatic** when his Prof. informed him that course work was over.
Explanation: In this example, Ram's ecstasy is modified by the opening phrase, "Tired with the hard work at the Institute". As ecstasy is not a person and cannot be "tired", it is assumed that it is Ram who is tired. By removing the subject closest to the modifier the sentence has been rewritten in the Correct usage column.	

Dangling Modifiers

Incorrect Usage	Correct Usage
One morning in Ahmedabad, **with two children following,** Mohini realised that she had not achieved anything in life.	One morning in **Ahmedabad, Mohini** realised that she had not achieved anything in life.
Explanation: The phrase "with two children following" modifies neither the first nor the second clause. The significance of this clause is suspect and can be deleted to make the sentence read smooth.	
Today in class, **with a mug of steaming hot coffee in hand,** Amresh answered out of turn and was reprimanded by the Professor.	Today in **class Amresh answered** out of turn and was reprimanded by the Professor.
Explanation: Once again, in the sentence presented above, the phrase "with a mug of steaming hot coffee in hand" does not modify either the clause before or after. Dangling modifiers can be added for poetic appeal. However, they should be avoided in concrete business writing.	

Warning! Dangling modifiers rob the sentence of specificity.

Conjunctions

Incorrect Usage	Correct Usage
Simran enjoys **hiking. She** often goes backpacking in summers.	Simran enjoys **hiking and** often goes backpacking in summers.
They were not the professional **actors. They** were the cricketers in disguise.	They were not the professional actors **but** were the cricketers in disguise.
Explanation: The independent clauses can be joined together with coordinating conjunctions (and, so, but, yet, for, or, nor) to show connects and avoid repetitively monotonous sentences.	

Active Voice

Incorrect Usage	Correct Usage
My first music teacher will always **be remembered by me.**	**I shall always remember** my first music teacher.
Explanation: The use of active voice makes the sentence more direct and straightforward.	
Attrition and poor organisational culture were **the causes for the drop in company reputation.**	**The causes for the drop in company reputation** were attrition and poor organisational culture.
Explanation: Use active voice, reverse the sentence structure and create the desired impact.	

Parallel Structure

Incorrect Usage	Correct Usage
Ravi likes dancing, singing and **to play** football.	Ravi likes dancing, singing and **playing** football.
The boss told Siddharth that he was lax because he never completed the work on time, often came late to the office, and **commitment was low**.	The boss told Siddharth that he was lax employee because he never completed work on time, often came late to the office, and **lacked commitment**.
Explanation: In parallel structures, the same level of words, phrases and clauses are used in a similar pattern. The parallel structures are joined with the help of coordinating conjunctions such as 'and' or 'or'.	

Transitional Words and Phrases

Words that indicate addition to the existing idea or are a buildup on the idea presented: Furthermore, moreover, too, also, in the second place, again, in addition, even more, next, further, last, lastly, finally, besides, and, or, first, second, secondly, etc.

> *Example:* I have to study this evening. *In addition (or additionally),* I have to go to gymnasium.

Words that indicate Time: While, immediately, never, after, later, earlier, always, when, soon, whenever, meanwhile, sometimes, in the meantime, during, afterwards, now, until now, next, following, once, then, at length, simultaneously, so far, this time, subsequently, etc.

> *Example:* Police were reviewing Ravi's case. In the *meanwhile*, he stayed in a jail.

Words that indicate Place: Here, there, nearby, beyond, wherever, opposite to, adjacent to, neighboring on, above, below, etc.

> *Example:* I like to stay in Hyatt International hotel as it is *adjacent to* Alpha one mall.

Words that indicate Contrast: Yet, and yet, nevertheless, nonetheless, after all, but, however, though, otherwise, on the contrary, in contrast, notwithstanding, on the other hand, at the same time, etc.

> *Example:* I accept that Formula 1 is a dangerous sport. *Nonetheless,* I want to try it.

Words that indicate Cause: Because, on account of, for that reason

> *Example:* I think he felt included in the team *because* he assisted as much as we did.

Words that indicate Effect: Therefore, consequently, subsequently, accordingly, thus, hence, as a result

> *Example:* Malini's car broke down on the way to the university. ***Consequently,*** she could not go to deliver the seminar on time.

Words that indicate Conclusion: Therefore, in sum, in conclusion, to conclude, finally

> *Example:* My Honda City broke down yesterday. I could not go to office. Moreover, the car is quite old. ***Therefore,*** I should buy a new car.

> "Cheat your landlord if you can and must, but do not try to shortchange the Muse. It cannot be done. You can't fake quality any more than you can fake a good meal."
> —William S. Burroughs

Use of Parenthesis

Incorrect Usage	*Correct Usage*
The concerns of Late **(Mr.)** McFettridge, **(erstwhile President, The Miller Tool Company (MTC))**	The concerns of Late **[Mr.]** McFettridge, **(erstwhile President, The Miller Tool Company {MTC})**
Explanation: Different types of brackets can be used to differentiate one parenthesis from another.	
Please submit the **NOC (No Objection Certificate)** at the earliest.	Please submit the **No Objection Certificate (NOC)** at the earliest.
Explanation: The acronym always follows the full form.	

Punctuation Marks

Incorrect Usage	*Correct Usage*
The things you need to carry **are:** bag, water bottle and umbrell(a)	The things you need to carry **are bag,** water bottle and umbrell(a)
Explanation: Colon should not be placed immediately after the verb.	
Cycling, riding and **dancing,** are his favourite hobbies in the academy.	Cycling, riding and **dancing are** his favourite hobbies in the academy.
Explanation: A comma cannot be placed between a subject and a verb	
The book is **widely-known** around the world.	The book is **widely known** around the world.
Explanation: The adverbs ending in -ly are not hyphenated when combined with adjective or participle.	

Some Common Mistakes

Incorrect Usage	Correct Usage
Please **explain me** what you have done with your books.	Please **explain to me** what you have done with your books.
I look forward to **meet you** in the party.	I look forward to **meeting you** in the party.
The **whole India** was celebrating Diwali.	The **whole of India** was celebrating Diwali.
Except Saurabh, everybody went to watch the movie.	**Except for Saurabh**, everybody went to watch the movie.
Although it was **dark, but** they went out to play.	Although it was **dark, they** went out to play.
It is **more hot** today	It is **hotter** today than yesterday
I am **good in playing** guitar.	I am **good at playing** guitar.
I have been waiting **here since two** hours.	I have been waiting **here for two** hours.
What is the **time in your** watch?	What is the **time by your** watch?
Susan is **incapable to collect data** by herself.	Susan is **incapable of collecting the** data by herself.

PUT ON YOUR THINKING HAT!

TOPIC

OBJECTIVES

Apply your mind to an exercise on good writing

Comprehend the misuse of words, phrases and clauses

Now that we have come to a close of the chapter, here is an exercise for you. Consider this example that is wordy and uses more than required transitional words and phrases. Can you make it briefer with fewer transitional words? As you plod through the exercise do remember what Ernest Hemingway once said: "We are all apprentices in a craft where no one ever becomes a master."

Firstly, glass provides a major advantage of chemical inertness that rivals even that of PET bottle. Moreover, the presence of a diversified supplier base and warehouses in multiple locations, in proximity to customers preferring glass bottle packaging, is another benefit presented by Ajanta's focus on the glass industry. Furthermore, it showed that the market share of glass packaging industry that is tapped into is a meagre 4.06%, indicates a huge scope for enhancing consumer base. Moreover, considering that 90% of the firm's revenues come from repeat customers, shifting to another sector could prove to be counterproductive in this front. However, recently, glass-bottle-packaging industry has been pushed to a precarious state owing to myriad challenges. The challenges primarily include physical constraints presented by glass as a material. Nevertheless, technological upgrades countered majority of the limitations except increased breakability and difficulty in transportation.

SUMMARY

Familiarity with the language can help in writing but is not sufficient to produce a meaningful and impactful written document.

The writer should cognise factors as reader orientation, coherence, logic and grammar. Focus on reader orientation and expectations is crucial as the recipient of the document should be able to comprehend the written text and take suitable action. Clarity in thought will help make the statements more assertive and render them a simplicity, specificity and brevity.

Coherence can be at the sentential or paragraph level. Beginning at the sentential level, focussing on simple constructs can enhance both the writing and the reading process.

Clarity in the thinking process will make the language specific and concrete, help the writer make a concerted effort in selection of right words to communicate, focus on what needs to go in at the head of the paragraph and to avoid use of strawman options and redundancies or dead wood.

Logic is the most important tool that a writer possesses to communicate. There are multiple logical errors that may inadvertently crop up in the writing process. This will weaken the persuasion and appeal in the text. Comprehension of these errors and methods of correcting them should be learned and consciously adopted.

There are multiple types of grammatical flaws, all of which may be difficult to script. However, some, which are commonly found in use as modifiers, active and passive voice, subject verb agreement, complex and conditional sentences, use of present continuous, split infinitive, parallel structure, transitional words and phrases should be addressed.

A grammatically error free text, without doubt, creates impact.

CHECKLIST

Do's	Don'ts
Ensure that you and the reader are on the same page	Assume that the reader is well versed with what you wish to communicate
Check if there is coherence in the text that you have written	Avoid checks for clarity and coherence in the text
Be formal in the writing process and adhere to principles	Use colloquial language in the written text
Follow grammatical rules	Avoid rules of grammar
Use punctuation marks to show breaks in sentence	Miss out on punctuation marks as they also assign a meaning to the written text
Develop a connect	Write standalone sentences and paragraphs

Be specific and concrete	Beat around the bush
Use the correct form of the tense	Use present continuous for all situations
Bring clarity in the writing by correct use of subject verb agreement	Use verbs incorrectly without first understanding their connect with the subject
Re-read the text to ensure that all issues related to logic and grammar have been addressed	Be in a rush to derive and conclude

RAPID REVIEW

A. Pick Your Choice

1. The word "likely" conveys
   - (a) probability
   - (b) certainty
   - (c) poetic justice
   - (d) adverbial fit
2. To indicate contrast, we can use
   - (a) meanwhile
   - (b) nonetheless
   - (c) moreover
   - (d) therefore
3. Furthermore is used to indicate
   - (a) addition
   - (b) conclusion
   - (c) effect
   - (d) cause
4. The preposition "in" can be used with
   - (a) between
   - (b) back
   - (c) move
   - (d) none of these
5. Parallel structures can be created by using words at the
   - (a) Same level
   - (b) Different levels
   - (c) Both same and different levels
   - (d) None of the above
6. Dangling modifiers are used for
   - (a) business writing
   - (b) professional writing
   - (c) poetic writing
   - (d) informal writing
7. Use of the article "a" and hence in the same sentence is
   - (a) grammatically correct
   - (b) can be accepted
   - (c) poetically appealing
   - (d) grammatically incorrect
8. In subject verb agreement, a collective noun takes a
   - (a) plural verb
   - (b) adverb +ly form
   - (c) singular verb
   - (d) verb+ing

9. The modifier, modifies the

(a) noun   (b) verb

(c) adverb   (d) transitional phrase

10. A colon cannot be placed immediately after a

(a) noun   (b) verb

(c) adjective   (d) adverb

B. True or False

1. The written text should have an "I-orientation".
2. Elaborations on a point should be crisp and brief.
3. Excess information is always useful.
4. To be on the safer side, we should always use tentative language.
5. There is no harm in writing each and everyone for emphasis.
6. Repetitions can be avoided with the use of conjunctions.
7. In concrete business writing dangling modifiers are a necessity.
8. An acronym should always be followed by the full form in parenthesis.
9. In an active voice, the sentence gains by being more direct.
10. The use of he or she makes the writing clearer and should be followed consistently.

C. Fill in the Blanks

1. While writing we should ensure _____ towards the reader.
2. In a genetic fallacy, the conclusion is based on the assumption that the _____, _____ or _____ is wrong.
3. To indicate probability, we can write _____ instead of "will definitely".
4. Repetition in the second clause of what has been stated in the first clause is referred to as _____ logic.
5. When we give only two choices when there is possibility of a third as well, gives rise to a _____ dilemma.
6. When the meaning is "nevertheless", the sentence should begin with _____.
7. "Into" refers to _____ or _____.
8. The punctuation mark, a _____ cannot be placed between a subject and a verb.
9. The word number is used as a plural when preceded by the article _____.
10. The word "consequently" indicates _____.

Answers

A. 1. (a) 2. (b) 3. (a) 4. (d) 5. (a) 6. (c) 7. (d) 8. (c) 9. (a) 10. (b)

B. 1. False   2. True   3. False   4. False   5. False
    6. True   7. False   8. False   9. True   10. False

C. 1. sensitivity 2. idea, product, person   3. may   4. circular
    5. false   6. however   7. motion, direction   8. comma
    9. a   10. effect

QUESTIONS FOR DISCUSSION

1. Write a brief report for your instructor. Share it with her and then discuss the same from the point of view of reader orientation. Has the report addressed the concerns? Is the quantum of information right? Does it appeal to the reader? If yes, why and if not, why not?

2. What are the advantages of active over passive voice? Discuss.

3. Ask a friend to share her report with you. Go through it carefully. Does it have appeal? What has she written or not written to capture your attention?

4. Rewrite a report written by a classmate. Identify the changes and discuss reasons for the same from the perspective of reader orientation and logic.

5. Share a report that has been written by you with your classmates. Ask them to go through the report and provide you with feedback on the text.

6. Discuss the significance of logic in the written text.

7. Why is reader orientation important? What may be some of the benefits of focussing on the reader?

8. How can different parts of a document be logically connected?

9. What are some of the common mistakes? Discuss using samples from either your own report or that of a peer.

10. How can coherence in a text be achieved? What are some of the important parameters to be kept in mind?

EXERCISES

1. Pick up any text that you have written. Read it again and check for coherence, language and logic.

2. Write a 200 word essay. Keep it aside and go back to it the next day. Remove dead wood.

3. Jot down five points on why you should be awarded the prize for the best student. Use one paragraph for elaborating on each point. Review the written document for coherence and clarity.

4. Write down 10 common mistakes you make repeatedly by reviewing previous documents written by you.

5. Script 10 sentences with dangling modifiers.

6. In an analytical report, identify the types of logic used to convince and appeal.

7. Identify grammatical errors, if any, in your written document.

8. Rewrite a report written by you. Identify the changes in the document and assign reasons for the same.

9. Write 150 words in the passive voice. Re-do the text in the active voice and assess the difference in impact.

10. Identify five logical errors in a report written by a friend. Restructure to make the text logical.

Index